If there's a worthy *Maintenance*, this book is it. Do not mistake *The Long Ride from Singapore* for yet another travelogue — it is much more than that. This is a tale of a man who is forced to come face to face with himself; Philip is a deeply honest writer whose prose is full of historical trivia, memories, thought processes, politics, sentiment, and most of all, belief. This book will make you laugh out loud, gasp, tear up and cheer up, just like I did.

Theresa Tan
Author of *A Clean Breast*

I have tremendous respect and admiration for these two surgeons, especially for Philip, who carried on despite tremendous odds on this journey of self-discovery. Beyond this, the important message of this book is the challenges faced by women with breast cancer in Asia. Many still hold on to the mistaken belief that this is a "Western" disease. In Malaysia we have the persistent problems of late diagnosis, the lack of uptake of breast cancer screening, and a belief in traditional medicines. This books speaks eloquently of how this "Asian-ness" affects breast cancer behaviour.

Dato' Dr Yip Cheng Har
University of Malaya
Past President, College of Surgeons of Malaysia

A chronicle of an unlikely pair of travellers who start out on this mission of telling Asian breast cancer stories when things start going seriously wrong. It is a fusion of a modern day Marco Polo and a Journey to the West on the famed Silk Road. Readers will find this difficult to put down without some thought of making mad endeavours themselves for a good cause.

Dr Gary Tse
Clinical Associate Professor
The Chinese University of Hong Kong

What happens when you spend your whole working life helping women to confront death, only to come face to face with your own mortality? What does it really mean to come face to face with fear? *The Long Ride from Singapore* chronicles Philip's journey, and the images jump out of the pages like a Chatwin book. It chronicles one man's courage to confront his own fears and find beauty and pleasure in all that life offers.

Dr Teo Soo Hwang,
Chief Executive, Cancer Research Malaysia

This book gives the inside story of a truly out-of-the-box effort to go one step further for Asian breast cancer patients and trying to understand their experiences. A must read for all involved in caring for these women.

Dr Ava Kwong,
Chief of Breast Surgery,
The University of Hong Kong

The LONG RIDE from SINGAPORE

Two Surgeons on a Motorcycle Journey Across Asia for Cancer

Philip Iau

Marshall Cavendish Editions

With the support of

NATIONAL ARTS COUNCIL
SINGAPORE

© 2017 Marshall Cavendish International (Asia) Private Limited
Text © Philip Iau

Published by Marshall Cavendish Editions
An imprint of Marshall Cavendish International

Reprinted 2018 (twice)

A member of the
Times Publishing Group

All rights reserved

No part of this publication may be reproduced, stored in a retrieval system or transmitted, in any form or by any means, electronic, mechanical, photocopying, recording or otherwise, without the prior permission of the copyright owner. Requests for permission should be addressed to the Publisher, Marshall Cavendish International (Asia) Private Limited, 1 New Industrial Road, Singapore 536196. Tel: (65) 6213 9300. E-mail: genref@sg.marshallcavendish.com.
Website: www.marshallcavendish.com/genref

The publisher makes no representation or warranties with respect to the contents of this book, and specifically disclaims any implied warranties or merchantability or fitness for any particular purpose, and shall in no event be liable for any loss of profit or any other commercial damage, including but not limited to special, incidental, consequential, or other damages.

Other Marshall Cavendish Offices:
Marshall Cavendish Corporation. 99 White Plains Road, Tarrytown NY 10591-9001, USA • Marshall Cavendish International (Thailand) Co Ltd. 253 Asoke, 12th Flr, Sukhumvit 21 Road, Klongtoey Nua, Wattana, Bangkok 10110, Thailand • Marshall Cavendish (Malaysia) Sdn Bhd, Times Subang, Lot 46, Subang Hi-Tech Industrial Park, Batu Tiga, 40000 Shah Alam, Selangor Darul Ehsan, Malaysia

Marshall Cavendish is a registered trademark of Times Publishing Limited

National Library Board, Singapore Cataloguing-in-Publication Data

Name(s): Iau, Philip.
Title: The long ride from Singapore : two surgeons on a motorcycle journey across Asia for cancer / Philip Iau.
Other title(s): Two surgeons on a motorcycle journey across Asia for cancer
Description: Singapore : Marshall Cavendish Editions, [2017]
Identifier(s): OCN 993033255 | ISBN 978-981-47-7930-2 (paperback)
Subject(s): LCSH: Iau, Philip--Travel--Asia. Hartman, Mikael--Travel--Asia | Exhibitions. | Breast--Cancer--Asia. | Cancer--Patients--Asia. | Awareness--Cancer. | Breast—Cancer--Treatment. | Fund raising. | Motorcycle touring--Asia.
Classification: DDC 616.99449--dc23

Printed in Singapore by Fabulous Printers Pte Ltd

Photo Credits:
All photos courtesy of Pierce Teo except page 6 (Cristi Mirica) and pages 302-303 (Lee Chuen Neng).

To Mike and Soo,
and all who give us courage

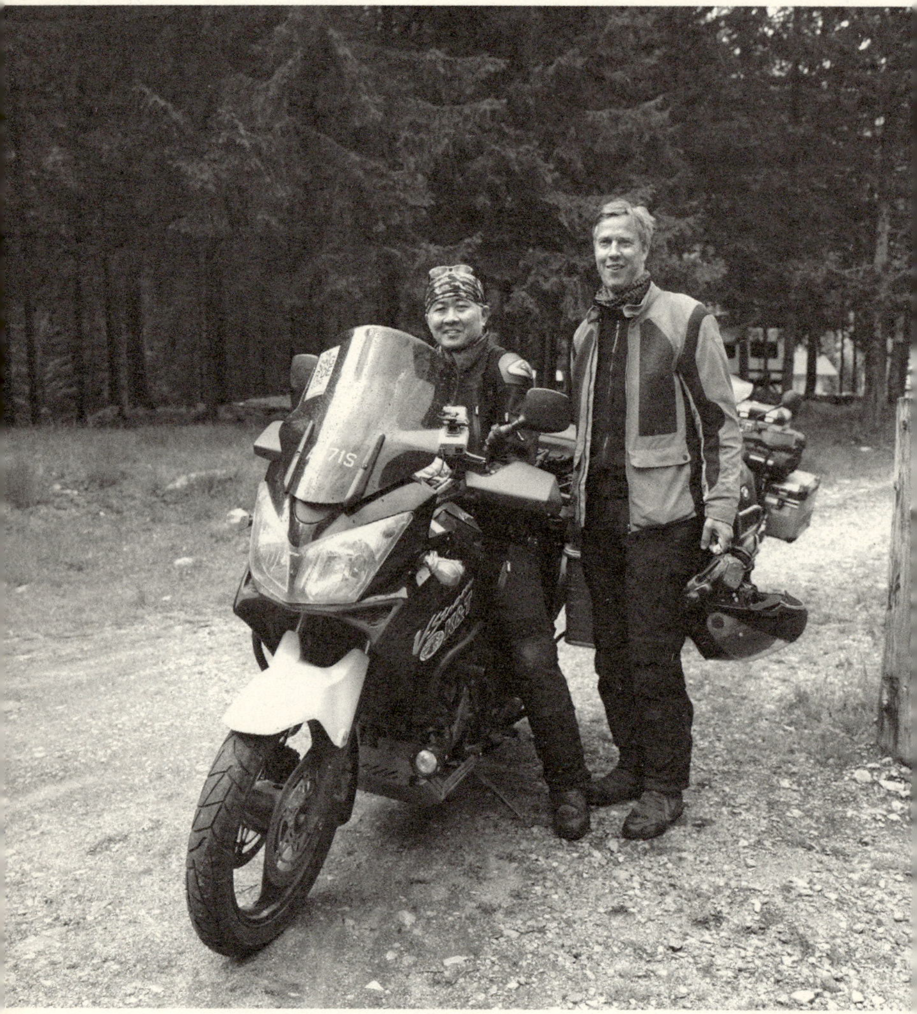

ACKNOWLEDGEMENTS

THIS BOOK WOULD NOT have got started without Professor Lee Chuen Neng (Boss). When the dust had barely settled, he turned to us and said, "Start writing the book."

My sincere thanks also to Mikael Hartman, who then turned to me and said, "You write the book."

To Viola, James, Jean and Jon, who on hearing I was about to get started, said, "You? Write a book?"

To Ovidia Yu for her encouragement and perspective. Her notion that we had already completed the physical journey and that the book writing would be easy by comparison is utterly untrue, but encouraging.

To Noreen Chan, Bettina Lieske, Chong Cheh Hoon and Rosalind Ng for their helpful comments and gentle but thorough butchering of the first drafts. It's turned from a book I wanted to write into one I want to read, thanks to your efforts.

To Pierce Teo and Jacqui Hocking for the photographs that grace these pages. Thank you for your belief in this outlandish endeavour. I think what that television producer said was quite true—Mike and I do have the perfect faces for radio—but you've made us look good somehow.

Most of all to She-reen Wong and the staff at Marshall Cavendish, for taking the chance on a first-time author who didn't even submit a book proposal, for the simple reason that he didn't know what it was. I just started to write, but you've made it into this book.

Sweden
Norway
Finland
STOCKHOLM
Baltic Sea
Estonia
North Sea
Latvia
Moscow
Москва
United
Kingdom
Denmark
HUNDIGE
Lithuania
HAMBURG
Poland
Belarus
Netherlands
London
Germany
Belgium
Prague
Paris
Czechia
BRNO
Ukraine
Slovakia
Austria
Moldova
France
Hungary
Romania
SIBIU
Croatia
PITEȘTI
Serbia
Italy
Black Sea
SUNNY BEACH
Barcelona
Rome
Bulgaria
Georgia
Caspian Sea
Madrid
DEREKÖY
ISTANBUL
DOĞUBAYAZIT
Spain
Tyrrhenian Sea
Azerbaijan
Greece
Turkey
TABRIZ
BATMAN
VAN
CHALUS
MARDIN
HASANKEYF
GORGAN
Syria
ZANJAN
Tunisia
Mediterranean Sea
Lebanon
Iraq
Israel
Iran
Jordan
Algeria
Libya
Egypt
Persian Gulf
Riyadh
United Arab
Emirates
Saudi Arabia
Mecca
Red Sea
Oman
Mali
Niger
Sudan
Chad
Eritrea
Yemen
Burkina
Faso
Gulf of Aden
Benin
Djibouti
Nigeria
Togo
Ethiopia
Ghana
Central
African
Republic
Lagos
South Sudan
Cameroon
Gulf of Guinea
Somalia
Equatorial
Guinea
Uganda
Kenya
Gabon

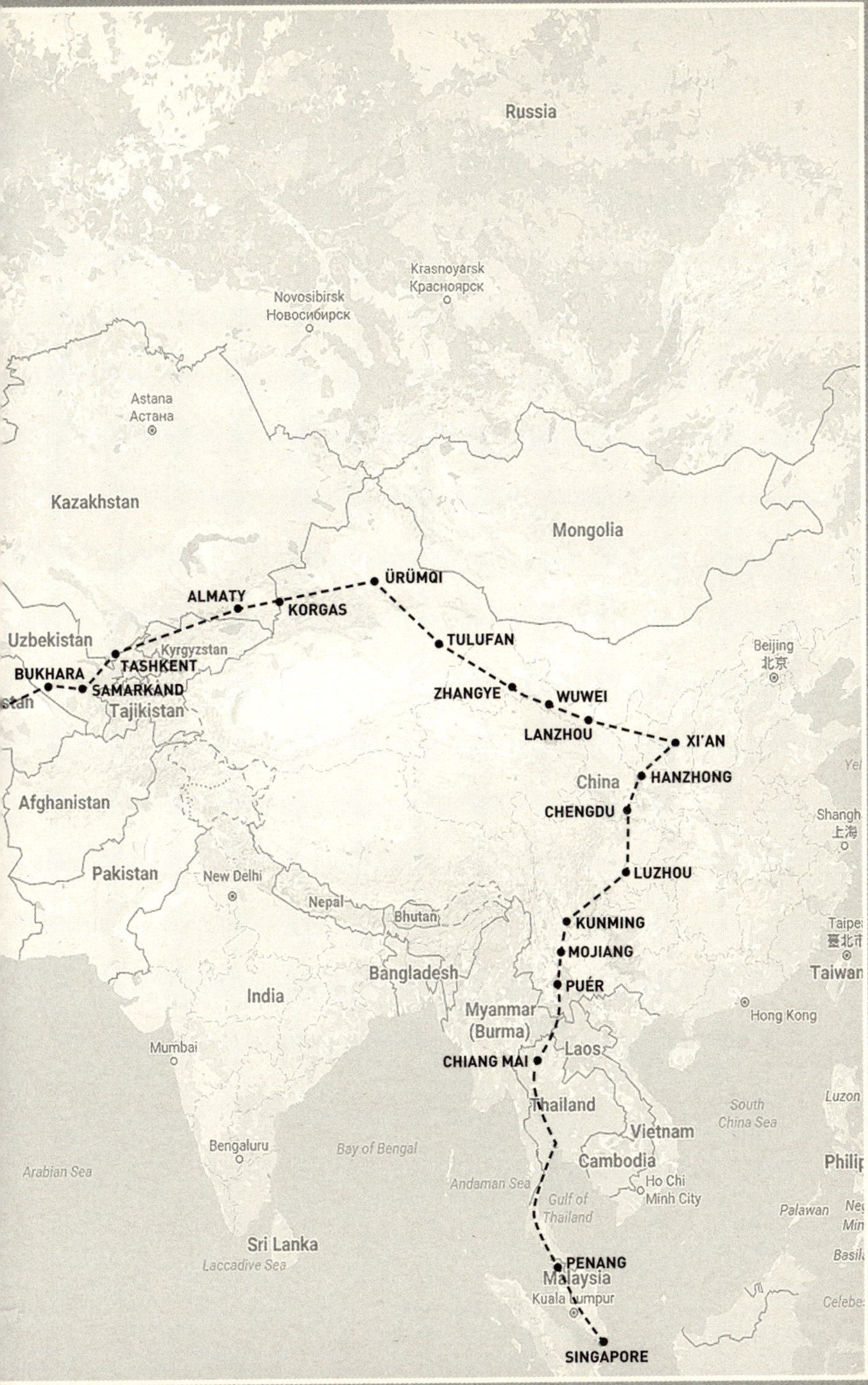

Russia
Krasnoyarsk
Красноярск
Novosibirsk
Новосибирск
Astana
Астана
Kazakhstan
Mongolia
ÜRÜMQI
ALMATY
KORGAS
Uzbekistan
Kyrgyzstan
TULUFAN
Beijing
北京
TASHKENT
BUKHARA
SAMARKAND
Tajikistan
ZHANGYE
WUWEI
LANZHOU
XI'AN
HANZHONG
China
CHENGDU
Afghanistan
Shanghai
上海
LUZHOU
Pakistan
New Delhi
Nepal
Bhutan
KUNMING
MOJIANG
Bangladesh
PUÉR
Taiwan
India
Myanmar
(Burma)
Hong Kong
CHIANG MAI
Laos
Mumbai
Thailand
South
China Sea
Luzon
Vietnam
Bengaluru
Bay of Bengal
Cambodia
Arabian Sea
Andaman Sea
Ho Chi
Minh City
Gulf of
Thailand
Palawan
Sri Lanka
Laccadive Sea
PENANG
Malaysia
Kuala Lumpur
SINGAPORE

Contents

INTRODUCTION — 13

One
WHY DON'T THEY COME? — 17

Two
THE BUDDHIST BIN LADEN — 24

Three
KISMET — 30

Four
SUPER KISMET — 36

Five
THE LONG RIDE BEGINS — 43

Six
PHILIP FALLS APART — 54

Seven
PROZAC RIDER — 72

Eight
ENTERING CHINA — 89

Nine
A KEY DECISION AT KUNMING — 106

Ten
NOT ALL FUN AND GAMES — 121

Eleven
NOT THE PLACE SHE LEFT   144

Twelve
TURNING POINT   152

Thirteen
THE RETURNING RIDER   165

Fourteen
GOODBYE CHINA   187

Fifteen
SAVED BY BLACK HORSE   210

Sixteen
NOT-SO-GOLDEN ROAD TO SAMARKAND   230

Seventeen
FATHER'S DAY IN IRAN   258

Eighteen
KILLER SHEEP, FALSE GODS AND
TRUE GODS   287

Nineteen
TRANSFARAGAN HIGHWAY AND
THE MANSION OF THE BEARS   323

Twenty
THE MONK IN THE GARDEN   349

Twenty-one
THE WALL AT THE END   360

ABOUT THE AUTHOR   367

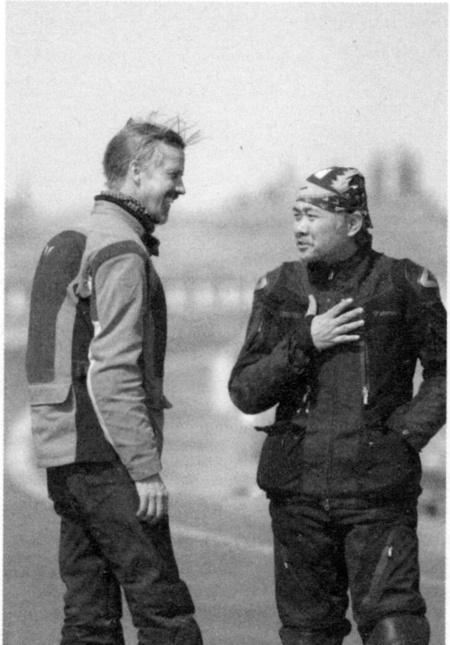

INTRODUCTION

LIKE MANY OF US, the Long Ride was conceived as blissful accident — its gestation a happy coalescence of modern hospital management, two hardworking Swedes and a free online video.

Total Performance Management (TPM) requires clinical leaders to sit down with senior clinicians to review key performance indicators. Our clinical leader, Professor CN Lee, is a cardiac surgeon known simply as Boss. The first hardworking Swede is Mikael Hartman, late of Karolinska Institute, Sweden, but for the last five years part of the Breast Cancer team at National University Hospital (NUH), Singapore.

Like most of us, Mike was TPM-ed on schedule. Unlike most of us, he had done superlatively well in clinical and research work. Perhaps unlike any of us ever, Boss had decided to reward him according to something he had seen online. This was where the free online video came in.

The online session in question was a TED talk. These are talks that try to spread good ideas worldwide. I never quite found out just which one it was, but apparently it was about how to get the best out of highly-skilled workers. Which Boss thinks makes up most of his department.

Anyway the idea was that financial rewards do not achieve the optimal results. At this point I understand Mike made a rather feeble objection, but we all know how these appraisal meetings go. Boss was on a roll. According to

TED, three things would have a higher chance of success: recognition, autonomy and a chance for further improvement. So as a reward Boss provided the most TED-esque form of recognition and autonomy ever seen in any surgical unit.

Boss said to Mike, "Next year, for up to three months, do anything you like, I will support."

"Anything?" asked Mike.

"Anything," replied Boss.

"Right. I want to take a bicycle from Singapore to Sweden to raise awareness of Asian breast cancer."

"Singapore … to Sweden … on a bicycle … tell you what," said Boss, "you send an email to Philip Iau and see whether it can be done. He's done this sort of bicycling madness before."

The email was sent as soon as the session was over, and I got to it later that evening. It did not include the details of the TPM, just the simple question of what it would take to ride a bicycle from Singapore to Sweden. By Google maps I estimated that it was about 19,000 km. Assuming average mileage on a touring bicycle was about 80 km a day for five days a week riding flat out, at 400 km a week it would take about 10 months to cover the distance. That was assuming a lot of things — no major illness, smooth border crossings, outriding banditry, stuff like that.

As a joke I added that what was missing from the calculation was an engine. This would enable him to cover about three times more distance. There would be more time to rest and see the sights. Instead of taking 10 months he could get it done in just over three months. Three months: exactly the time Boss had given Mike. I had no clue.

Up to that point it had been a simple mental exercise, but

having said that I mentioned that if such a thing was possible and a ride was on, I would really like to go. As Boss had said, I had done madness like this before: mountain biking in Indonesia, Taiwan and South Africa, and more recently taking my own newly acquired adventure motorbike to Thailand.

Oh, then there's the other hardworking Swede. A certain Erik Ohlson, aged 25 years, had completed a bicycle ride from Stockholm to Singapore in November 2012, just one week after the aforementioned meeting with Boss. How long had he taken? Nine and a half months. Distance travelled? 19,000 km. It was chillingly close to the estimates that I had given, and mysteriously made Mike's proposal seem not so crazy after all. It would need a lot more preparations, but Boss took this as a sign. Kismet, he called it.

That was how it all got started. Over the next two years I would often wonder how an undertaking based on such flimsy reasoning could grow into something that had taken over my life, and what on earth any of it had to do with breast cancer in Asia. I'm still not really sure, but was told that this book might help.

ONE
WHY DON'T THEY COME?

It may have already happened to any one of these women and I honestly cannot tell which one. About 1 in 12 women from the New Case Clinics will have breast cancer. That's the average I've seen, having run these clinics for 18 years. I have 11 patients to see this afternoon and as each walks through the door I'm sure we're both thinking the same thing: *Is she the one?* Before the physical exam and the rest of the diagnostic procedures there is just no way of telling. Still, it's good to know that for the large majority I should be able to give them the all-clear.

The women who need further workup are seen again on the following Wednesday at the Results Clinic. Again the majority will be told that the biopsy has shown no cancer and it was all a false alarm. The Results Clinic is run with breast care nurses who will help care for the few women who will be told that they do have breast cancer. These nurses, some of whom have been down the same road themselves, form the heart of this clinic.

Running the Results Clinics can be difficult. In the time that I've been doing this I've told so many women that their worst fears have been realised. Over a hundred women a year. Most of them have never ever had a life threatening disease before, nothing even remotely like this. Some of my colleagues and friends have asked me, maybe with a bit of voyeuristic envy, what it is like seeing so many female breasts. I tell them it's something like telling over a thousand women they have cancer.

There really are all kinds. From busy young executives with their constantly yammering handphones, to near deaf great-grandmothers wheeled in on wheelchairs — I've shouted it in their ears before. I've told schoolteachers, nurses, housewives, hawkers, new grandmothers, administrative assistants, factory workers, domestic helpers, wives and girlfriends, wealthy Indonesians with their Burberry togs and inflexible hairstyling.

A particular group stays in my mind: young mothers — trying to keep a grip on their feelings, listening for words of hope while their overactive children wonder why their misbehaving in the doctor's office has suddenly gone unchecked. Those are the ones that the breast care nurses have to specially watch out for. In a few minutes that young mother is going to look up and realise just what her cancer means to the lives of those children. How up to a few minutes ago she had assumed she would always be there as they grew and had children of their own.

How to break the news properly is something that I wish was more science than art. There must be a proper way of doing it because I've seen it done so badly. The breast care nurses will tell you that while some doctors are just awful at it, others make a bearable mess. They ought to know. They have the patient and the bearable mess to clear up after the Results Clinic, often for hours before the woman feels composed enough to go home. Then there'll be the follow-up calls, where sometimes our nurses find that even after days the women just can't bring themselves to tell anyone. I'm not sure how they can call that mess bearable.

There are times when I can tell I'm making a hash of it, occasionally even mid-sentence when I'm going through the results with her. The key is to constantly listen, even while speaking. Listen to what she's saying and what she's not saying, and for heaven's sake learn to react. Sometimes what's needed is just to slow down, use plain language, or stop sounding like an expert and start sounding like someone who wants to help. I know the news will hurt, but when I don't do it right she looks like the words lacerate. Then there are times when I think there's just no good way.

Where I had my training, doctors could only be let loose in the Results Clinic when the breast care sisters thought they were ready for it. It sort of made sense because they were going to have to deal with the aftermath. That was the Nottingham Breast Unit when I was there as a clinical fellow in the mid-1990s. I remember feeling a little puzzled when Ms Linda Winterbottom, the senior breast care sister, finally felt I was up to it.

By that time I had been there for about six months and I wasn't really sure what made her change her mind about me running these clinics. *I seemed more understanding and empathic since coming back from a visit back home*, Linda had said. *It must have been a good holiday with the wife and kids?* I didn't have the heart to tell her that I had gone back to help my wife Viola and her family bury their mother. By the time she had gone to the doctors, her breast cancer had already spread to her spine.

Maybe the death of someone you love makes you better at breaking the results to total strangers. Do they sense that you know even a little of what they and their families are going through? I know it can make the Results Clinic a lot harder to run, and harder to stay completely objective.

AT THE RESULTS CLINIC the following Wednesday we've outdone ourselves. Of the 11 patients from the previous week, I've got three new breast cancers: a large, diabetic Malay housewife, a Singaporean Chinese retiree in her late fifties and a recently married executive in her early forties with a penchant for running marathons. They can't be more different from each other. I really don't know what these three did differently from the remaining eight who had received their all-clears the preceding week.

After the last patient is taken away by the breast care sister, Mike sticks his head in my clinic room. Aside from consulting on each other's cases we have a ritual of after-clinic beverages. More and more we're talking about what the Long Ride should be about.

"Coffee?" he offers.

It's been a lousy afternoon. "Yes, absolutely."

When he sits down Mike tells me he's been having the same sort of week. Four cancers, one so large there's no way even a layperson could mistake it for anything but a cancer. "Right," I say, taking the coffee in. I'm thinking about treatment options for his patient, but Mike has something else entirely on his mind.

"So if she knew," he asks, "why didn't she come sooner?"

"I don't know," I reply, "but sometimes I have this pain in my back teeth and I manage to convince myself I don't need to see the dentist. I hope it'll go away."

"Yes, but at the most you lose a tooth. This thing can kill you."

"Maybe that's why she didn't come," I counter, "it's too much to take on board."

Mike mulls on this for a while. I can tell it isn't good enough. We sip our coffees in silence.

"This is the thing about Singapore I really don't get," Mike says finally. "You have all this prosperity, all this education, all these wonderful hospitals but the women don't come. A Rolls Royce of a national breast cancer screening programme provides care at a Hyundai price and women don't come. Singaporeans seem to be the most Westernised of Asian countries, but still very Asian when it comes to accepting cancer screening, or even cancer education."

He's right. Of the three women with cancers that I had seen just minutes earlier, none of them had gone for their mammograms even though they all qualified for subsidised mammographic screening. They had all come with a breast lump. A mammogram would have discovered their cancers months, possibly years earlier.

"So if good care is available, why don't they come?" Mike asks again.

"I don't know," I admit, "maybe it's cultural. Part of being Asian compels us to not look for trouble when we feel fine."

"Well we need to sort it out soon," Mike points out, "your country's breast cancer numbers are going to be the same as my country's numbers within one generation."

I know he's right there too. It was the whole reason why our national breast screening services started over 10 years ago. The data was undeniable: Singapore has one of the fastest increase in breast cancer rates ever seen anywhere — from 1 in 30 women to an anticipated 1 in 10 in the space of 40 years.

"So if it's such a clear danger, why don't they come?" Mike has a way of picking at a sore.

"I don't know," I say again, "I don't think the problem is a surgical one though."

"No ... it's not a surgical problem," he agrees. "We really don't know anything about what to do about it, do we?"

"No ... I guess we don't."

Silence for a moment. Mike exhales slowly and stretches out in the chair, a sure sign something's brewing.

"We should find out," he says finally, "on this ride."

"OK ... but if the problem is not surgical, then we are going to need to get help."

"Yes, we're going to need to collaborate with people who study these things. Cultural influences. What are they called? Ethnographers? Multi-culturalists?"

"I think anthropologists are the people we're after," I suggest.

"Know anyone?" Mike asks.

"Nope. Last time I hung out with an anthropologist I was an undergrad. And she told me the main interest in her department at the time was how to design train stations to prevent criminal activities. So she decided to look for work elsewhere and left. Nice girl too, but we lost touch soon after that."

"What?"

"You know," I explain, "things like the colour of the walls, lighting intensity, not providing loitering places … stuff like that. It affects human behaviour. Apparently."

"Really? That's pretty amazing," says Mike.

"Yes, I know," I agree. I've always wondered what happened to Cynthia Chou.

"That we can know so much about crap like that and so little about what we really should know everything about."

TWO
THE BUDDHIST BIN LADEN

THINGS STAY THAT WAY for a few months. We know that we want to make this three-month ride from Singapore to Sweden for Asian breast cancer. We're calling it the Long Ride. Aside from that we don't know much else.

The reason why things can't move ahead is because this is all new ground. What can a Long Ride do for breast cancer? Mike and I are both surgeons so I suppose we could run courses, hold public forums, maybe raise funds for research. All of that is going to take work: to get collaborators on board, plan programmes, set dates and most importantly, decide on the route.

Boss knows we've got enough work to do without having to sort all this out at the same time. His solution is to give us a deadline, which he sets for one and a half years away, sometime in the second quarter of 2014. That would give us enough time to accumulate the necessary leave and to get things sorted out.

I'm not sure how he's managed it but after a meeting with the senior hospital administrators Boss has persuaded them to let us take three years' worth of annual leave at one go. I get the feeling he's made some promises to push this through. I can see the problem they might have with it. There has to be some breast cancer-related activity to make this ride more than just a biking holiday. Before we get to that, I need to plan the route.

Soon every spare hour away from clinical work, research meetings, administrative duties, postgraduate teaching and medical conferences is spent with Lonely Planet guides, online adventure motorcycling websites and Michelin maps. It's starting to feel like a second job. After a few months, Boss can sense me flailing. He's starting fortnightly early morning meetings just to make sure I am making progress.

After months of poring over maps I decide that there are three possible routes I would consider riding from Asia to Europe. The only prerequisite that Mike and I agree on is that it should be entirely overland. If we succeed, the bikes will have to be shipped back from Stockholm but for the outward journey we'll be on the road throughout. No ships or planes.

The southern route is the most attractive. This will take us through Malaysia and Thailand before Myanmar and then into India. We'll enter Nagaland and then through Sikkim into Nepal on picturesque mountain roads before crossing the border with Pakistan into Lahore. After that, the famous Karakoram Highway to Kashgar in China before coming to

Kazakhstan and the rest of Central Asia. It has all the nice ingredients: fabulous riding roads, known collaborators in India and Pakistan who want to come onboard and the shortest time in China.

The two backup routes both stay longer in China. The southern China route turns west from Kunming through the Himalayas into Everest Base Camp, while the northern route through all of Yunnan and Sichuan and Ganxi and then into the vast flatlands of Xinjiang. The southern route is uncertain: there are rumours that the road to Everest Base Camp may be closed to outsiders.

On the whole, China isn't the most popular route for bikers. There is the myriad of offices to deal with to get a Chinese registration for the bikes and a valid Chinese driving licence for ourselves. We would have to pay and feed tour guides who are nothing more than government minders making sure we don't wander off on our own. The worst, however, is that bikes are not allowed on highways – covering the distances needed on country road will make it harder for us.

Boss and Mike have left the final decision to me, and I decide to push for the India option at this morning's pre-dawn meeting. There is just one small detail that I hope they don't uncover, but I'm hopeful that since I seem to be the only one reading up on this part of the route I might get away with it. I hear Mike's voice just as I enter Boss's office:

"Just what the hell is a Buddhist bin Laden?"

Ah, I think. *They've uncovered the small detail.*

Since coming to live in Asia, Mike's had to repeatedly adjust his views on what Asian culture really means but a Buddhist terrorist seems to be the ultimate oxymoron.

Even as early as 2012, there had been some inkling that Myanmar might be a problem. It was reported that some new kind of ethnic cleansing was underway. In Myanmar, of all places, led by Buddhist monks, of all people. In a place called Rakhine, hundreds of Muslims were apparently killed in broad daylight. Like many others I had never heard of the place and a quick check of the maps led to some relief. This was in the southwestern corner of Myanmar, away from my proposed route.

It's March 2013 now and for the most recent atrocities, I don't even have to take out the maps. I know where Meiktila is. It's on the main road from Yangon to Mandalay. I actually have a GPS fix on the place. We'll have to turn right at the second junction into town to head north. There are pictures of Muslims being led out to the streets and butchered in broad daylight. Hundreds killed, thousands of homes and businesses torched. This is not going to work out.

What miniscule hope I have of claiming ignorance is comprehensively buggered by an issue of *Time* magazine lying on Boss's desk. The Buddhist bin Laden has made it to the front cover of *Time*. So the game is well and truly up. Without Myanmar there is no overland route into India that doesn't involve China. The other Chinese routes would make a lot more sense than entering and leaving China twice.

"Just as an academic point," Boss asks as he hands out the coffee, "what are the chances of failure?"

"Based on the blogs I've come across," I reply, "about one third of intercontinental bike trips like this fail. But when I say fail it's actually quite hard to define. A lot of European bikers set off trying to get from say, London to Sydney. Then they discover just how beautiful northern India is and don't bother to go further. Is that failure?

"Another thing we should keep in mind is that no one else has our kind of strict time line. Almost everyone takes at least six months, usually much longer. So if something goes wrong they can wait at a place for a week or two for the parts to ship out to them. We don't have that luxury of time."

"So ..." Mike says what's on all our minds. "Given that India is out of the question, and the costs of riding through China, can we get support from the University? Do we still go?"

"Well, I can tell you two things," Boss says, "even without these problems, I have real doubts we are going to get any support from the University. What you're trying to do is just too outlandish, which to them is the same as too dangerous. I don't think they're going stop you, but don't expect any special leave or anything like that.

"Secondly, I don't blame anyone for thinking it's selfish. You have got a route and that's one thing. But so far there is nothing to say that it's about breast cancer. It's just two middle-aged surgeons going on a motorcycle ride when they should be working. You'll need to work hard at making this more than a bike trip."

"And we need to give up on India?" I ask.
As usual, Boss happily provides the kick in the behind I need. "Get over it," he says. "Which other way?"

"China," I concede, "going through Kunming. But that road from Mojiang to Kunming is a real challenge very early in the ride."

Boss doesn't look too disappointed. "Tell you what. I

know a four by four driving group that can help us sort out the arrangements in China. I'll get in contact with them. You worry about how we can get more breast cancer collaborations on the route. And we need to start telling people about what we're going to do."

It's not quite the way I expected the morning to turn out, especially that bit about China. Involving the Chinese authorities means that an itinerary will have to be drawn out and stuck to no matter what the cost. There would be no chance of wandering off, or staying a little longer anywhere if we want to. It is becoming less and less of a biking adventure and more and more like work.

A few days later, Boss introduces me to Hung Tuan, the leader of the four by four group, who briefs me on the route they're proposing. It's just as I expected. All the cities and hotel stops are laid out, with the distances that have to be covered each day. They had done this before and promised an interesting time. And yes, what I heard about that road leading to Kunming from Mojiang is true. Last trip a Subaru Forester actually broke an axle on that road.

Three
KISMET

Boss takes charge of the fundraising. We decide to have funds administered by the University Endowment Fund. That way there is a clear understanding that none of the funds we raise will go to paying for the ride itself, but future Asian breast cancer research. I hear talk about charity dinners, art and wine auctions, possibly even a film crew coming along. It's a world I know nothing about.

"You don't have to worry about any of that," Boss says.

"Right then. I'll start with hotel bookings and the visas and travel documents and shipping for the bikes and …"

"Well, to be honest you don't have to worry about that either," he says.

Enter Connie. Boss brings her in as our ops manager. She'll take care of all that. She had been shortlisted to the administrative pool in our department but for the time being we are her priority. At our first meeting she asks us for a copy of our passports, driving licences and bike ownership papers. *She'll take care of the rest, don't you worry.*

"What you do need to worry about," Boss says to Mike and me, "is getting collaborators. I'm a cardiac surgeon and I'm not familiar with the breast cancer scene in other countries. I can introduce you to the deans and CEOs of different universities and hospitals, but the final approach has to be made by the two of you.

"And don't leave it too late either. Without the collaborators this ride is just a ride, not a Long Ride for Breast Cancer. Without that distinction we can't go to press. And without going to press we can't raise funds. So get going."

Boss says it's a lightning rod for publicity. People will want to know what it's about when two bikers show up from far away. I figure we don't know what the local needs are, so all we can do is provide a menu of options and let them decide what is best. With the four by fours carrying some of our luggage I figure we could help run a local congress, maybe conduct undergrad and post grad teaching. If the film crew eventually materialises, we can showcase what the locals are doing for breast cancer.

"That won't help us in our primary goal though. We want to try and understand how we can help Asian women overcome cultural inhibitions to come early to get their cancers treated," Mike points out.

"Yes," I agree, "we still don't have any anthropologists coming forward. I've checked the social science faculty's website. No one is doing this kind of work, and I'm not hopeful about finding an anthropologist who wants to come on board. We may want to consider changing tack. We could use the ride to increase awareness about breast cancer in Asia."

"What, you mean like health fairs and public symposiums, stuff like Breast Cancer Awareness month?'

"Well, I was thinking of awareness in another way," I explain."We could use the ride to tell people outside Asia what it's like as an Asian woman with breast cancer. Tell breast cancer stories, so to speak. Barriers to seeking treatment, social inhibitions, cultural factors. Increase the awareness of specific problems Asian women face."

"That's good," Mike agrees, "but we still don't know what to ask. How to phrase the questions."

"Well, something will come up," Boss says. "For now, what you need to do is tell as many people as you can about this trip. Who knows what that'll lead to. Most great ventures don't succeed because of good planning, but from dogged persistence. Trust the kismet."

"Sort of throw everything on the wall, see what sticks?"

"Exactly."

So WE START TELLING everyone about our plans. Colleagues past and present, family, medical students, church meetings, everyone. The idea is that hopefully someone will know someone else who might be interested. Over the next few weeks we get some leads and send out feelers but there doesn't seem to be any real interest.

In a sense I don't really blame them. Why would anyone commit the time and effort to hold a collaborative meeting with two riders whom they've never met before, who might very well not even make the proposed dates? Bike rides don't exactly have a reputation of keeping to schedules.

EIGHT MONTHS BEFORE WE'RE supposed to leave, and only the Mount Miriam Cancer Hospital in Penang, Malaysia is confirmed. I was an invited speaker there last year and made some sort of impression. There is also Rebecca, a young breast surgery consultant from Luzhou, who is keen to have us come by but is still checking with her bosses. Rebecca had spent some time with our unit earlier in the year.

Connie has sent out the route, aims and the tentative itinerary to people we've worked with in some of the countries we were going past. There are about a dozen hospitals all told. Some interested noises had been heard, but no one's committed yet.

"So ... eight months to go and it's one confirmation and one maybe?" asks Boss.

"Yes, but we are waiting on about another possible half dozen or so. I think the problem is that there may be many people in the country who are willing, but they are too far off our route and we can't afford the travelling time."

"How many do you think is enough?" Mike asks Boss.

"Well," Boss replies, "you are pushing yourselves as taking up the cause of Asian breast cancer. That you are supposedly willing to undergo some hardship to tell their stories. That's why the university is letting you go. So there must be a representative sample. We don't have India, which means we must get more centres in China. I think all in at least five working stops. By the way, how do you intend to tell the breast cancer stories, do you think they will give you access to their patients?"

I haven't a clue, I think. I don't even know what to ask. I need a miracle, or preferably a series of miracles, in quick order.

I'm starting to realise that the only way for something like this to work is by knowing people. Or people who know people. At her brother's fiftieth birthday Viola and I meet Antonio Corbi and his wife Wendy, complete strangers who think that what we're trying to do with Asian breast cancer on this long ride is a great idea. By now we're used to spreading the word and getting this sort of response, but theirs is not the frozen, I-pity-the-missus kind of smile. They really want to help.

Antonio used to run his business in Almaty where he knows Nina Abramovich, who knows people in the cancer hospitals in Kazakhstan. Through her we manage an invitation to their annual oncology meeting. I suspect that she even managed to persuade them to alter their dates to match with our planned arrival after leaving China.

I haven't met Dr Theresa Tan for ages, but she's heard about our Long Ride through the grapevine. She's now a fellow in the University town and reacquaints me with Dr Tan Lai Yong, who was a few years ahead of me in medical school. He is best remembered for the 16 years he spent in rural Yunnan, setting up local enterprises, teaching village doctors and spreading the word of sustainable local communities.

Lai Yong introduces us to Dr Loh Cheng who has taken over some of his work in China. He knows people from the cancer centre in Kunming and soon we're arranging dates and programmes. Over the course of the next three weeks, we get confirmation from Almaty, Luzhou, Kunming and another previous collaborator from Chiang Mai. With Mount Miriam in Penang and Karolinska that means six collaborative meetings. It's enough to go to press.

The distribution of these collaborators means that our Ride will be in three parts. The first part will be hard riding and academic work through Malaysia, Thailand, Laos, China and the first part of Kazakhstan. We have to try and make all the appointed dates, given the trouble it's taken to set up these collaborative meetings. The second part is through the "–stans" (the rest of Kazakhstan, Uzbekistan and Turkmenistan), where we have no collaborative meetings. It will be very much a bike ride through some of the nicest roads anywhere. The third part is through Europe proper where we have collaborative meetings with Mike's old colleagues in Stockholm. Mike says that Europe can easily be covered in a week, but I have my doubts.

Four
SUPER KISMET

ONE OF THE BIG discussions that Mike and I keep having is what bike he should get for this ride. I've got a Suzuki V-Strom, which is not quite top of the line (that would be a BMW GS Adventure), but is known for its solid dependability. Mike, on the other hand, has to go buy a bike.

I tell him rule number one for riding in a group: Bring the same bike. That way, there's only one set of spares to bring, and we only need to learn how to fix one bike. He has a look at the V-Strom and says, "Well, maybe not." He wants something a bit more refined. I tell him bring a Japanese bike then, there are lots of interchangeable spares, and mechanics all over Asia can fix Japanese.

Mike listens to all this quite politely, but I can tell he's already made up his mind. Pretty soon I'm looking at a gleaming red BMW GS Adventure. It's secondhand with major mileage but it's a Beemer, so all is well. I try not to roll my eyes too much. I don't think there's a BMW mechanic for about half the countries we have to get through, and spares are going to be really expensive. They don't even use the same tools as anyone else, much less share components.

I decide to re-familiarise myself with some basic roadside repairs: fixing punctures, oil and air filter changes, replacing broken foot pegs and brake and clutch handles. There are also some more complicated fixes to learn that are unique to the V-Strom. Every bike has some sort of Archilles Heel and it's good to know what to do when things go wrong. This I do with Ah Chye, my longtime bike mechanic down at Desker Road.

One morning after discovering just how many connections there are to replace the stator and alternator, which are the parts most likely to give trouble in my V-Strom, I ask Ah Chye whether he thinks I'm bringing the right bike. I mean, we've been through a bit together and I trust him.

"This bike," he declares in Chinese, tapping his knuckles on the V-Strom's fuel tank, "I have no problems. This bike will make it."

"That's great," I reply. It's good to get some vindication from an expert.

"The rider, on the other hand…"

"Wait, whaddya mean?"

"The bike will make it. It will make it because it's simple. Because it's simple there's less things to break down. And even if it did break down it's easy to repair. You got the hang of it in a few sessions. Also, parts are available practically everywhere. Remember, you even have a stator that's off a Yamaha FJR.

"Most Japanese bikes really have many interchangeable inside parts whether it's Suzuki, Yamaha or Honda. Which means that mechanics that can fix one can usually fix the rest. Your problem will not be the bike."

"What then?" I ask.

"The problem," Ah Chye says, "will be you. You and your friend. I see you here, but your friend is not. That means you are very different people. You want to be prepared for everything; he may be a little less thorough. And that will give you problems."

"Nah, Mike's going to take lessons at a BMW workshop." Or so he says.

Ah Chye pauses for a moment, cleaning the grease off his hands with a rag. "It's not your friend I'm worried about. It's you."

I didn't expect that. "Me? Why?"

"Anyone can see you're not enjoying this," he explains. "The most important thing about a bike ride is to enjoy it."

"What do you mean? I enjoy riding bikes, otherwise would I be doing this?"

"Maybe not so much not enjoying, that's too strong," Ah Chye corrects himself. "You're not excited about the ride. You were a year ago, now you're not. Now you're just planning.

"You must enjoy it, otherwise when things go wrong, and something *is* bound to go wrong, you won't have any reason to want to go on and finish. You can only get to the finish if you enjoy it.

"This is a once-in-a-lifetime ride. You don't look like

someone who's going on a once-in-a-lifetime ride."

I guess Ah Chye's right. I am starting to miss the forest for the trees with all the planning and research strategy and whatnot. I suppose that if some of the loose ends could be tied up, I could start enjoying it again. So I spend what energies I have after the pretty long work hours trying to tie up the loose ends.

But I was wrong. The loose ends are never completely tied up. The only thing that got tied up as the trip drew near was me. And I should have worried a lot more about me than about the bike. And I never did quite start enjoying it until much later on.

IT'S OCTOBER 2013, WE'RE less than six months from the start of the ride and still in need of a miracle. We have these collaborators lined up, but what are we going to do with them? Thanks to Boss' efforts the ride is already raising funds for breast cancer research, but what else? Are we just going to go there and have health talks? It seems a little thin.

Ever since that exchange with Mike, I have been dogged with the question of what Asian women really need to come forward for their breast cancer care. Despite all the efforts of the Health Promotion Board and various volunteer groups, less than 40% of at-risk women in Singapore ever attend mammogram screening. Less than 15% ever go regularly.

We wonder why women don't come for screening or accept complete treatment and the rest of it, but have we actually asked them why? When I look up the published literature I find an underwhelming number of publications. We have found out a lot more about breast cancer, but hardly any more about the breast cancer *patient*. We aren't the only ones who are not asking. Practically no one has asked. At least not in a way that is practically useful in helping them come forward.

So I run the idea past Mike. Perhaps we can use this ride to start some sort of international study that essentially asks Asian women about their breast cancer experience? Maybe if we can identify real or perceived barriers we can start to take them down.

"Interesting," Mike says.

"Yes I thought it might be," I reply, "but it might not get published anywhere high though." There is a complex system that grades the quality of scientific publications. Cell lines and pharmacogenetics do very nicely, but studies about cultural factors affecting breast cancer behaviour won't.

"No, it might not," Mike replies, "but it is what's needed. How do we begin? What kind of questions do we need to ask that might be useful?"

"Not an effing clue."

It sounds bizarre but as an experienced breast cancer clinician I am having trouble getting my head around how to understand breast cancer patients.

AFTER A MORNING SESSION with Ah Chye I return to hospital by train for the afternoon clinic and feel that I need a little extra something to get into the swing of things. For the first time ever I walk into the Coffee Bean at the Kent Ridge train station and get a large cappuccino.

As I'm leaving, I see Cynthia Chou. Now to understand

what an accomplishment it is for me not to get a large cappuccino all over myself, you need to know a little about Cynthia Chou. She is the anthropology honours student that I used to hang out with as a medical undergraduate over twenty-five years ago. The one I told Mike was the only anthropologist I had ever known personally.

"Cynthia?" I blurt out.

She turns to me. "Uncle Robert?" Ah well, that's a good start. Robert was Dad's name. Well, it *has* been that long. Don't think I would have mistaken her for her mum though.

After a hug and an awkward silence she gets her coffee and we find a table to catch up. The last time I had heard from Cyn she had submitted her Masters thesis and was about to head out to study the Orang Laut. This is a maritime race that once occupied large bits of the Sulawesi. Studying them meant long periods away from any phone or mail service, which is when we sort of lost touch.

Cyn starts to fill in the blanks. After finishing her Masters she put in for a scholarship for her doctorate degree with the Orang Laut idea but this was not taken up. It was, however, reviewed and accepted at Cambridge, which actually has a department called the Study of Vanishing Cultures. This lead to years of fieldwork throughout Sulawesi, where she lived among the Orang Laut and became part of their community and established lasting links.

Later she took up an associate professorship in Copenhagen, where she met James, her husband who was the Rector at Leiden University. He had since retired and they both live by the sea just south of Copenhagen. James is a world-renowned authority on the Chinese language.

I tell her about the Long Ride and how I had spent the morning learning how to fix the V-Strom. When we get to the bit about how I'm desperately looking for an anthropologist-collaborator, Cyn's face lights up. This is right up her alley. The University of Copenhagen has an active interest in trans-ethnic studies and even has researchers who are embedded in different cities in Iran, Malaysia, Turkey, China and Mongolia.

Before I can get over the shock, Cynthia proposes a collaborative study between our universities. She is especially keen if our ride can open up opportunities to meet patients in China, where James can come as interpreter. Later on I would discover that there is a memorandum of understanding between the NUS and the University of Copenhagen. That means it's far easier to access funding and joint publications.

I tell Boss and Mike at the next pre-dawn meeting. It's such a load off my mind. This makes our ride more about breast cancer than we ever imagined before.

"Incredible," says Mike, dumbfounded.

"Kismet," says Boss.

"I'll tell you something," says Mike. "We're meant to go. There's something much bigger than us that's involved here. And if we just let things happen, they will happen."

Five
THE LONG RIDE BEGINS

It's 18 march 2014, the day we start riding from Singapore to Sweden.

The last few weeks before leaving have been one numbing shock after another as things miraculously fall into place. The most significant of all: Boss is coming along. He's got some overdue leave and should be able to join us for about two months. In fact, he's bought an Isuzu four by four which some of his friends at Hope Technic, a local engineering firm, have rigged to take a large motorbike on a tailor-made rack off the back end. It seems like overkill, but you never know. The whole thing is smiley yellow and we christen her The Bumblebee. She will serve as our formal support vehicle, driven by Neo Chian and Sonny until boss takes over somewhere in China. Neo Chian is a retired army officer and

Boss's Bumblebee

should keep us grounded until Boss shows up.

To decompress from the stresses of the preparation phase and transit to the actual start of the ride, Mike and I decide to leave a few days earlier than planned, just the two of us to Penang, the site of our first engagement.

Three hours later, I'm soaked to the skin and freezing on the North-South Expressway in Peninsula Malaysia. Rain here takes things seriously. It doesn't usually last long but while it's here highway visibility is down to less than a hundred metres, cars make unpredictable stops to avoid water obstacles and stuff gets blown off the back of trucks, or into your path from roadside repairs.

This provides interesting if slightly random things to avoid. Over the last half hour I've evaded a traffic cone, a tarpaulin sheet and a toilet lid on the overtaking lane. It hasn't rained for some time here and there's a lovely slippery layer of grease over the road surface.

There is simply no such thing as waterproof kit for this kind of weather. Over the intercom Mike reviews his new thousand-dollar riding jacket:

"Hello Phil," he says, "you staying dry?"

"Nope. Welcome to bike touring in the tropics," I reply.

"Good news is that this shouldn't last long." It's true. After touring around these parts I've discovered it's more sensible to wear a mesh jacket rather than anything that claims to be waterproof. In an hour or so the rain usually clears and under a tropical sun the mesh allows the headwind to blow everything dry. For now it's pretty chilly though.

"Well, I'm here to tell you that my thousand-dollar jacket is really, really waterproof," Mike says.

"You gotta be kidding."

"No, really. It's keeping all of this water in. The water rises from the waist upwards. None of it drains out until it gets to the sleeves, then it just flows freely over the armpits into the gloves. Quite something. Nothing escapes even at the elbows. If I could get to my shower gel I might smell fresh and breezy by the time we arrive."

I glance back at him through the mirrors. It's late in the morning, but all I can see back there is grey gloom. There's no trouble picking him out though. The GS has a characteristically shaped headlight, and Mike has switched on the two auxiliary lamps that I suspect can be seen from space. He's got one hand on the throttle and the other hanging down one side, for drainage, possibly. He looks like a limp teapot.

Well, at least he's not cold. My V-Strom has good enough protection from the headwind but in a thunderstorm the wind shifts direction all the time. I'm noticing that when overtaking heavy vehicles the bike has a tendency to twitch as I put on the speed. Maybe I haven't quite balanced things out. That's unlikely though, I've been doing this sort of riding for some time now and after finding a balanced loading plan I haven't changed it over the years.

We're heading to Kuala Lumpur, or KL, where we have to spend a night before we collect the visa for Uzbekistan and head up to Penang the next day. At this rate we should reach KL just before the evening rush. After an hour and no sign of the rain letting up, we decide to pull off the highway at Tangkak and get ourselves warm. We should still be able to make good time.

The only reason why covering distances like this is possible at all is because of the wonderful North-South Expressway. This runs the length of the Malay Peninsula and is an engineering marvel. It is the smoothest, most well-thought-out piece of road from Singapore to Sweden. For the possibilities it opens to the biker it's the closest thing to a magic wormhole. You can leave Singapore after an early breakfast and get to Thailand before teatime if you want to.

All that smooth perfect tarmac has its own hazards though. As we come up in the early morning it isn't unusual to pass a wreck on the central divider, or sometimes clean off the highway into the surrounding trees. No skid marks means only one thing — someone's fallen asleep and gone off.

I remember once when Viola and I were heading up to Cameron Highlands and were on the highway near Segamat just as dawn broke. We passed what looked like a ridiculously large accordion in a shallow gully on the side of the highway, through a gaping hole in the crash barrier. No skid marks, and the emergency services did not seem in too much of a hurry trying to get the driver out. Truth is, Malaysia has some of the most dangerous roads in the world, with over 20 deaths per 100,000 population per year, compared to, say, the United Kingdom's 3.8 per 100,000.

When it rains in the tropics, it really rains.

After an hour in Tangkak the rain lets up a little and we get back on the highway again. The exit for KL is about an hour away. It's still dark and wet but the visibility has improved considerably. The roads are still soaked and the traffic seems to be moving even faster than on a dry day, as though to make up for the lost time.

By the time we get to the KL exit it's only a drizzle. There's a way of doing this. In Malaysia, cars don't really slow for the exits, but rather brake well into the curve, wet roads or not. Where bikers are concerned car drivers also like a "sniff up the arse", coming within inches of a biker's panniers. All this is taken as Good Fun. Point is, these curves need to be taken at a bit of speed.

As I lean into the left turn I see a pair of high beams behind me as someone comes sniffing. It's a blue pickup that's gone right through Mike, who's had to give way and gone wide. I can see his Beemer's lights in the right mirror. When I glance forward again, it happens. Someone's left a thick cord of rope, or maybe a metal cable, right across my lane. It's probably blown off the back of some truck in the storm. With the gleam of the wet road and the rain on the visor, I only see it when I'm practically on top of it.

Don't touch the brake; the sniffing idiot behind won't be expecting that. Just lean in and watch the apex. As the front wheel hits the cord, it bumps up and I'm just on the rear wheel. Then the rear wheel hits, loses grip in the wet and starts to come forward. As the front wheel tracks again, I counter steer and the big bike twitches for an instant then hauls itself back on line. I think that if I wasn't already completely soaked I would have wet myself. The curve loosens up and soon the pickup's well behind us. Mike comes on the intercom again:

"Interesting riding, you alright?" he asks.

It's an effort to keep my voice calm. "Yeah, I'll be happy to get off this highway though."

A thought enters my mind, and stays for a surprisingly long time: Months of preparation, spreadsheets of dates to make and lectures to give, it could all have been buggered right then and there. All anyone would have heard about is that you got as far as K effing L. Now that's something worth thinking about.

After a night in KL, we get our Uzbek visas done the next day and head out on the highway again the following morning. As we pass the exit to Cameron Highlands at Batu Gajah, Mike gets on the intercom:

"OK, it's all new for me from here," he says.

"Sorry, what do you mean?"

"Never been further away from Singapore on a bike,"

Mike says. Then I remember. Viola and I had taken him to Cameron Highlands last year when he first got the Beemer. I look at the odometer. We've done just over 600 km, with another oh, about 20,000 km to go.

OUR FIRST OFFICIAL ENGAGEMENT is with the Mount Miriam Cancer Hospital in Penang. Our cameraman, Pierce, and all his equipement will be joining us there in the Bumblebee, piloted by Neo Chian and Sonny. Although we didn't get to meet him until the week before we left, Pierce would prove to be an invaluable asset. Not just for his photos and friendship, but also in getting two old codgers on bikes up to date with twenty-first century Internet access. With his head of shocking blonde hair, he was easy to find and a willing dogsbody whenever we needed help.

Two more friends, Yu Seung and his wife Rosalind, will be joining us on their bikes as well and riding up Thailand with us. Yu Seung is an experienced long distance rider with an encyclopedic knowledge of motorcycles and How Things Work. Rosalind is an unstinting supporter of breast cancer work who has returned to her very active life after her own diagnosis a few years ago. Together they are just the perfect people to have on the ride. For a while we had seriously considered doing the whole ride together but it was impossible for them to get away for so long and still keep their jobs.

I'm looking forward to Mount Miriam because it will be our first contact with breast cancer patients and their carers. Mount Miriam Hospital is a not-for-profit cancer hospital that has been caring for cancer patients for nearly 40 years.

Mike arrives at Mount Miriam to a shower of pink confetti; I'm just the sidekick.

As with all our collaborators, we have left it to the locals to determine how to make the most of our visit. In Penang, they've gone gala. We get to spend a night at the luxurious E&O hotel in Georgetown, then make the 11-km ride to the hospital the next morning escorted by the local big bike club all dressed up in pink. At the hospital there are television crews and a welcome committee followed by a tour of the facilities. After that, it's back to the E&O for a public health symposium.

We arrive at the hospital in a shower of pink confetti, with leathered up bikers over-revving their engines and all the hospital staff waving and crowding our bikes. It's our first experience of being celebrity riders and takes some getting used to. I feel like I've crashed an Elton John concert.

During the tour I discover that when the hospital started out, nuns were running what would be considered nowadays as a hospice service, taking in patients in the terminal phases of cancer, who could no longer manage at home. At first the nuns did everything on their own: ward administration, cancer counselling, clinical care, the lot. Some of the original nuns still serve, not so much in ward work but providing a distinct service often neglected in cancer hospitals: grief counselling for relatives and pastoral care for the terminally ill. They seem to be a comfort regardless of the religious beliefs of those under their care.

After the tour we head back in convoy again to the E&O for a breast cancer public symposium. Mike and I have been asked to give a lecture each and after this I'm required to facilitate a session where some of their breast cancer patients share their stories to the public.

It's my first time in such a role and it's not an entirely comfortable one. The patients who have come forward to share their stories are all articulate, well educated and not without means. And yet all have come late with their diagnosis, requiring radical surgery and chemotherapy. I only have a few minutes with them before we take the stage, and all I know about their history is given in a few brief handouts.

Looking through their charts I realise that many have an outside chance of surviving their cancers despite the treatment they've received. In our brief introduction before we go on stage I find that despite this they are all still very positive. They want to encourage people to come forward for screening, and to accept complete therapy in order to maximise their chances of survival. It's a good message, but something still troubles.

It's what Mike said all those months ago. Why didn't they come sooner? Why did they put trust with traditional healers with their empty promises and ineffective therapies?

Soon I'm sitting onstage next to a woman who delayed

coming for two years before going to the doctor. When we were introduced over morning tea she had said that she would be willing to answer any questions, but I still hesitate. Now she's sharing about the importance of finding support, about not keeping the problem to yourself but getting to care as soon as you feel a breast lump. The answers are all familiar and quite well-practiced. There's 15 minutes more to go and I have nothing left to ask that everyone doesn't know her answers to. Maybe it takes as much courage to ask the right questions as to give the honest answers.

I finally decide there's no other way to do this. "So why did you wait so long?" I ask her.

She looks startled. "I'm sorry?"

There's no backing out now. "You felt the breast lump for two years before coming forward. Why did you wait so long?"

She stares at me in silence. Like I said, sometimes words can lacerate. I guess I'm not going to be invited back here again. Have I sounded more like an interrogator than a facilitator? Unnerved, I back off.

"Right," I change tack desperately, "so when you went to the doctor, what did he do?"

She's still uncertain, but only for a moment. "No, that's a good question," she says. She's recovered now and looks me straight in the eye. "I waited because my husband and I were going through a bad period then. There was another woman, and he was threatening to leave. My son was still in school then and I needed him to stay to see my son through school."

Oh God.

"I knew that it was probably cancer because over the

months it didn't go away," she continues, "I knew that the treatment would have to remove my breast, but that would give my husband an excuse to leave. I needed my son to be a little older before he left."

I don't know what to say, but sense that she's not done yet. "What happened then?" I ask.

"I never told my husband about my cancer, but he left anyway," she laughs ironically. "But I haven't been alone through this. My son has been wonderful, and so have friends I've found here and in the support groups. I wish I had come earlier, but I can't do anything about that now. Except to tell other women."

After the symposium she comes up to me and thanks me for facilitating. She's says she's never talked about the reasons for her delay until today. I apologise for forcing her to make something like that public without any warning.

"No, you don't have to apologise," she smiles again, drying a tear as she continues, "you remember that silence on the stage just now?"

I nod, staring at my feet. "It seemed endless," I tell her, "that's why I lost my nerve and moved to another question."

"Well, that's the silence that kills. The silence of women who don't come forward when they feel something's wrong, because of all these fears. Thank you for giving me a chance to say that."

I was wrong. It takes a lot more courage to give an honest answer than it does to ask the right question.

Six
PHILIP FALLS APART

IT SEEMS LIKE MADNESS to leave but we have to go. What I would really like to do is stay at the wonderful E&O hotel for another night; it's been a pretty trying day already and baking hot outside. As it is, I don't even get to finish lunch. As soon as the symposium ends, I get the things down from the room to the bike, load up the panniers, one last photo session and head out to Hatyai.

The reason for the rush is that we have to get to Chiang Mai, some 2,000 km away with one border crossing in between, over the next four and a half days to make our obligations there. We don't have the luxury of another half day in Penang, no matter how warm the hospitality. For the first of many times over the next three months I discover how difficult it is to leave.

This time it's four bikes on the road, with Yu Seung and Rosalind linked to us through intercom. We cross the Penang Bridge and find ourselves back on the mainland again, heading up through Kedah to the Malaysian-Thai border. This is rice country and the highway is completely flat, lined on both sides by mile after mile of paddy fields. It is blindingly hot, but we stick to it, trying to make good time to the border at Bukit Kayu Hitam. In the end we needn't have worried, we clear customs with another three hours of daylight to cover the last 60 km into Hatyai.

Outside the customs complex, the Thai highway system begins, but it's nothing like the North-South highway in Malaysia. Here it's one lane each way, but most of all it's an open highway system where anyone can wander on to the road from either side.

It's been a long day, both physically and emotionally, and it's an effort keeping up with the others. I find that I'm starting to fixate on the road surface, made worse by the firm suspension and hard tyres I have. I'm not sure why I'm doing this but I find myself scrutinising every defect and squiggle in the asphalt.

Just outside of Hatyai I see an impossible pattern of parallel grooves in the road. On reflex I down shift and lag behind the other three bikes. It's impossible to tell what could have caused these ripples in the surface in the losing light. They run in parallel rows along the length of the road, across most of its width. It's only after I've slowed enough that I realise there's nothing wrong with the road at all. I've been fixating on the shadow of the telegraph cables by the side of the road, cast long by the setting sun. Odd, that — never made that mistake before. It's the first sign of real troubles ahead, but I had no idea.

We arrive at our hotel in Hatyai just at last light and after a very satisfying dinner we bring out the maps to see what is required tomorrow. It'll be the 24th. We have to get to Chiang Mai by the 27th in order to meet our next collaborators, the Faculty of Medicine of Chiang Mai University, on the 28th. Four days to cover about 1,900 km. We decide to make Chumphon tomorrow, just under 500 km away. Shouldn't be a problem. If all goes well we'll be there for a late lunch; there's a good beach to chill on.

Heading out of Hatyai the next day we realise quickly that until we get to Europe it is going to be typical Asian roads, not at all like the world-class highways in Malaysia.

No one seems too concerned about the Highway Code of keeping to lanes, checking blind spots, signalling before filtering, maintaining vehicles in good working order, or keeping to speed limits. There doesn't seem to be any rules about limiting the number of family members on a bike, or restricting the motorcycle-based transport of livestock or household furniture. As the miles go by Mike and I start a wager on who's going to spot the most unexpected cargo being transported by motorcycle. Mike wins it hands down. He's the first to call out a biker transporting another motorcycle, by motorcycle.

I find myself starting to notice little niggling things about the bike. Part of it might be due to the tyres I have on, which are meant more for poorer road conditions. They have large chunky bits and sharp cut–offs that are not ideal for cornering. Unfortunately, while these Thai highways may seem fairly straight on the map, in reality that's not quite true. There are dead straight bits which lead on to right-angled turns and I am finding that off-road tyres don't quite let me bank as I should.

Another problem is the heat, which Mike happily tells me is now 41 degrees, thanks to the thermometer on the Beemer. Not that we can do anything about it. Must make the distance, or we'll have too much to cover tomorrow.

What saves the day are the roadside Amazon Cafés. I have never tried one of these before, preferring the local coconut and sugarcane stalls, but Yu Seung and Ros are seasoned travellers on Highway 41 and swear by these things. They are air-conditioned, have meditative fountains (which somehow seem quite attractive now) and the iced tea is fabulous.

As we pull off Highway 41, it is 10 km to Chumphon and the sun is setting in our mirrors. Dinner is by the sea with this wonderful landward breeze before I stagger to bed.

The next day I'm hoping for a bit of an easier time on the bike. Yu Seung says that the beaches at Phetchaburi, some 300 km away, are some of the nicest in Thailand, where the wealthier class from Bangkok come to play. We would not be seeing the sea again until Iran and the Black Sea coast, so it would be the last bit of sand and surf before heading through the Asian land mass.

It's hard to explain why I'm already feeling a little out of sorts even as I load up the bike. There is no reason for it; it's a short day to the beach. Mike and Seung spend the time on the intercom chatting on about what they have planned if we manage to get there while the sun is still out. Pierce thinks that he can set off his drone and have some stunning shots of the bikes on the beach. I just want to get some rest.

As we get on the highway again my road fixation seems to continue. For some reason I'm not happy with my bike, and the frustrating thing is that I can't quite figure out what it is. She just doesn't feel right. Is it my imagination? Am I getting fixated on the fear of failing somehow, or is it just being too tired and the mind making stuff up? The others don't seem to be affected, and I find myself losing the thread of the conversations on the intercoms.

Yu Seung, Ros and Mike definitely seem more relaxed about things. They are certainly riding better and seem to be having a better time of it. In contrast I'm set on looking for where the dangers are and what's going wrong. It isn't so bad when we meet together at the drink stops. The worst part is when the tea is all drunk and the loos all visited. I'm getting more and more reluctant to get on the bike and on my own again. Alone and in the helmet and on the road I notice that I am starting to play things over again and again, and to constantly worry about whether I'm making enough speed or keeping my friends away from their beach resort.

Then on one of the right-angled turns, something happens which is new and very dangerous.

I feel the rear wheel wobble.

Can't be! I had taken off the rear wheel during those last tutorials with Ah Chye to learn how to change the drive chain. There was definitely no wobble then. Over the intercom I ask Yu Seung to have a look at the rear tyre and he sees no problem at all. I ask him to hang back for the next few curves and he doesn't see anything amiss. This could be because by now I am so spooked by the idea that I may have an unstable bike that the speed's dropped all the way down — nothing much wobbles at 60 km/h, but I'm pretty reluctant to test things harder.

Progress is slow and Mike, Yu Seung and Ros stay with me to help me sort out what's wrong. Gradually my speed comes up to normal again until finally on one of the turns just south of Hua Hin the rear wheel loses grip entirely and starts to come out before I counter steer and get it back on track. Yu Seung calls out even before I say anything:

"Yep. I saw that. That rear wheel's wobbling, but very slightly."

We pull over just south of Hua Hin behind a gas station. I get the V-Strom on the main stand and the boxes off. There is a definite wobble on the rear wheel, but the tensioners seem correctly set. Probably a worn bearing, but we haven't a spare. It's not something that you expect to go wrong this early and in the middle of nowhere. Besides, you can usually ride through it until the part's available, but with my thoughts on the way the bike feels, I figure we better fix it now.

I've been given phone numbers to call by some of the more experienced riders in Singapore just in case something like this happens. Soon I'm speaking in English to the chairman of the Thai chapter of the Tri-nations big bike group. After I send him our GPS location and explain what the problem was, he tells me to sit tight for about half an hour. Turns out that a Thai mechanic called Song has a shop not far away in Cha-Am. The necessary calls are made and he is on his way over.

Now that's a real relief. Not just that help is on the way. I don't understand why I'm losing trust in my bike after so short a time, and until Seung confirmed that wobble, I was starting to think it was all in my head.

The V-Strom undergoing major surgery in Cha-Am.

We have a simple roadside lunch and a short siesta when Song shows up with an orange pickup. He expertly rolls the V-Strom on the back and we're off to his shop. In five minutes the rear wheel is off and the bearings inspected. Almost to my relief I see what the problem is: they're both worn over. We get replacements from another shop a little up the street. The whole thing is done in under an hour and I take the bike for a short spurt up the road. The wobble is gone and the bike does genuinely feel better. I really hope that I'll start having a better time.

On the last 100 km to Phetchaburi we're caught in a torrential rain and have to halve our speed. Thai roads in the rain are really something. Because it is still the hot season it hasn't rained for some time and all the grease is smeared over the road with the downpour. There's no way of seeing where the bad patches are or to tell between a puddle and an open manhole.

I find myself keeping to the slow left lane and as the rain gets heavier I lose even more speed as I feel the tyres hydroplane again. On one horrid right hander as I make the right turn, I'm actually steering left with the rear wheel coming forward and a lorry overtaking. Yu Seung's been good enough to hang back with me and even he thought that was interesting riding.

With the three hours lost to getting the bike fixed it is just before sunset when we arrive at the lovely resort that the support crew has picked out. They have made much better time getting here, and are relaxing with drinks in hand when we show up. Ah, the joys of motorcycle touring! I was so hoping for a pampered afternoon, but instead it is already nightfall when I stagger to dinner.

Over dinner we talk things over with the support crew. We know that we have two days to make it to Chiang Mai, some 900 km away. I feel I'm slowing down everyone and we need to discuss the options. To make the last day's riding we would have to make at least Nakhon Sawan, preferably Phitanoulok. At Chiang Mai there will be a day without riding when we have to give lectures at the medical school. Hopefully that rest from the saddle can get me to unwind. I need to get something off my chest with the rest.

"Listen people. I don't know what's wrong with me. I've never been so tense on a bike before. I know part of it is to do with these tyres and maybe that bearing, but they really shouldn't be affecting me this much. I just wish we had more time to unwind."

"Not sure what you're on about," says Seung, "it was a worn bearing. After that we all had to slow for the rain anyway. You're doing alright."

"Well I'm grateful you feel that way, I just think I'm holding the group up. It's not quite the tour of famous Thai beaches we planned."

We decide that we should stay as a group. I would either try and keep up, or they would slow, or beyond a certain threshold we would have to make the decision to put my bike on the back of the support vehicle and I would take a break. Suddenly Boss's precaution of that bike rack doesn't seem so much of an overkill after all.

As I get to the hotel room all I'm sure about is being really tired, but there is almost certainly something else. There has to be. I've taken this bike, even more heavily loaded with the missus in the back, up similar roads before without any trouble. There's something on my mind and with enough rest and quiet I might possibly get to the bottom of it, but there isn't time to do anything but ride.

UP AT DAWN AGAIN the next day. The first 10 km or so from the beach to rejoin Highway 41 is really quite idyllic. There is something quite therapeutic about going through villages and hamlets with the sights, smells and sounds of people just getting up for another day — smoke fires, roosters crowing, doors opening, that wonderful hacking sound that rural folk make when clearing their throats in the morning.

Back on Highway 41 it's not long before we are in the thick of it again. It's a single lane each way until you get to a traffic junction when it can open up to three or four lanes. When the light turns everybody tries to find their space as the lanes revert to the single arrangement. This means tankers, lorries, pickups, bikes, bullock carts. In addition there is also a painted shoulder on the side of the road. That's where bikes are supposed to be, not on the road proper. It's probably appropriate for the 75cc local *kap cai* motorcycle, but an impossible arrangement to keep on bikes our size and speed.

What this means is that Thai drivers are not quite prepared for you to be on the road with them. You certainly cannot expect them to respect your personal space. So if you shift out to overtake, the oncoming traffic will have no qualms about going through you; you're not even supposed to be on the road, much less overtaking. And if you're too slow, the Thai driver coming up from behind might not bother about overtaking; he'll just go through you — you're supposed to be on the shoulder.

With bikes like ours there's a clear solution to this, which is to make use of the power available. Keep the revs in a sweet spot, stay right on the tail of the vehicle in front, looking for that overtake. Clear road ahead means a quick out and back in again. Thai drivers are pretty cool with you if they see what you intend to do, and if you make it clear, hey man, it's live and let live. Thai drivers are a pretty chilled lot if you don't behave like an idiot.

Like a broken record I'm running though the same thoughts as I had yesterday. Why am I not going fast enough? Where would we be now if I wasn't holding them up? What was that little shift in the grip? My fixation with the road surfaces has gone to another level altogether. I've scrutinised so many of them that I've developed my own classification system:

a. Ridges — these are found at the traffic junctions where trucks have to wait for the lights. Their weight carves out two furrows with this bit of intact tarmac in between. The problem is that on a bike it isn't easy to balance on these ridges as I slow down for the lights. The bit between the ridges tends to be melted asphalt when the combination of the hot sun and the baking from the overhanging truck engine turns the tar to goo. I can hear chunks of it come off the tyres and onto the bike when I move off.
b. Ripples — these are found just after the lights when trucks use some of that massive torque and push the asphalt back like a throw rug off the road. It makes for interesting riding when the lane markings are also rubbed off in the same process as I try to jostle with other cars and trucks for a place on the road as we move off.
c. Patches — where the asphalt has been ripped away entirely leaving the black basal layer. This looks as if a maintenance crew has taken it away because it tends to take up precisely one lane, sometimes two (then I'm in real trouble). Because this layer is softer it gets furrowed and over time the furrows are filled with oil, grease and whatever trucks spill on the road for fun.
d. Ropes — I really don't know how these are made but they look like lashes on the road, as though someone has flogged it and there is a groove that whips all over the lanes. Most of them are harmless although it's difficult to tell which are the dangerous ones when you're travelling at speed, so I tend to slow down. They don't usually cause much trouble although occasionally they get the

Thai cooking: on Thailand's famous Highway 41

bike to "skip", which is all right because she usually corrects herself. Ropes can't be seen at speed and just thinking of them, which I am having trouble avoiding, tends to keep my speed down.

I start looking for these defects in the road as soon as we get onto the highway, which is difficult because it's a scorcher and the air over the baking tarmac shimmers and blurs the surface. It isn't until much later that I realise that I'm not in control of these thoughts; they just come.

Most of all, I feel a sense of foreboding, that there is something in my mind that I haven't had the chance to find and sort out. After a few minutes on the highway this morning I realise it's not going to need looking for. It's going to make its appearance all by itself today. Today there's something new: fear. It's not in the forefront just yet, but it's there in the shadows.

It's like one of those horror movies when the expendable minor character (usually the black dude) walks into a dark room with a thunderstorm outside. He mucks about looking for the light switch and then suddenly a flash of lighting shows — just for an instant — this godawful nine-eyed, tentacled horror towering behind him. The plot usually takes a predictable turn soon after. My problem now is that I'm getting a lot of those flashes. I'm frightened of the speed, the road, and most of all, of overtaking.

Now those who don't ride will think, *well, what's so surprising about that?* Adventure biking means hurtling down horrid roads in a foreign country at ungodly speeds. A good dose of fear is probably what keeps adventure riders alive.

I'm here to tell you that's utter rubbish. What keeps a rider alive is calmness and instinct. Riders need to be in a kind of Zen state. Calmness is the very opposite of being excitable or panicky, which is what I am now.

Instinct has two parts. A baseline, anticipatory part arranges for the least dangerous situation while engaging in very hazardous activity — checking mirrors, moving out of blind spots, taking the right line. The other part of instinct is reacting to unplanned changes: always instant but never sudden. Calm, instinctive riding is what keeps riders alive.

Fear is when you stop trusting all of that. When you doubt your ability to make those instant alterations, when you needlessly re-check what your senses are telling you, when you prepare for contingencies that could not possibly happen, and overreact when a small change is all that's required. Fear makes you tense up, tensing makes you tired, being tired makes you slower, and being slower keeps you on the bike longer, and the cycle just goes on. Good bikers are not fearful. Fearful riders don't live long enough to get good.

What I'm sensing very quickly after the fear is bewilderment. No, really, today's ride has hardly got started but I'm completely out of sorts. I mean, what the HELL doesn't even begin to capture this moment. When was the last time I couldn't manage? In Afghanistan we had rocket attacks on our position pretty much every night towards the end and I kept working. That horrid night when we took four major casualties in one hour and I can't remember how many walking wounded — I sorted things out and everyone got out alive. I'm the man with the plan. I don't do scared. This is something entirely new.

Here on this Thai road the worst part is that it does not feel as if the fear is ever going to go away. If anything it is starting to feel like it might go all the way to panic, like going down one of those pool slides where there doesn't seem to be anything to grab hold of. When was the last time I EVER panicked? And I can tell that very close behind that panic is despair. That after all that planning and promise I'm going to fail.

Just before lunch I find myself behind a truck on second gear going up a hill, unable to bring myself to get out to the overtaking lane. Mike, Ros and Yu Seung are so far ahead they aren't even within intercom range. I'm trying to remember when I last felt like this. When was the last time I let fear interfere with what I needed to do? I know I don't have a head for heights but that's usually within some control. If I really want it to go away I can put it at the back of my mind. This is something different. I have no idea where it comes from or why it's here or how to make it go away.

Thankfully the truck turns off at the top of the hill and I have a nice stretch of road ahead. I open up the speed but nothing more than 70 km/h, beyond which I have the sensation that this is travelling awfully fast. If I weren't so shit scared I would be laughing my head off. This is all so crazy. Doing 70 on this bike is between second and third gear and there are six forward gears available. Soon I see the three of them waiting at the side of the road under a tree for me. We are already way behind schedule and Ros signals for me to keep going. They soon overtake me anyway, Mike and Yu Seung going ahead while Ros sweeps behind me.

As we come up the next batch of slow traffic I can see what they're doing. They aren't just slowing down for me; they're nursing me through the overtaking. They would stay out on the outside lane and tell me when it's clear to come through. Soon they realise its not the coming out I have a problem with, it's picking up enough speed to clear the trucks and come back to my side of the road. I tell them to go ahead, but Ros still sweeps behind me. I hear her on the intercom:

"You alright, Phil?"

"Er, not quite. It's not the bike though," I reply. It's a choked up, guttural voice I hardly recognise.

"Yes, I can see you're riding really upright, and really tensed up. What's up?"

"Oh man, that's not the half of it." I decide that maybe if I actually tell somebody what I'm going through it might make things better.

"Right," I tell her over the intercom, "you see that mark in the road ahead? Those ridges? Well, I'm pretty convinced that if I take that at any speed at all the bike will lose traction. That bend in the road that we just went through? The only reason I made the bend was because I was going this slow. Anything faster and I would have come off."

Silence. Then Ros, bless her, trying to be as gentle as possible, "Er, what mark on the road?"

Oh hell, you mean there's nothing there? I've made a classification system on something that isn't even there? Whatever it is that I've got, I've got it worse than I think I do.

"OK you hang in there, Phil, I'll be back." Effortlessly she overtakes everything ahead of me to get back within comms range with Mike and Yu Seung. Pretty soon Mike's gone ahead while Yu Seung and Ros hang back with me.

"OK Phil," Yu Seung says, "just relax. I can tell you're holding your breath. We have lots of time. Your bike's fine, there's no more wobble, we'll get where we need to go, Ros and I will stay with you."

"That's great, no, really, I appreciate it, but I think I'm in big trouble here, not the bike."

"What do you mean?" asks Yu Seung.

Again I talk about the road markings, about the way the bike seems to be travelling so fast.

"What, you mean that small bump in the road?" It looked like a lot more than a small bump to me, maybe even a patch of oil.

Bikers are pretty practical minded people. They really do try to help. Over the next 100 km or so, Seung and Ros hang back with me in the stifling heat and do everything practically possible to convince me that this is a safe road. They ask me to point out a dangerous patch as soon as I see it and then they take it at normal speed with no consequence.

They watch my bike like hawks to see any sign of instability. At one point we even switch bikes, with Yu Seung taking my V-Strom in exchange for his 650. The lighter bike does seem a lot easier to handle but I still can't get up to my usual speeds at all.

By the time we get to Nakhon Sawan it's nightfall, and the decision is simple. The three of them will ride on to Chiang Mai tomorrow. It's going to be an early start so we have to rack the bike up tonight. I'm not really up for dinner and despite their tiredness everyone gets out their head torches and we assemble the bike rack at the back of the Bumblebee, with the panniers on the roof.

When everything's packed away, I have a quiet moment with Mike.

Not overkill after all – the V-Strom finding its place on the Bumblebee

"It's not quite the Thai ride we were hoping for," I start. I don't think I've ever felt so weary.

"Nope. You're having anxiety attacks but it's really nothing to worry about. I've seen it many times before. Usually it goes away after a few days. Recovery is expected especially if treatment is started early. And there are drugs we can get at Chiang Mai that will almost definitely make it go away."

"Trouble is," I point out, "we don't have a few days. There's pretty tough riding every day, and I've just made your ride tomorrow longer than it needs to be."

"Really, not to worry. Tomorrow's tomorrow. Get some rest and we'll try again after Chiang Mai."

Seven
PROZAC RIDER

THE NEXT MORNING WE start out right after daybreak. Without me to slow them down, their progress is much quicker. Within two hours the temperatures start to soar again and is rarely below 40 degrees all the way to Chiang Mai. The working hypothesis is that I'm simply worn out from all the preparation work and trying to keep on schedule.

When we get to the hotel in Chiang Mai we have a warm welcome from the other members of the four by four group who are already in the lobby waiting for us. To save their travelling time they had come up directly from Singapore over two days. This adds another four vehicles to our convoy.

It's good to see them. They're old hands at crossing borders and we'll have to cross from Thailand to Laos and then into

China in two days after we finish in Chiang Mai. After that we'll be spending the longest period in a single country: over four weeks in China. During that time we will be entirely dependent on a group of fixers that they are familiar with.

I had planned for a nice break in Chiang Mai before the tougher roads of Laos and southern Yunnan. Diana, an old friend since my mountain biking days, had taken up residence here since retiring a few years ago. It would be good to see a friendly face after the events of the last few days. Now over some of the best Thai food and Chang beer, Diana is giving me a worried look. We're having dinner with her husband David and some of his business associates at this restaurant on the bank of a manmade lake at the outskirts of the city. A cool night breeze blows in from over the water. Diana has been speaking to Yu Seung and Ros on the way up and has heard about my troubles.

"What do you think the problem is?" she asks.

"Not sure. For one thing I've made the distances too long. Really tired but can't stop because of the meetings we've lined up."

"Why not just rest? You look really bad. And the weather this week is hot even by Thai standards."

"Nothing I would like to do more," I reply. I feel pretty torn up about the whole thing. I had let Diana know months before about the dates and even planned a bit of off road riding around her home just outside of the city. I can't remember whether it was Chiang Mai that moved their dates forwards or Mount Miriam that had moved theirs back, but the result is this cramped schedule.

What was supposed to be a nice few days of rest and

catching up with an old friend suddenly seems so full of things to do. Tomorrow we are to give lectures at the department of surgery of Chiang Mai University (CMU), there's an afternoon programme that has not been confirmed yet and then dinner with some of the faculty. Somewhere in between I'll need to get the tyres changed to hopefully help my riding, and maybe find a way to get the tar off most of the underside of the bike.

All that is for tomorrow though. Now there's a nice feeling around the table. Mike, Ros and Yu Seung are pretty serious mountain bikers themselves and it's very much a gathering of kindred spirits. Diana soon has us wondering if we'll all wind up spending our retirement years here, with her tales of unlimited mountain biking routes, in perfect temperatures if we come at pretty much any other time of the year. The cold beers make the hours pass quickly and before we know it we're the only ones left in the place. I'm just happy to not be riding tomorrow. Diana's been telling the rest of the gang about our adventures in the past together, especially one particular episode which resulted in a torn shoulder, three fractured ribs and a mild concussion.

"Ah," Mike says to Diana, "so it's all your fault."

"What is?"

"You never warned us what a shite biker Philip is."

THE NEXT MORNING MIKE and I are dressed in our suits and neckties. A CMU van picks us up from the hotel to the Maharaj Nakorn Chiang Mai Hospital for our lectures. The CMU and its associated hospital are the main provincial university and tertiary hospital for most of northern Thailand. It serves a population of about five million people. About two million are in the city proper and the rest in surrounding rural areas. Essentially they handle with one hospital what five general hospitals manage in Singapore, with far greater travelling distances and other barriers to care.

My contact person with CMU is Prof Malai Muttarak, the past head of radiology. I've had the pleasure of working with her in setting up multidisciplinary breast cancer conferences throughout Asia. Last year I was very happy to have one of their trainees, Dr Phananporn, stay with us for a few months to see how she might help to bring our multidisciplinary care model back to CMU. Phan, as she insists we call her, has in good measure that natural grace that seems unfairly bestowed on northern Thai women. I remember an unusual interest in breast cancer work among the male surgical residents when she was with us.

This morning Phan is presenting the cases at the tumour board after our lectures for discussion with the local faculty. After the first half dozen or so cases, something strikes me: I feel like I'm at my own tumour boards back home. Most of the patients have presented to their doctors with relatively small cancers, many of them detected by mammograms. With the access to modern chemotherapy and hormone therapy, an excellent prognosis can be expected for most of these ladies. I'm curious how these women got their mammograms done, and what made them come forward so early. Phan explains that most of the patients are from the city, and that mammograms are commonly available through private medical insurance. Many others were detected during "opportunistic" screening, when portable mammograms services would go out to the community at regular health fairs and public education programmes. I remember Malai telling me her involvement in bringing the breast awareness message out to the offices and schools. This level of awareness and the consequent probability of long survival are the results of decades of good work.

This is in sheer contrast to patients who come from rural areas outside of the city. Breast cancer is almost always painless until the very late stages when cure is often already out of reach. At that time, the spread of disease to other organs may lead to non-breast symptoms such as headaches, bone aches, breathlessness and abdominal pain. Rural folk tend not to present to medical care until there's pain, and often after they've been to their traditional healers, sometimes for years. That so many of them perish at their incurable stage of disease soon after going to the hospital in the city does not help improve their opinion of modern medical treatment.

After lunch we are given a short tour of the surgical intensive care and the cancer unit. Unexpectedly, Mike says that he has something to attend to, and I'm on my own on the rounds.

Sister Song is in charge of the surgical oncology intensive care ward and possesses that demeanor that seems to pervade senior ward nurses the world over. An acute surgical ward is a busy place but there is an aura of calm and order about her. She has that neatness, both in dress as well as clarity of thinking that sends a clear message: The nice thing about anything she can't manage is that it probably doesn't exist.

A small teaching round starts with some surgical and

medical oncology residents as Sister presents the cases. After the morning sessions it's not quite what I expected. The first case is an emaciated woman, her face angular from wasted facial muscles, neck muscles standing out in her effort to take each breath. Her skin and sclera are yellowed and a tube sticks out between her ribs on the left side, draining light yellowish fluid into an underwater sealed bottle under the bed.

"Admitted two days ago, metastatic breast cancer from the villages, for palliative care," Sister Song says. We talk about comfort care, the role of palliative chemotherapy and end-of-life issues.

The next case is a patient whom one of the trainees had seen earlier: "This lady was admitted from the villages with investigation for abdominal pain, and found to have locally advanced breast cancer."

After obtaining consent she lifts the patient's hospital blouse away. A cratered ulcer has replaced the right breast, but what is more worrying is the abdomen is grossly distended with fluid. Most likely spread to liver. We talk about comfort care and the role of surgery in metastatic disease.

At the third bed Sister Song is momentarily flustered. It's an unusual sight in the busy ward: the bed is empty. She had intended to demonstrate this case of advanced breast cancer from the villages, but the patient had died suddenly in the early morning, possible pulmonary embolism.

As I'm led out of the wards I catch our reflection in the intensive care windows. I had not realised it before, but compared to the Thai doctors and nurses I look huge. The men don't even come up to my shoulder. That only exacerbates the feeling I've been having since the round started. I'm useless here. It's that phrase we hear again and again: "From the villages."

I have a depressing feeling that as we enter the Asian landmass from its southern back door, we are going to keep hearing it: from the villages. And it will always be the same thing. Women presenting late to their doctors, beyond the reach of effective medical treatment.

After the rounds we meet Mike at the hospital lobby and get into a CMU van. We have one of the surgical trainees who speaks some English accompanying us and he mentions that we are being taken to the new Women's Health Centre. He tells me that this is what Phan has helped to set up since returning from her time with us. I guess we're going to sit in on some clinics. This should be interesting; I wonder how much of what we do has to be adapted to local conditions. As we round a corner we see a particularly impressive spanking new yellow themed building decked out in pink buntings and balloons. A thick red carpet rolls out from the main entrance under a pink archway, with a seven-piece traditional music group standing by. I point it out to Mike, who is sitting in the row behind me.

"Must be waiting for some VIP," I tell him.

"Yeah, maybe even some royalty ... have you ever seen anything so pink ... er, hang on ..." We both notice our Long Ride logo on the buntings at the same time.

Our van turns into the driveway, and before we can close our gaping mouths we come to a stop at the head of the red carpet, and the side door of the van slides open. On their cue, the band strikes up traditional Thai music.

We both sit dumbfounded, staring out of the van at

the camera crews and what looks like a very well-dressed welcoming committee coming towards us. I hope that if I blink hard enough they might disappear but there they still are.

"Um, I think it's for us, Mike," I manage without moving my lips. "Did you know about this?"

"Yeah. Like I knew we were going to open a building but failed to mention it. What do you think?"

"What do we do now?" I feel like telling the driver to make a break for it. A quiet roadside tea would do me good right about now, but the driver has already gotten out for a smoke.

"Well we can't stay in the van, Phil. I'll be right behind you."

I step onto the red carpet and a very attractive nurse drapes a garland over me. I keep telling myself I can do this. *You've seen this done before, Phil, just pretend you're royalty.* There is a row of staffers on one side of the red carpet who is being introduced to me by our helpful resident, and I can just make out Malai inside the building. Short-term goal: Try to get to Malai without falling over. There are camera crews and lights everywhere.

I can't really remember much of what happened next. I think I started shaking hands, because that's what I've seen royalty do. This doesn't go too well. Thais aren't much for hand shaking. They do this *wai* thing. A very graceful upward steepling of the fingers under the chin with a respectful bow. Halfway down the row I think that this is so much more appropriate than shaking hands and start to follow suit, right about the time they start hand shaking. Instead of the *wai*, it

Mike, a very proud Malai and me.

must have dawned on them that I'm more of a *farang* after all. Towards the end it was both the handshake and the *wai*, or the *wai* then the handshake. I think Mike was following behind me, doing his best to keep a straight face and not to record this whole thing.

It is the grand opening of the Chiang Mai Women's Health Centre. And it is quite something. There are a lot of very important people. Speeches are made, and I cut a ribbon, then *wai*-ed everyone. We then watch a traditional dance by some delightfully sweet Thai children before Malai takes us around on a tour of the facilities.

I can tell Malai is especially proud of this place. The emphasis appears to be on breast and cervical cancer screening, but also antenatal and menopausal care. What she is particularly proud of is the one-stop breast service, with on-site outpatient clinics, digital mammography and ultrasounds, and pathology reads. It would make anyone proud.

There's another reason why it's such a special day. At the end of all the official business we pass the child dancers in the lobby waiting for their rides home. They still have their costumes on. When I point out one of the dancing girls in the troupe who was especially graceful, Malai lifts up the girl in her arms, turns to me and says proudly, "My granddaughter!" I think that made her day as much as anything else.

We meet Yu Seung in the hotel lobby after the CMU van drops us off. We had left the bike keys with Seung for the day and he had the bikes sent to this professional bike cleaner and also made arrangements for a tyre change for me. By the end of the day we had the cleanest bikes in Chiang Mai and the cleaners had an experience they would talk about for a long time. The Suzuki also has a new pair of Pirelli Scorpion Trails, the tyres I use as a default back home. I'm so happy and grateful that I actually take a bit of a ride around Chiang Mai before heading back to the hotel.

After dinner with Malai and Phan, Mike comes to my room and shows me what he's managed to get hold of in the hospital. It's a two-month supply of Fluoxetine 20mg tablets, with a shorter prescription of sedatives.

"Prozac? You think I should start taking Prozac?" I have never been on any kind of anti-depressants before. Now, don't think I'm offering any kind of resistance. Right now I'm willing to try just about anything.

"Yes, definitely." Mike answers. He had discussed things with the Chiang Mai doctors and they had also concurred that it was probably the best thing.

"OK, when do you think I should start?"

"Now. It may take a week or so to work. Steady state takes a bit longer. You may have to take it for the rest of the ride. We can get some more from Singapore when Viola or Boss joins the ride."

"You've prescribed this before?" I ask.

"Yep. Remember what you have isn't uncommon, even if it is scaring the sweet bejesus out of you. It's quite common among professionals, although nobody likes to talk about it. I have known people who have been on it for years. Not in Singapore, much more open and accepted in Sweden and Norway."

"Right then," I agree, "we're certainly not as open about this in Asia. Not sure how many people would want to know their surgeon was on a neuroactive drug. I remember reading something about Prozac. That it essentially blunts the peaks and troughs. If you're depressed it makes you less depressed and if you're high it brings you down."

"That's about right," Mike says. "On the whole it makes you *nicer*."

"Ah right. Side effects?"

"Well it's on the insert. Mainly about drug interactions, which is not a problem because you're not on anything else.

By the way is Viola coming up anytime soon?"

"No, I think we're planning to meet only in Istanbul, although she is thinking of coming up to Chengdu."

"Ah good. It's just that I think it might also treat premature ejaculation."

"What?"

"Never mind ... how are you feeling after the rest? Ready for Laos?"

"Actually I feel pretty good. The bike's riding a lot better with the Scorpions. I think we've come to the end of the hot bit, I'll be quite happy to never see Highway 41 again."

THAT NIGHT I TAKE my first Prozac and feel ... exactly the same. *Well, give it a little time,* I think.

When I get up in the morning I'm sitting upright in bed before I even know I'm awake, with a very definite sense of dread, but about what, I'm unable to sort out. It's still dark outside. Inexplicably, my first thought is that I must have been awoken by a trauma call, that means I need to get my sorry self to the hospital in thirty minutes to stop someone from dying quickly. Then I remember where I am.

Out of the habit of the last two weeks I get out of bed and into the big riding pants, slip on a clean T-shirt—there was time to do the washing over the last two days—socks and boots and then the wristwatch. A quick glance at the time stops me in my tracks: It's 4:30 am in the morning. I'm wide awake and for some reason, I think that I need to rush, that there's someone dying. It's impossible to get back to sleep again, so I sit on the edge of the bed and try to sort things out in my head.

Dialogue with self:
- *Why am I up?*
- *Oh, that's easy. To get ready for the first day on the bike.*
- *Let me re-phrase. Why am I up so friggin' early?*
- *To have enough time to pack and have a good breakfast.*
- *Er, it's all packed. All that's needed is the toilet bag and clothes bag on the bike. Panniers all up. Tyres and fluids were checked at the mechanics yesterday.*
- *Well, you don't want to keep people waiting, don't want to slow them down. It's 300 km to the Thai-Laos border, and then another 240 to Luang Namtha near the border with China. Big riding day today!*
- *It's two hours before they even serve breakfast. The alarm clock hadn't even gone off but something's woken you up. And it doesn't take two hours to load a bike. What woke you up? What's really going on?*
  [Pause]
- *I'm sorry, I haven't a clue.*

Just for good effect I take another Prozac and get ready very slowly. By the time I get to the lobby, Mike is already there, munching away at the packed breakfast. Ros and Yu Seung have news. They'll be heading off on their own and not crossing into Laos with us. I am quite sad about this. They've been an invaluable help coming up and I was hoping for some proper trouble-free riding before parting ways. I have not been my jovial self and the furthest from good company and was hoping to make it up to them.

After a few minutes it's back to just Mike and I on the bikes again. The sun's barely come up and Chiang Mai still lies silent. Being up in the hills means it's about perfect riding temperature and it's one of the nicest riding roads in Thailand today – Highway 118 between Chiang Mai and Chiang Rai. I haven't ridden for three days and am feeling fresh. I know that just a little time out of the saddle would get me into the groove again.

The roads are better here, and there is that smooth, wonderful grip from these Scorpions. Through the intercom we start the usual chatter. There is a sense that things are going to get better, and we can start the ride proper now. Highway 118 is dead straight heading out of Chiang Mai and at this time in the morning almost entirely empty. It's the best time to ride, before the heat really starts to turn on, and the only aberration I notice is that Mike seems to be going quicker than usual. I'm catching up with him only at the lights. I guess it's the sensible thing to do, try to get as much done before the heat comes up again.

Before long we enter the Khun Chae national park. This is where it really doesn't feel like Thai riding at all. The roads here follow the ridgelines; sweeping curves take us through one canyon to the one beyond. At the sharp ascents there are still those bits where the heavy trucks have rubbed off the surface asphalt but on the whole it's good surface. Tall conifers lining the sides of the road provide shade from the rising sun, and through them we can see mountain streams and glittering waterfalls.

We're not in a big rush but we're making good time. I'm trying to keep under 100 km/h until the new tyres are broken in, and Mike is keeping behind me. By late morning we are almost 150 km from Chiang Mai already and the day is starting to warm up.

In any group riding the guy in front always has the advantage to get away. He spots the road and the overtaking chances first, and the following bike will have to bide his time while the first guy pulls ahead. The first sign of trouble is when I notice it's harder to stay ahead of Mike.

"You alright, Phil?" asks Mike on the intercom.

"Yeah, so far so good. Can feel myself tightening up though," I reply.

"Yeah, I can see that too."

"Really? How?"

"You start breathing hard, and then you stop breathing. I can hear it on the comms set." The mouthpiece is so close to my face that he can make this out.

The road is starting to have its share of slow trucks and buses and I don't seem to be managing them as smoothly as I should. Then, while overtaking a truck up a steep hill, I'm late in getting back into my own lane, pulling in at high speed at the apex of the hill. Immediately ahead is a steeper descent then I'm expecting, with a sharp left turn. Larger street barriers and chevrons on both sides of the road indicate this is an accident area. I touch on the rear brake a little harder than I should and gear down, making the curve but losing too much speed. The truck I've just overtaken now can't slow down because he's heading downhill now, right up my mirrors, it seems. In a moment of terror I can't make the simple countermeasure of opening the throttle and getting out of trouble. Out of pure self-preservation I head to the shoulder and let him pass. Mike gets on the intercom as he flashes by:

"You alright, Phil?"

"No, definitely not. Something's just happened. Not sure what it is." I can barely recognise my own voice. Something definite had made me hit those brakes as hard as that. I've felt it before and it takes me only a moment to work out when. It's what woke me up this morning. Difference is that now I'm wide awake when it happens and I can clearly put a finger on it. This morning the nine-eyed tentacled beast had retreated before I saw it. Now it's not even trying to get back into the darkness. The dread isn't for someone who might die if I don't wake up. It's the conviction that *I'm* going to be killed.

This is completely different from being afraid. This is being frozen. Can't breathe, can't take my eyes off scrutinising separate bits of gravel on the road surface, can't even make myself look into the mirrors for sheer horror of what might be coming up behind me. All this even after the bike's stopped.

Mike doubles back to me on the road shoulder. I've already stopped for a full five minutes and I see him walking up to me in my mirrors, but I can't move. The visor's fogging up from my heavy breathing and it takes an effort just to lift the helmet off.

I forcibly hold my breath to stop the hyperventilating. I'm making these strange gagging noises, trying to choke back the tears. Mike comes up and stands next to me, hand on my shoulder, saying nothing. After a few minutes I get off and side-stand the bike. The day's properly hot now and through the trees we see one of those really inviting streams. Mike calls for the support vehicle to pick up the V-Strom and we settle down by the stream to talk this through.

There's nothing to do but wait for the truck. We take our

boots off and soak our feet into the cool waters of the stream. I wish I could just stay here, the last thing I want to do is get back onto that bike again. Mike takes out a chocolate bar. I really wish things had worked out and that a rest was all I needed. Clearly it's a lot more than that.

"Better put the bike back up, Mike, it's a long enough day for you. I would like to keep trying but it won't be fair to hold everyone up."

"Yeah," says Mike. He has the knack of saying just the right thing at the right time, but he also knows he can't sort this out for me. "Don't worry about this. You know, it's early days yet, you've been on treatment now for only two days," he says.

If it takes a week for that Prozac to kick in, that means I'm going to miss all of Laos and probably not get on the bike again until after Kunming. All that wonderful road in Yunnan. A week seems like ages, but if I had only known then just how long it would take before I rode normally again, I might have even turned back to Singapore instead of going on.

Eight
ENTERING CHINA

Our ride turns from the ordinary to the epic on entering China. Malaysia, Thailand, Laos, even Cambodia and Vietnam, can be reached by bike from Singapore without too much trouble. Border crossings across those countries are relatively straightforward, getting the bike there and back is really just a matter of how much time you have, and living is definitely cheap.

All that changes here. The border crossing is notoriously difficult, almost impossible to cross on a strict timeline without the help of local minders. This is where Irene, a local tour operator that our four by four crew has used before, will be invaluable. A real stickler for details, we had met her in Singapore some six months before leaving when she finalised the routes with us and outlined some of the challenges.

To ride our own vehicles in China means having to sit for a written driving test and getting a temporary Chinese license for the bike. Travel in private vehicles isn't allowed without a local guide. Bikes are not allowed on the highways and can only take the local B roads. Which means our group of bikes and four by fours will have to be divided. Two groups of vehicles and therefore two groups of minders, all adding to the cost of travelling for a whole month. There'll be lots of local laws to deal with later; these are just the highlights before we even get started.

Even though I really don't feel like it, Irene suggests that I ride across. It would be a lot easier than having to explain a bike on a rack, looking suspiciously like an import rather than a tourist's bike. Now as we come to the Laos-China border we catch a glimpse of what life is going to be like for the next month. The Laos side is cleared quickly enough before we enter no-man's land between the two countries. This unshaded area has an overfilled car park with all sorts of vehicles spilling over to the surrounding bush, in no particular order.

Our convoy pulls into the car park, out over the curb and finds a shady spot on some clay soil at the side of the road. We can see that the last 1 km before the Chinese border posts is just rows of container trucks packed tightly as far as the eye can see. None of them have their engines running. The road runs up a little slope with a dirt track to its left.

The four by four people have done this before and for the first time we hear something that'll be a routine for the next few weeks. Whenever there's any kind of trouble: call Irene. Our liaison is Hung Tuan, the leader of the four by

Mike and the bike: the best way to see China up close.

four group, who is already on the phone with her. Turns out she's already waiting on the China side but can't get through. Apparently there are some truckers who are working out the order of the queue to get into China and since it's the same narrow road that truckers leaving China have to take, we can expect protracted negotiations.

It's never a good sign when you see truckers turn off engines and leave their cabs for a game of cards under the trees. Here we have them watching soap operas on mobile phones, drying laundry and brewing up tea, mostly under their loaded trucks to get out of the sun.

After about an hour someone comes by to take our passports and the papers for the bikes. When they're returned, Hung Tuan says the bikes can cross. The problem is how to get through the trucks. I think I actually saw one of the truck drivers taking out his watercolours.

Mike and I start the bikes up and decide to take that dirt track by the side of the road. This leads to another car lot where we squeeze our way through gradually narrower gaps between container trucks. Before long we come to an improvised roundabout managed by a completely bewildered Chinese customs official. There's road-widening works all around. To the right and completely out of place at this dusty construction site of a border crossing is a duty free shop that looks right out of downtown Singapore. It's all gleaming glass and aluminum, with larger than life posters of Diane Kruger pursing her lips, impossibly pale Japanese models and Chinese cigarette advertisements. In front of it, under a pink umbrella, is our guide and fixer for the next month.

Irene is physically quite diminutive. She stands just an inch over five feet, and the pink umbrella and parking attendant's sunhat don't make her more intimidating. Since we first met in Singapore she's always reminded me of Dolores Umbridge, that teacher from Hogwarts who always appears in pink and constantly takes, er, umbrage. Like Ms Umbridge, first impressions of Irene can be most misleading. She would turn out to be the main reason we ever got through China so smoothly.

Now she greets Mike and I with bottles of cold water and introduces us to the duty free shop manager, who is very happy to see her. Then she excuses herself, opens the umbrella and steps out towards the customs official at the roundabout. Mike and I settle on the curb by the bikes, sip bottled water and watch How Irene Clears Traffic. We get all our four by four crew in thirty minutes.

Hung Tuan says it's the fastest turnaround he's ever seen on the China-Laos border; Irene must be in rare form. After the four by four crew do their best to empty the duty-free store of cigarettes and booze, we head off for Jing Hong in Mengla County, some 200 km away.

CHINA IS A DIFFERENT WORLD from Thailand and Laos. Just before the border on the Laotian side, people are still living in mud and attap huts without running water, with firewood stacked outside the door. Once across the border it's hard not to notice how quickly China is leaving her neighbours behind, and just how in your face it all is.

Whereas in Thailand and Laos there are broken bits of road that seem to be in disrepair for ages, everything in China is in the process of being renovated, repaired or improved on. The road repair teams physically move faster. I notice for the first time that women do manual labour here — including the heavy lifting and shovelling, and the workers have their lunch in teams. They even eat faster, scarfing down great scoops of rice and some simple vegetables. No after-meal siesta, it's back to work.

After crossing the border we get our first taste of the Chinese expressways. They all seem to run a hundred metres in the air, across valleys and everything else. There isn't a lot of wind protection and not a single other biker at all.

Travelling in convoy with the four by fours, I sort of know that I'm not going to be able to keep up. This time it isn't the road markings; this is almost perfect expressway. I just feel that 100 km/h is awfully fast. Otherwise I'm feeling pretty good and excited about finally riding in China. I'm starting to wonder if I should push it to see if I can shake it off and start riding again … that's when it happens.

Someone's left a bit of road surface in exposed concrete and I hit it at speed. The bike wriggles for a mere second before correcting, but I really thought that I was going to come off. Again the difficulty with freezing up and I slow enough to have Mike on the intercom again, this time just to call it quits. We call the Bumblebee and have the V-Strom back on the rack.

It's all a little strange. That change in the road surface had frightened me and it was an effort to not hit the brakes hard, but I wasn't completely rattled. I've failed to have a full riding day again, but somehow I'm not completely bothered. It should be a crushing blow but it isn't. It just isn't fun anymore; everything has become a bit of a drag. As I resume my place in the back of the support vehicle, I wonder if one of the effects of Prozac is not giving a damn.

That night in Mengla I'm still pretty detached over the whole thing. It's time to have a chat about this and to make some decisions. Essentially I'm getting tired of trying and failing. Maybe I should just stop here and head back, or send the bike back and carry on in the support vehicle. As a result of my problems the support vehicle is being used as a primary form of transport for my bike, not as a backup. If something happens to Mike that needs him in the vehicle, as is its original purpose, one of the bikes would have to be left behind. I'm ready to hear what everyone has to say about this.

Mike's view is that it isn't time for any hasty decisions. There is still a lot of riding to do and my anxiety attacks have a really good chance of sorting themselves out, even if I don't feel that way now. Neo Chian has confirmed with Irene that the next few days are going to be pretty horrid roads, all the way until after Kunming. In Kunming there'll be another medical congress to sort out. He suggests that I use the time to just rest and see how I feel over the next four days. If I still feel like sending things back after Kunming we'll make arrangements from there.

I get the message. No one is going to pull the plug on my ride. I will have to do it myself, if it really needs to be done. I'll stay off the bike until after Kunming before trying again.

The next thing to decide is whether to tell people about this. I'm in charge of the blog and have been keeping people updated on our progress. There are a couple of hundred hits a day, increasing every time a new blog post goes up. I've told Viola that there have been some problems but not just how bad they really are. Not the terror attacks, or the waking up frightened at night. I'm not sure people would even believe me. On one hand, I feel that we should tell things just as they are; on the other hand, this ride is supposed to be about breast cancer. The only other disease that is more of a taboo is mental illness. It's completely unexpected and could take some wind from our sails.

Mike thinks I should put it on the blog. There are people who are just starting to sign on and we're still in the process of building trust, of being real people to them. This happens to real people, so we should put it out. I'm not too sure just how to do it, but tell him I'll update the blog over the next few days.

After our meeting I go up to my hotel room and look at the kit strewn all over the place. I'm still living out of five bags. It must be the medications working, because it doesn't bother me at all that I'm seriously contemplating how to re-organise the luggage if I'm not required to ride anymore; what to send back with the bike and what to bring along. Then I update the blog, pop a sleeping pill and go to bed.

I'm awake again at four in the morning. Again with the feeling that so many things need to be done, when in truth there is really nothing to do. Just chill in the support vehicle. I'm starting to be redundant. What is the use of a rider who can't ride?

Out of habit, again I put on the big bike trousers and the riding boots. They are easier to wear than they are to pack up and carry, I reason. In truth I think it's my last defiant gesture at failure. I spend the time until breakfast making up a song list on the iPod. There isn't any need to check out the bike, it'll be racked up as soon as we finish breakfast.

Our convoy leaves Mengla and heads for Mojiang in a slightly unexpected order. Mike is the only rider, I'm with our photographer Pierce and his assistant Soo Lin in our own Toyota Land Cruiser with our guide Li Ma (we call him Mister Ma), clearing the way for Mike. Sonny and Neo Chian drive the Bumblebee support vehicle with my V-Strom racked up in the back with the rest of the four by four convoy. They are taking the "high roads" as expressways are called here, while we're on the trunk roads.

Irene's made special arrangements to get Mr Ma, who is one of her more experienced guides. He is a Yunnan native in his mid-forties, a stocky five-foot-four with that look of indestructible dependability that always reminds me of the Gurkhas. I don't think that I would ever see him without a hat on. He seems to have spent his life outdoors, first as an alpine guide, and then as a trekker mainly for nature groups and camera crews for movies and documentaries.

When he started a family recently, Ma decided to take on less challenging tours like ours to spend more time at home. Still, I don't think that in all his thirty years as a guide he's ever had a biker under his charge spending his first day in the back seat, with the bike on a rack a hundred miles away on a highway. Ma's good enough not to ask for details; I think in his mind he's decided that we're good sorts doing something worthwhile, even though at least one of us is in way over his head. "Don't worry," he tells me. "At least I can give you a proper guided tour of Yunnan you wouldn't get if you were on your bike."

About half way to Mojiang we enter the outskirts of Pu'er. This region produces some of the best tea in China. Now that's quite a claim, says Ma, but he agrees, partly because as a Yunnan native he is quite partial to the *hei cha*, or black tea. The best tea, he says, has been grown for centuries on the slopes of six mountains in Xishuangbanna, the county we have just come through. What follows is a detailed discourse on the different kinds of colour, flavour, fermentation processes, and how to bring the best out of *Pu'er cha*. I get the impression that Yunnan natives take their teas as seriously as a sommelier his pinot noir. One thing for sure, we're going to stop to drink tea in Pu'er. Not at some tourist place, Ma says, I know this corner shop.

Soon we're off the main street in a quiet part of the town. It's about two in the afternoon when we arrive and the lunch crowd is fading. Ma stops the car on the pavement, greets the landlord heartily, places our order and goes back to clean the Toyota as the tea is brewed. Soon we're sitting on knee-high rattan stools having tea and stretching our legs out at the side of the road. The sun is shining and the tea is perfect. Things couldn't be better. We are having *Pu'er cha* in Pu'er!

That's when Mike notices this guy selling meat and rice on the side of the road. Well, I'm sure it is meat because it still has some of the hair and hide on. That at least makes it mammalian; other than that, it's difficult to say, just dark brown slabs soaked in thin gravy. I think it might be large muscle, liver or lung, because there are large blood vessels in it. I'm not sure if it's smoked, steamed, left to ripen, or all three. It's served with black sauce and what looks like ground garlic, and white rice.

"You guys hungry?" Mike asks as he makes his orders with sign language, "because that looks pretty good."

"No, not really," Pierce and I reply, exchanging glances. Even by relatively wide Singaporean definitions of street food, this is a walk on the wild side. Of course, we have no idea what Swedish standards are. I mean, I might not be too keen on reindeer and blood pudding, but I understand they fly off supermarket shelves in Sweden at the end of each year.

Soon Mike's tucking away with chopsticks and oil dripping off his fingers, Pierce and I looking on with our Pu'er tea. Ma, who is already pretty impressed with Mike's BMW, is looking at him with even greater admiration now.

"This is great," says Mike, "what is it?"

"Well …" I say, trying to make the best of the situation. I've heard of roadside toilets in the Chinese countryside and maybe something encouraging now will help in the mind-over-matter battle I anticipate Mike will have to face shortly.

"The precise English translation is a little difficult …" I start.

"Yes," Pierce agrees, drawing on a cigarette thoughtfully, "I'm pretty sure I don't know what the English word for … um … that is."

We ask Ma what our Swedish friend is eating. He has no idea. He's seen it before, but has never been hungry enough to try.

"But broadly speaking," I say, turning to Pierce, "I think the closest thing I can think of, is ham. Wouldn't you say, Pierce?"

"Yes, quite possibly the closest English translation for whatever that is, is ham."

"Well, this is great ham," said Mike, licking the curdled fat off his fingers, "you should try some."

Incredibly, Mike survives the regular incubation period of staphylococcus poisoning, or whatever microbe that flourishes on road kill. It's the start of Mike's exploration of local roadside cuisine. He discovers a few constants: That if it looks like meat, it probably is. That its Chinese name, at least to Ma, Pierce and myself, is difficult to translate into English, except that it's a sort of ham. In the course of the next few days Mike gamely puts away ham soup, steamed ham, ham and black chilli, ham noodles, even ham dumplings. The game is up when one of the less well-known ham stews has a ham's head, which really does look like duck.

Soon we pull into Mojiang in really good time — it's still daylight. In fact, we arrive around the same time as the four by four convoy despite the smaller roads. Unfortunately there really isn't so much to do in Mojiang around dinnertime and the lack of any real Wi-Fi service means that we don't really have any response to the emails sent the previous evening.

It would be a common theme in Chinese cities where we have such short stopovers. Never enough time to work out what makes each city unique. Mojiang does make the effort though. Its main claim to fame is the annual international festival of … wait for it … twins. At least that's what I thought I heard the concierge say when I made enquiries. He might also have said meat dumplings, the two things sound very close in Mandarin.

The next day we head to Kunming, some 230 km away. I'm really looking forward to it. I've made some hectic arrangements to put together a one-day breast cancer seminar with the local Third Affiliated Hospital. The whole thing is based on goodwill and reputation, and the most remarkable thing is that it's goodwill by association. As far as I know the good people of Kunming have never even heard of us.

The one that they have heard about is Dr Tan Lai Yong, who has spent over 15 years in this part of China before returning to Singapore. The contact that Lai Yong provided us is Dr Loh Cheng. He has continued much of Lai Yong's work and also been the liaison for many visiting Singapore doctors helping to train local medical residents. Together we've been able to put together a programme of lectures, ward rounds, a public health symposium. The highlight is the half dozen or so breast cancer patients who have agreed to interviews by Cynthia and James, who should already be in Kunming ahead of us.

***

EARLY NEXT MORNING THE four by fours take to the expressways while we are on typical Yunnan country roads. Twisting, unmarked, no railing, varying surface, sheer drops on one side as the other side hugs the contour of the hills. I lose count at 200 hairpin turns before lunchtime. Ma is sweeping the road ahead for Mike, taking the corners wide and using his horn whenever needed. Looking back I can see Mike through the clouds of dust. He has the full-face helmet on but I can still see the huge grin on his face. This is real biking country.

I feel a tinge on envy, but I'm quite happy to be in the Cruiser — Yunnan roads are interesting enough as a passenger. For one thing there hardly seems to be any flat ground in Yunnan. Most of the cities and villages are by the riverbanks, surrounded by towering hills and terraced fields of paddy, tobacco or tea. In fact there is hardly any straight road. Over the hours things would take a sort of rhythm. Twisting roads up one hill, equally exciting roads on the way down, then tear through the river valley where we might take the main road through a small village, then up the next hill.

The road surfaces are a wonder. In cities like Mojiang there is near perfect tarmac. This turns into potholed asphalt interspersed with simple sandy track as we leave the cities. After that in the villages you take what you get ... loose gravel, mud track, cement, concrete. One interesting downhill is surfaced with bathroom tiles. Many of the roads have been cut through the very hillsides with rocky overhangs. Landslides are commonplace, as are the road repair crews. Occasionally there are small waterfalls from run-off water, straight off the side of the mountain and onto the road. Dramatically beautiful, but the thin layer of moist mud and moss gives no traction at all.

We share these roads with every imaginable kind of motorised vehicle. The heavy trucks are the most interesting, with the uniquely Chinese habit of cooling the brakes with water. I suppose this is so that the brake shoes don't melt and lock up on these overloaded trucks as they go down one twisting downhill after another. As the lorries make their tentative descents I can see the steam rising off the wheelbases, leaving two strips of greasy water on the road, right on the line a biker would take around a bend.

The real wonder is how Mike keeps going. He's not only eating the dust we are throwing up but everyone else's dirt as well. At a lunch stop I catch Ma having a closer look at the Beemer, giving it a respectful wipe down. I think he is wondering what's keeping it going through all that. It isn't just the dust either. I'm making a list of what Mike has managed to evade while tearing down country roads. Ducks, chickens, dogs, goats, cows, children, and a variety of seemingly home-made vehicles. One of them looked like a hybrid between a Ferguson tractor and a sitting room, sofa set and all.

The only time I ever see him slightly disconcerted is in the

Proof positive that China now leads the world in hybrid car technologies.

tunnels. According to Ma they were built before the roads, and sometimes even before cars. The tunnels are narrow, unlit, unsurfaced and with no real indication of how long they are or what the form is if you meet something coming the other way. If that happens the biker definitely has the advantage, he can squeeze by in water channels on the side of the road. The biker would also be a little more motivated to get through — the fumes can build up in these intra-tunnel gridlocks very quickly.

One thing makes up for all the dangers on these country roads. This is the best possible way to see China. On the expressway speeding over everyone and everything, you could be anywhere in the world but for the license plates. Here by the trunk roads though, is where China puts its feet in the ground. In fact I'm getting the impression that in China it is all about the land.

I don't think I have ever seen a people so intimately intertwined with the soil. I suppose being in a rural agricultural area this is hardly surprising — we're surrounded by cultivated land — but there is more to it than merely using the land. For one thing, much of the work seems to be carried out by hand. Rice is planted by hand, one stalk at a time. The soil is turned by hand and hoe, and after rice is harvested it's all threshed by hand. Tea is harvested by finger, not just by hand. The whole lot of it is carried on man-packed, or sometimes woman-packed bushels. Every inch of the fertile hills is used in an endless landscape of terraced fields. These are furrowed by either water buffalo or sometimes just by man-pulled ploughs. The mud dykes that separate the layers of fields are molded and jammed together by hand and spade.

Terraced fields everywhere we look in Yunnan—it's hard to find any flat ground.

Even the villages that we're going through consist largely of thick mud-walled houses, although occasionally in the larger towns we see a brick mill. Bricks are made from packed earth and tiled into large furnaces, the whole operation done again by hand.

It's a two-way thing: the land has marked the people here just as much. The Yunnan villager has an indomitable look about him. They are friendly to a fault, but always on the go, with something to do before long. They are not very tall but sinewy and leathery, always with a hand on some farming implement, a sack or a basket, over the shoulder. I notice that everyone does their part in the work, even the women and children, although in the villages the very elderly smoke what looks like a small chimney for a pipe.

By pure chance we have come during the Qingming festival. This is when Chinese all over the world venerate their ancestors, particularly by the tending of family graves. We can see these scrubbed gravestones dotting the landscape, the surrounding shrubbery newly trimmed back. In Singapore and Malaysia the graves are at the most 100, maybe 150 years old; before that there wasn't any notable Chinese presence. Here,

A head for heights: This isn't the view from a plane, but on a bike hanging on to a twisting road with no railings.

the ancestors have been about their business for far longer.

As a result of the re-parceling of land through the running centuries these family tombs and gravestones seem to be placed at random across the land. It gives me the impression that the people were buried just where they died. This may be at a vantage point overlooking the valley below, or by the entrance to a farm, or even in the middle of a paddy field. Some of them look centuries old. They might stand alone or in a clump of a dozen or so, decorated with brightly-coloured ribbons, or occasionally, the odd smouldering joss stick. Even when you're gone you return to the land, and your descendants continue working the land you toiled, all around your bones.

It's easy to imagine that on a good day centuries ago some ancestor might have finished his day's work and wandered up the hill for the view with his smoking pipe over his shoulder (they are that big around here). After a few last lungfuls he quietly shuffles off his mortal coil, so they just buried him there, where he liked to be. In the life thereafter he would have much the same view as the one we're having, which isn't so bad.

NIne
A KEY DECISION AT KUNMING

When we finally get to Kunming it's just about nightfall and we see the four by fours lined up in front of the luxurious Crowne Plaza hotel, including the Suzuki still strapped on the back of the Bumblebee. On the highway it had taken them just over three hours from Mojiang. We had taken 10 hours on the small roads. Mike is literally grey with dirt and fatigue; I'm exhausted from just not getting regular sleep and trying to decide what to do next.

Irene and Hung Tuan have informed me that Kunming is where some decisions have to be made. The key question is where to send the bike. If I feel up to it we could send it forward in the journey so as to take the stress off the support vehicle and the crew. Even after a few days it's clear that the rack can't take much more of a beating. We can meet up with it again in about a week or so after we clear the mountains and take up riding again then.

The disadvantage of sending it forward is that it would be really difficult to send it back out from so deep in China. If I couldn't ride safely by then, we would be in big trouble. Of course, it would also mean the end of my ride.

The alternative is to leave it in Kunming and have Irene and her people send it back out to Thailand. Irene has already started exploring this possibility and discovered that because of some bureaucratic requirements, the bike has to leave the country on the same day as the rest of the convoy.

This means that it will have to be held somewhere in China until the end of April, and then ridden or taken out through Laos into Thailand. From there we can only keep a bike in the country for a month before getting back to Singapore. That would make it end of May; I would still be in Turkey if everything went according to schedule, which means that I will need help to get the bike out of Thailand. Both options are very involved, with all sorts of things waiting to go wrong.

With all this on my mind it's good to see Cynthia and James in the hotel lobby. It seems like a lifetime ago when we chatted at their home in Copenhagen after breakfast about working together. In truth it's been just over six months. In that time what had started as after-breakfast banter has grown legs, arms and some body parts. Thanks to Loh Cheng's contacts the two of them are here, ready for the first interviews with Chinese breast cancer patients the next morning. Hopefully this will provide the basis for more detailed studies on how Chinese breast cancer patients perceive their illness.

Loh Cheng joins us before long and together we sort out

the details of the next day's arrangements. Two sessions at two separate hospitals. The first will be a public health symposium with local surgery and oncology lecturers and breast cancer support groups. The second is to staff and trainees at the university department of surgery. Thankfully Loh Cheng will be available throughout and can act as interpreter for the presentations. As this goes on Cynthia and James are going to meet breast cancer patients and their carers for their interviews.

AFTER WE IRON OUT the last details, it's a quick dinner before I head up to my room. I'd really rather get to bed but it's a rare opportunity of good Wi-Fi in China, so after a shower, out comes the laptop. I've got some replies from the messages I had sent a few days ago.

Viola says that I have to send the bike forward, it's a no-brainer. After all that planning and fretting, calling it quits now is just ridiculous. Which is sound reasoning, I guess, but I suspect another unspoken reason is that there is no way I am going to put her through this a second time. There are no more tries for the Long Ride, either finish it or don't bring it up again.

Boss has also replied and he says that I should stop riding and bring the bike back. I won't be managing panic attacks in the safe sterility of a psychiatrist's office. We don't have the luxury of several weeks of waiting for the medications to work, or for the attacks to somehow resolve. The only way of knowing if I'm ready to ride again is to actually get on the bike somewhere in China. And if I'm not ready and overreact to any number of possible dangers? The risk is not worth it.

Boss points out that what's more important to keep in mind is that the Long Ride is not about motorcycles. It's about breast cancer awareness. If I arrive safely in Sweden on a *tricycle*, but have a better idea about what it's like for women in Asia to have breast cancer, that's a successful mission.

After balancing both views carefully, I conclude that life would be a lot easier if wife and Boss have the same opinion.

After this I read a series of emails and text messages that I know is going to keep me awake all night. All have offered their commiserations but a few, including some from psychiatry colleagues, mention that my problem is not such a big surprise. This kind of throws me off. I've never pictured myself as the poster boy for panic attacks. I have been in danger before; far greater, malicious, directed violence, and never experienced anything even remotely like this.

"It's got nothing to do with the threat of violence or injury," they say, "it's the threat of failure. Your problem isn't that you cannot handle the danger, your problem is you cannot handle *failing* ... You're paying the price for caring too much about the outcomes. Your personality trait that makes you prone to these anxiety attacks is your unrelenting high standards."

"I tell you it's all to do with your father," says another old friend, "he's that albatross that has been following you all these years. You've got to let him go. He's gone now and can't give you any approval he didn't give you for all those years when you needed it. You need to stop doing things to live up to these imaginary standards you think he's set for you."

It's all pretty bewildering. I don't know which confuses me more. The idea that I've been prone to panic attacks for so long without knowing it, or that people who have known me well enough sound like they were almost expecting it.

All this time while I had become better and better at cutting people up, or making very quick decisions on who to cut first in order to save as many as possible. What I do for a living requires me to be the very opposite of the kind of panic-stricken, overwhelmed insomniac I have become. The very thought is just so bizarre. Having high standards is what brings success, not panic and failure. And as for unrelenting high standards, that isn't my problem, it's my trainees' problem. These people are talking out of their hats.

I'm not sure it's all hot air though. What is most unsettling is how much insight these colleagues of mine have. Which sounds silly now, considering how they *are* mental health experts. I'm really starting to wish I had paid more attention to my undergraduate psychiatry lectures. Through WhatsApp I start a chat group titled, "Philip Falls Apart". A few of them are still awake.

They ask me to describe in detail what troubles I'm having. When I mention how I'm fixated on the markings in the road, at first they don't understand; markings on the road sound pretty dangerous. Then I point out the fact that they are not really of any consequence at all. As Ros and Yu Seung had demonstrated, they're safe at almost any speed.

"Right, that's cognitive disorder," the shrinks reply.

"I'm sorry?"

"The road markings are there, right? So it's not some sort of hallucination. You're not making it up in your head. The problem is that your mind's interpreting them incorrectly. You see what's there, but you give it too much significance."

Then I describe how crippling it is to think about each corner I've taken, even days afterwards, and to constantly berate myself about how I could have done better. Or how I could have overtaken quicker and not held people up. The really odd thing is that I don't want to think about it; the thoughts just keep coming like some sort of automatic recall. It's very strange to realise that I've spent hours in Ma's Cruiser ruminating over something I had no intention of thinking about at all.

"That's called retention and magnification," they say.

"Well," I inform them, "I'm having retention and magnification that wakes me up scared shitless in the middle of the night. I feel like I need a urologist rather than a psychiatrist."

I mention that I feel I'm the main reason why we are taking so long. Mike had looked more dead than alive today when we got into Kunming.

"Isn't it true that you're not the only thing that can hold things up?" my friends ask. "Like today for example. The four by fours took three hours and even with Mike travelling alone it took you 10 hours. The point is that you weren't even riding, so how can you have held things up? Any number of things can cause delays: road conditions, detours, long breaks after meals. Not just you. You over-magnify your personal accountability to everyone's negative outcomes. That's magnification."

It's already well past midnight when I get through my Wi-Fi-mediated psychiatry consult. *Bugger*, I think, *they understand what I'm going through after all*. It's not just me having to figure it out, they seem to have a handle on it, although we haven't quite got to the part about just what I should do about it. Just getting to talk about what I'm going through with someone else has made me feel better.

I'm not sure if it's the medication but I feel a bit less bewildered by everything now. Although I don't quite agree with all the mental health mumbo jumbo as yet, the idea that someone else clearly has more insight about this than I do is reassuring. It isn't a random chance event, it can be somewhat explained and maybe even sorted out. What I want to do is stay online and work things through, but it's a full day tomorrow so I sign off to get some sleep.

WHEN I WAKE UP again at four in the morning I admit to myself for the first time that it's not all mental health mumbo jumbo. I'm sick, actually mentally ill. It is just not normal to be this tired and wake up thinking about how I am slowing everyone down when I'm not even riding. It is very frustrating because I'm not making any progress at all in getting a good night's sleep despite the sleeping tablets. Mental illness just isn't the sort of thing that I expected to happen this soon. I mean, I am sort of counting on dementia but that's for much later on.

The big question is how long I am going to take to get over it. There is no way of knowing. If medications are all that is required, then it'll be a simple matter of dosing and pharmacokinetics, but somehow I feel that it's going need more than just taking happy capsules and sleeping pills.

Right now I have more urgent problems. I'm pretty sure that with something like 12 hours sleep over the last four days, I'm going to crash before the day is over. I anticipate around lunchtime. After all those hectic arrangements I'm hoping that Kunming won't be one big disappointment.

Breakfast is nothing more than weak tea and porridge. I'm wondering what it would take to get a proper cup of coffee that means business in China. Still, it's good to see Mike freshened up after yesterday's long day. After the usual morning pleasantries, there's something I want to clear up with him after last night's mails.

"Mike, I've been told that these panic attacks aren't much of a surprise to lots of people. Do I strike you as the panicky sort?"

"Nope," he replies, slurping up some ham noodles. Amazing, his ability to eat at a time like this.

"Ah, good." Well, I'm glad we cleared that up. I watch as he uses sign language for the waiter to bring him seconds.

"So ... why am I having them now?" It needs saying. It's sort of been hanging in the air.

"You need to let go. You've got too much on your mind. When you ride, just make it about riding. Not about schedules and the rest of it. If we make it, we make it. If we don't, we don't. Just live for that moment. Otherwise it's just going to overload."

"But someone's got to plan ahead," I reply. I remember the trouble it took communicating with Loh Cheng from Singapore just to get today's programme settled.

"Yes, that's true," says Mike, "but that's before the ride. Once the ride starts it should be just about riding. Like how it was yesterday riding through all that wonderful scenery. Sometimes we pass something that looks really interesting but in a moment it's just gone and that's where it should stay. Just gone. It's all for the moment."

"A bit like a Zen state?"

"Exactly."

I know what he means. I have taken solo rides up Malaysia and Thailand before and that was the precise state I was in. Hours, sometimes entire weather fronts would pass, and I could stay in some state of mental homeostasis. He's right. It's all the planning that's gone into this trip that's made me forget this. All the routes and lectures and meetings and border crossings and the rest of it. I hadn't made the switch when the planning ended and the ride started.

There is something else I want to check with him. I think it's the lack of sleep that's making me free-associate.

"Mike, do I bring up my Dad often?"

"No, although … actually maybe you bring him up more than others. I mean, you've told me what he did and you mentioned on the way here how you used to take holidays in Malaysia before … actually … yes you do bring him up quite often, but I wouldn't say he's on your radar all the time. Why?"

"Oh, nothing. Trying to work out something I was told. By the way, got in touch with Boss last night. He says to stop riding and send the Suzuki back. In fact he said if we just sold the Suzuki in China somewhere that might be the best thing. Save a lot of trouble. What do you think?"

"Your call. But I would say that you can expect these panic attacks to stop in a week or so when the drugs start to work. What's more, your treatment was started early, which is also a good predictor of successful treatment, and you are clearly showing insight. You're trying to work things out, as you said."

That's just Mike through and through. I'm slowing him down, he's going to have a whole lot less to worry about if I stopped riding, but he's leaving it to me. I'm feeling better.

"Oh, by the way," Mike says as he heads up to his room for his lecture things, "you should eat something. You look like crap."

WE MEET JAMES AND Cynthia at a teaching hospital for the health symposium. Both of them take one look at me, exchange glances and Cynthia speaks up:

"Philip, you look just awful."

"Actually, I'm not feeling terribly on fire to learn about breast cancer today." Which is a pity, because it's a good programme. I sit down behind them at the back of the hall and try to stay conscious until lunch. The sequence of talks for this session has two local speakers before Mike and I go on.

At first I think there must be some mistake. A local speaker is presenting the trends for breast cancer incidence in different cities in China over the last 50 or so years. By sheer coincidence she's using the same PowerPoint template as Mike and I are. Breast cancer incidence in Singapore has doubled in just under a generation. So that a woman born in Singapore between 1935 and 1945 has a 1:30 chance of breast cancer, compared to one born between 1960 and 1970, who has a 1:16 lifetime likelihood of the disease. These trends are similar to all the major cities our Chinese counterpart is presenting — Beijing, Nanjing, Shanghai, Kunming,

Mike and Loh Cheng help me demonstrate how to field questions from the floor while completely asleep.

Chengdu. It's not data that I have come across before and it should mean something more to me now, but I'm way too out of it, wondering how on earth I can possibly stay conscious for the programme and network with people who have come to meet us. At this stage coherent speech will be an unexpected bonus.

In the late morning a van takes us to the Third Affiliated Hospital where I give a lecture and we're brought back to the hotel after lunch. Cynthia and James will meet us later after they've finished their interviews with the cancer patients. I thank Loh Cheng for putting together a wonderful programme. We do not have the time now — we are due to leave Kunming for Zhaozishan tomorrow — but promise to keep in touch for future collaborations.

That evening when we get back to the hotel Mike and I sit down with Irene and Hung Tuan to sort out the bike arrangements. Despite what Boss has said I am going to send the bike forward. Irene already has the answers. She recommends that we take the bike off the support vehicle and into a van, which will take it to our hotel in Chengdu. That is 1,600 km and some eight days away so there are some costs involved. We agree on the price and the arrangement is for the van to be brought later this evening.

I really need to get my head down and ask Mike to wake me when the van comes so that I can help get it loaded. He tells me not to worry and that he'll get it sorted. He can see that I'm barely on my feet and will just be in the way. I am to pop a tablet and go to sleep and see him at breakfast.

When I get up it's after 10 hours of sound, dreamless sleep and the bedside clock shows 4:30 am. One thing I can say about the Crowne Plaza in Kunming is that the beds are fantastic. I'm rested, alert and have perfect insight as to why I've woken up frightened to death. My heart is pounding in my ears and I feel breathless. My guts feel all knotted in a tight ball and there is a faint taste of vomitus in my mouth, because most of it is on the luxurious bed sheet next to me. I'm clear about what has brought this on.

It is the thought that when I get up to ride the bike in Chengdu, I won't manage to get out of the car park lot, much less tangle with Chinese city traffic. Whose mad idea was it to take that kind of risk?

For a moment I wonder why Mike hadn't woken me up to pack the bike. Then I remember. Oh hell, I've already committed to the risk! The bike's already all packed up and ready to leave deeper into China in the morning!

Dressed in just a T-shirt and shorts, I head down barefoot

to the hotel lobby. Everything is dark and quiet and I head out to the line of four by fours next to the canal at the back of the hotel. There she is, my Suzuki, still strapped to the back of the Bumblebee! The wave of relief is overwhelming and I sit down on the curb in pure gratitude.

Wait a minute. What does this mean? Well, that's pretty obvious, isn't it? It means I'm out of this ride. There was some doubt before, but now I know deep down inside that I really don't want to ride anymore. I'll have to come clean and tell the rest. After sitting outside in the night air for an hour I head back in and call Mike in his room and ask for a short meeting. When I get there I notice an uneaten room service dinner next to the bed. He had sent one up last night in case I woke up hungry.

Mike explains that Irene had managed some sort of bread delivery van, which was far too small. A larger truck will be coming after breakfast. When I tell him what I've decided, he's silent for a moment, then suggests that we should sound out Neo Chian and Sonny. After calling to wake them, we meet in their room.

"OK, here's the thing," I start, "I don't think I want to ride anymore. Boss may be right, I did promise the wife that I wouldn't take any unnecessary risks and I think sending the bike to Chengdu, where I would have no choice but to perform, is taking a needless risk." I'm starting to convince myself, but my guts seem to revolt against the whole idea of quitting. What I am saying makes me feel physically sick. I have trouble standing up straight.

Neo Chian has a patient look. If he has an opinion about my decision, he doesn't show it.

"Only you can decide whether or not you want to ride, and whether or not the risk is worth taking," he says. "Are you sure this is what you want? We will support whatever decision you make. Don't think about putting us through any trouble, that's what we're here for, to support whatever decision you make."

"Actually, I'm pretty certain." There is relief in the thought that I don't have to think about this anymore, but I certainly don't like the decision that I'm making at all.

"Ok, we'll let Hung Tuan and Irene know at breakfast and sort things out. You get some rest and we'll see you later."

After breakfast the confusion begins. It's supposed to be a short day, less than 200 km to the mountaintop at Zhaozishan. Thank goodness for that because Irene really has to pull out all the stops to help this clearly neurotic rider take care of his bike. The revised plan is to leave it at her own home in Kunming, where it will stay until the rest of the convoy reaches the China-Kazakh border so that we can coordinate when to get it out of China. Another van has arrived but again it is too small, so when the third van arrives patience is wearing thin. We're holding up the rest of the convoy.

I'm out of sorts. I have trouble doing two simple things I have to do: disconnect the battery and call Diana to prepare to receive my bike in a few weeks. Eventually everything is settled and I'm back in the back of Mr Ma's Land Cruiser. Mr Ma is the only one who asks me directly why I've decided to send the bike back when the problem is expected to be a temporary thing. I don't think my reply in Chinese made any sense to him but I can tell what he's thinking without him having to say a word: *This is the ride of your life. You shouldn't quit for what ifs*. Instead what he does say is that I'm welcome in his Land Cruiser and at least he can tell me more about what we're going to see than if I was on a bike.

Now what I need to do is get used to the idea of not riding again. This actually isn't very hard, there isn't much of a reminder of failure anywhere; the riding kit is packed into the back of the Bumblebee. The bike isn't even on rack; as far as I know it's safely tucked away under wraps in Irene's place in Kunming.

The only thing I really have to worry about is the next medical seminar, which is scheduled at Luzhou, some five days away. I take a sedative and try to sleep away the nagging feeling that I may have just made the easier decision, rather than the right one.

Ten
NOT ALL FUN AND GAMES

JUST OUTSIDE DONGCHUAN THE landscape changes dramatically. In the space of a few minutes the towering precipices and plunging canyons give way to gentle hill country. It reminds me of Devon, with the wheat and potato fields instead of the ubiquitous paddy fields of the last few weeks. What is even more remarkable is how the colour of the soil has changed to a rich brick red. It looks like a giant quilted blanket has been placed over the previously uncompromising landscape, smoothing it all out to rolling grassland with separate squares of green, red and brown.

As we drive up a steep hillside Ma notices an old man with a walking stick wearing little more than shorts and a blue headgear. He's shuffling along the side of the road, puffing light blue pipe smoke in his wake. We're nearly

2,000 m above sea level, there's a definite chill in the air and here's this old bloke walking around in his underwear.

Ma checks his watch. "I think we've got time," he says, "we'll pull over for a few minutes."

We pull up a hundred metres or so ahead and I help get the coffee going. Mike's already off the bike and looking at the open landscape—a panorama of red and green and yellow wheat fields as far as the eye can see.

Ma starts digging deep inside the back of the Toyota and pulls up a plastic sack of used clothes. By now the old man has come alongside the car and I notice the sockless feet in split shoes, thin cotton shorts and calloused hands. He's incredibly thin. Ma speaks to him in his local dialect and some everyday Mandarin I can barely make out:

"Not feeling cold?" asks Ma.

"Was colder in the winter," pointing at his bare legs with big toothless grin and happy puff of blue smoke.

"Well, choose something you like then," Ma says, opening up the sack full of sweatshirts, track bottoms and scarves.

"I bring them from my friends in Kunming whenever I get up here with a tour group," Ma explains, grinning as some farmworkers come off their fields to have a look.

Most are women dressed in more elaborate headgear and scarves, but not a lot warmer. Ma explains that these are the Yi people. They make up a large part of the population in this part of Yunnan but are completely distinct from the Han Chinese. They keep to their old customs, and often are disconnected from the progress in the towns and the cities. This is just Ma's small way of helping.

We help them choose what's available and tell them how beautiful this place is. They just grin happily, the way women do when helping each other choose clothes. Pretty soon the coffee's drunk and we have to get back on the road. Looking back I see the old man resume his climb up the hill, he's started a new pipe now with his dark-coloured Hitec track bottoms and a grey hoodie with that familiar print across his chest: DKNY.

BEFORE WE GET TO Luzhou, the hills and valleys of Yunnan give way to the broad flood plain of the Jing Sha He (golden sand river). There are no ancient homesteads here, just modern mini-cities that straddle the river. Wide expanses of farmland are replaced by newly constructed multi-storey residences that line the hillsides and spill down to the riverbanks.

Unlike the sense of peaceful perpetuity that we have become accustomed to, here in the flatlands there is a sense that the land is under strain to move forward. Road widening everywhere, hillsides being terraced not for paddy but taller and taller buildings. Everywhere the din of machines throwing up clouds of dust and smog. Most of all we miss the mountain air. It would be more than a week before we have clear skies again.

As we leave Yunnan and enter Sichuan the Jing Sha He changes its name to the Yangtze. This river is so much a part of the Chinese psyche that it's simply called Chang Jiang — the long river. The shift is more than just geographical; Sichuan is the heart and soul of Chinese history and culture. We're not in the provinces anymore.

Ma starts getting positively eloquent, even slightly teary-eyed. He plies us with Tang poetry and ancient wisdom from the period of the Warring States, bringing to life all those proverbs and stories I learned as a boy. After rattling off his favourite poems of Zhuge Liang, one of the most famous of ancient China's sages, Ma asks what I hope to see in Sichuan. Apparently, the route that we are on now isn't one bikers usually take. It's not exactly biking country — the cities and towns are too close together, and there seems to be a permanent haze over the whole place.

Ma's definitely right about this place not being high on the list of must-ride routes. Here it's start-stop traffic, long queues as road works reduce roads to one lane each way, and crowded villages trying to become small cities. Mike's still calmly taking the lot in his stride, but he's not smiling much anymore.

This part of the journey is not so much about the biking though. We're here for the conference with the breast section of the Luzhou People's Hospital. Dr Rebecca Lin, one of the

Ah, the romance of bike travel — some parts of China seem like one giant construction site.

new generation of breast surgeons, spent a few months with us two years ago. When she heard about the Long Ride she was one of the first collaborators to come on board.

We know Rebecca as a capable, hardworking English-speaking surgeon in a discipline that is dominated by older men. It's an old story, but perhaps one more prevalent in this part of the world. These aren't typical senior doctors either, but very established, long-serving general surgeons. General surgeons who don't have a unanimous opinion that breast cancer work should be a separate surgical discipline. Rebecca's got an uphill task of changing things and appreciates the help. In all our dealings we make it a point of emphasising that it's mainly through our positive impressions we have of Rebecca during her time with us that has brought about this collaborative meeting.

In many ways it is an ideal collaboration, the kind where everyone gets to benefit. For us, Luzhou gives us access to patients who might otherwise not be available for interviews with Cynthia and James. James is especially keen on learning about renewing his ties with the local people. Although he's spent most of his life in Europe and the US, he was born not far from Luzhou and considers them very much his people.

Mike's made good time despite the road conditions and we pull into the Jiu Cheng Hotel at about two in the afternoon. Just as well, we need to have the suits and shirts laundered before tonight, when we have to attend a formal dinner. We see James and Cynthia in the lobby, looking relaxed and very much at home, having arrived two days ago. They've already met up with Rebecca and started on their interviews. James, ever the linguist, is intrigued at how much the local dialects have changed in such a short time. They tell us that there is a street right in front of the hotel where we should be able to get what we need.

I head out with Mike and Pierce and find the laundry easily enough. Qianjingshia street is a leafy avenue with one lane of traffic running each way, lined with shops clearly not dressed up for tourists. Besides the laundry there are a few tailors and boutiques, bicycle mechanics, a GP clinic, a coffee shop doing a roaring trade in dumplings and a few bookshops. It reminds me of Geylang back home, circa the early 1970s. As a boy, Grandma used to walk me out there to get lunch for the family and keep me out of trouble. Funny I should remember that now, haven't thought of her for years.

After leaving the suits at the laundry we take a walk down the road to use up the two hours they need to get our things dry-cleaned. It's the GP practice that captures my attention.

At first I think it's a modern day opium den. There are a dozen or so men sitting on stools outside the practice, puffing away on their rolled-up cigarettes. Large public health posters hang from the panels behind them, including a rather graphic one of the perils of tobacco.

Peering through the clinic's front glass I see a waiting area that has a half dozen or so small stretchers and couches. They're filled with smoking men sitting or lying on their sides, their arms attached to intravenous drips hanging by their stands. As I watch, another man comes over with his own IV, puts down his cigarette for a minute and at the first try, successfully sets his own IV drip.

This is too good a chance to miss. I don't smoke cigarettes but do enjoy the odd cigar or pipe. I've actually brought a pipe along, after being advised it's one of the best ways to break the ice with strangers anywhere. So I light up and sit down on an empty stool outside.

I turn to the nearest man on a drip, pass some pleasantries and ask what he's here for. Oh, headache, he says. Ah, right. The man next to him is here for a backache. He says the drip's the real goods. The third man has got a fever and sore throat. No, no diarrhea, why do you ask? I'm not sure which I'm more surprised by: that any of these conditions should need an IV, or that all of these patients have actually set their own IV lines. "Always get it on the first try, or it can be an unpleasant mess," they tell me.

I decide to hang around here while Mike and Pierce go down the road for some bubble tea. It's hard to explain but I feel quite at home here, in a place I've never been. It's an odd pleasure to be able to speak to complete strangers like we're sort of related somehow. A few older men, intrigued more by my pipe than by me, come by for a seat and a smoke and that's all right. In fact I've noticed that I've been talking more to the natives since arriving in Sichuan.

So we shoot the wind like old friends while my laundry gets done and their IVs get run. Across the street is a woman's clothing store selling what can only be described as rather formidable brassieres. Like the kinds we used to look out for in early James Bond movies.

Then it hits me. It's the accent, the Sichuan accent! The same lilting Mandarin we used to hear from Grandma when she taught us Chinese before we even went to Chinese school. Grandma used to teach us Chinese out of the Epistle to the Romans. I haven't heard it since she died years ago—there're very few Sichuan families in Singapore. Cynthia's husband James speaks Mandarin exactly the same way, which is probably one of the reasons I enjoy his company so much.

Sichuan Mandarin has a warmer, friendlier musical quality than the harsh, martial tones Nanyang Primary School tried to replace it with. The only other parallel I can compare this to is the Dublin lilt versus Received Pronunciation's clipped sentences. One is as welcoming as a warm pub on a cold night, the other gives me flashbacks of the Principal's Office. Fascinating though, how language can bring me back despite not having used it for decades.

My Sichuan Mandarin is put to the real test that night at the formal dinner. This is at the very respectable hotel restaurant, which has some very large round tables. It's our first formal dinner since Kunming and is very different from the semi-casual air that pervades the provinces.

Cynthia, James, Health Secretary Chen and me, before the wallpaper came to life. Note the shot glasses at each table place.

Here there's a complex formula that has overcome the insoluble problem of who gets which seat of prominence around a perfectly round table. I find myself sitting to the Sichuan Health Secretary's left, with James and Cynthia to his right. Mike is sitting next to a very pretty interpreter on the opposite of the table, with Pierce, Rebecca and other dignitaries filling up the other seats.

As expected the food is excellent and nearly flammable, but it's the booze that is the real threat. The Health Secretary relates an old proverb: When the wind blows across the valley, all of Sichuan envies Luzhou. The reason is the *bai jiu*, or white wine. In these parts it's called *yao wu qi san*, or 1573, after the year when China's longest-running distillery started putting out the stuff not far from here.

It looks harmless enough, but so does tar remover. At each of our places at this opulent dining table is a sizeable crystal shot glass and as the evening really gets started I see what this is for. 1573 is taken neat and all in one go in these parts, with again a complex formula of who offers the toast to whom. Usually the number of hosts and guests at each table is fairly evenly distributed so that everyone leaves uniformly happy, but I'm at a disadvantage here. James, an old hand at this, has politely demurred on account of medications he's taking (what medications I never heard mentioned till now), and Mike is understandably distracted in his own little world with the interpreter.

By the time the Secretary, his assistant, the chief of the hospital, the surgical chief and his assistant have their way toasting with me, the Sichuan food doesn't seem too spicy anymore. In fact, I really can't feel my tongue. Soon it's my turn to stand up and go round the table and reciprocate all the toasts individually, but I discover I really can't feel my feet either. An unanticipated problem with a round table is that I don't know when I've done a complete round. The trick I had in mind was to watch out for when I arrived to my own empty seat, but someone else has filled it on his own round of toasting, the cunning bugger. No matter, we'll just go round again, everybody seems happier at seeing me a third time, and I feel fine.

When it's time to go Pierce helps me make my way out of the restaurant and to the lobby to see our hosts off. Funny thing, I tell Pierce, that they're the hosts and yet they're leaving and we're staying. It's because this is our hotel, Pierce patiently explains. And a wonderful hotel it is too, almost magical.

I hadn't noticed just how vivid the wall paintings were when I was coming in, but they look wonderful now. Even the floral patterns on the carpets seem to shimmer with a life of their own below my feet. Then the most wonderful miracle of all. The Secretary and his delegation walk through the revolving glass door, without the door revolving at all, and leave the building.

Next morning way too bright and early the van comes to take us to the People's Hospital in the heart of the city for the lectures. It's a relatively light schedule. After our lectures Mike and I will be brought back to the hotel while Cynthia and James run interviews with some of Rebecca's patients.

The audience consists mainly of surgeons, oncologists and other cancer workers from Luzhou as well as other parts of Sichuan. Once again a local speaker goes through the epidemiology slides. This is often used as a general introduction in medical congresses, so the audience gets some perspective of the size of the problem at hand. Something stirs — I've seen these before. Then I remember: it was a week ago in Kunming. There was something I wanted to think about then but was a little too out of it to follow through. Now it hits me. I want to dwell on this for a bit — it's been bothering me for a while.

The similarities between major Chinese cities and Singapore are alarming. A woman born between 1930 and 1940 has an approximate lifetime risk for breast cancer of about 1:25 to 1:30. That woman's daughter, born, say, between 1960 and 1970, has a lifetime risk of 1:16. And if present trends continue, and there is no reason in the world to expect otherwise, the next generation, born, say, between 1990 and 2000, will have risks of about 1:10, so called "Western" rates. What the data shows is that breast cancer, contrary to common perception, is definitely not a Western disease any longer.

Most of the known risk factors have to do with reproductive factors. Having fewer children, having them later in life and not breastfeeding, all increase the risk of breast cancer. So do obesity, possibly increased protein and calorie intake, and prolonged use of hormone replacement therapy. Of course there are women with many children, all of whom they breastfed and then stayed slim and never used hormone replacements, who do still get breast cancer. There is no satisfactory explanation for why it should happen to them, but at a population level, what is known to affect breast cancer risk seems to account for most of the rise in incidence.

How has the Singapore woman had a change in risk exposure? For twenty years starting in the 1960s, we had very effective population control measures thanks to the Stop At Two policy. At that time we were a tiny country with no natural resources, limited housing and an unskilled workforce and this was completely necessary.

These population control measures involved considerable social engineering and early imprinting. I remember as a kid having public health posters explained during Civics class in primary school. These depicted the multiparous as those with unkempt homes, women trapped with childrearing and kept away from fulfilling their full potential at work. On the other hand, families with two children were obviously better off. Two children could fit under a transparent umbrella and share an apple while staying dry in the rain. There was a darker side to it as well. We had about 20,000 full term deliveries in the largest maternity hospital when I came through in medical school. The number of pregnancies terminated that year was not that much lower.

There is one other country which had an equally urgent need to slow population growth, and we are sitting in it. Remarkably, all this was put in place at very much the same time as Singapore. The Chinese went one better: In the cities, couples were allowed only one child. There were the same other risk factors as well, and the results were predictable: the same astronomical rise in cancer incidence.

The one stark contrast in the situation between Singapore and China is what keeps me entranced for the entire morning session. The difference in scale: In Singapore we have five million people. China has 1.3 *billion*. Ma tells us that in China, a city is not considered properly populous unless there are over 10 million residents. Luzhou itself has as many people as Singapore. Guangzhou 8.5 million, Shanghai and Chengdu have 14 million apiece, Beijing a whopping 21 million. In Singapore breast cancer is the leading cause of cancer death in women, accounting for about one fifth of deaths from all cancers, or about 300 to 400 deaths per year. I did not see any data on breast cancer mortality in China this morning, but it should be in the tens of thousands. That's every year. I suddenly feel the need for a strong drink.

THE CONGRESS IS OVER by two in the afternoon and after a more controlled re-acquaintance to 1573 at the farewell lunch in the hotel, I go up to the room to sleep it off. We have the rest of the day off but tomorrow is going to be an early day. There's about 300 km to cover on country roads before getting to Chengdu, where Boss will be joining us for the rest of the ride.

I look for any response to the blog posts. Based on what Mike and I had discussed earlier, I had provided as much detail as possible of what we are going through, unpleasant as it is. On a venture called the Long Ride half of the riders not riding sort of begs an explanation.

I don't think I feel particularly embarrassed by it. Bewildered and frustrated, yes, but the support from Mike, Neo Chian, Hung Tuan and the rest of the crew makes it more like a problem to sort out rather than something to be embarrassed about, or kept under wraps.

Which is why this afternoon's long list of emails in response to the blog posts comes as such a surprise. There are messages from all sorts of people: surgeons, scientists, physicians, fellow bikers and engineers, many of them with the same problems with anxiety attacks.

My experience seems to resonate especially with a younger biker who had to fight his mind to get back on the bike after a proper smash up. We have a long and very encouraging chat online. Others have different shades of the same basic problems. There're a host of different triggers: public speaking, grant applications, tricky surgery, an emergency call in the middle of the night, or just generally not living up to expectations they have set themselves. Many struggle with letting go of unreasonable goals.

Sometimes their difficulties in letting things go spill over and despite their best efforts, they had take out on their spouses and colleagues. They're labelled as "difficult to work with". They know it but can do little about it. One of them puts it better than I ever could: "Everyone says I should learn to relax, why don't I just relax, but why can't *they* see that *I* just *CAN'T*?"

All of them go through their own dark purgatory. Some bring it up to psychiatrists, many do not and just grit through. Just like me, they have thought retention, magnification, cognitive disorders, unrelenting high standards, the lot.

I sit in my hotel room, stunned. Soon after the surprise comes the relief. Hang on, there's something important here: *I am not alone! This does happen to other people!* Just knowing that this can be sorted out, that there are many others who have gone through this before and emerged better for it makes all the difference.

It strikes me how ridiculous this all is. Some of these people I've known for years, and until now I had no idea what their troubles were. How difficult must it have been to keep going and pretending that everything was all right? They are stable, calm, capable, trustworthy people in positions of responsibility. They have literally held lives and limbs in their hands. People that I could and would trust without a second thought, not the sort to go falling apart in any kind of situation. Then the penny drops.

Alone in my room in Luzhou I think I actually say it out loud: "You big, effing idiot Philip, what kind of person do you think *you* are?" This is not about some character flaw, or failing to meet some silly grade, or anything that makes me less of a person than I am. This is a mental illness.

More importantly, some of my friends, with the help of emails and WhatsApp, are starting to give me useful practical advice on what needs to be done. I have long suspected that although the Prozac helps, I need something else to get back besides just popping pills.

It's called cognitive behavioural therapy. The basic premise is that the way we feel depends on how we perceive things. I am feeling anxious and fearful because I'm perceiving things incorrectly. Due to certain character traits — fixation on high standards, fear of failure, difficulty in trusting others, a very low opinion of what I can trust myself to do — I'm putting the wrong emphasis on what I'm seeing.

Everything I do right is ignored, and everything I do wrong is emphasised and magnified. Every little hiccup is taken as some sort of major calamity, and it isn't helped by the schedule that we've set. There is no time to rest and get quiet and try and sort the lies from the truth.

One of the things I've been advised to do now is to monitor my thoughts and question their legitimacy. This isn't easy. The first hurdle I need to get through is accepting that my mind has broken down.

I'm one of the sanest people I know. The mind is something I've taken pride in. It's sorted out all sorts of things for me, and part of the pleasure I get at work is from people asking me what I think, what my mind can conjure up to help move things along and help this patient.

The basic assumption is that it'd do its thing: See the world around me as it is, discern and retain the valuable, discard the needless and hold in abeyance the rest for further consideration. The working relationship I have with my mind is that the more I train it the better it gets. Take in more factors, weigh them faster, discern greater subtleties, decide quicker and make fewer mistakes.

Now what I have to accept is that all of that's not true. At least not right now. And that's no real surprise to a lot of people because of my character traits. And by the way I'm not alone with this, there are lots of people with exactly the same problem, but we don't talk about it because it's not talked about. And just in case I think all this is bollocks and that I have a handle on things, try and remember what happened the last time I tried to get on the bike. In fact try to remember what I feel about riding at all, or where the bike is now, and where I am. It's nearly 1,000 km away in Kunming so something must be seriously wrong.

OK, now that that's settled what I have to do is learn how to develop second thoughts: the thoughts you think about how you think. So if a thought comes into my head, I learn to ask if it is true, what is the objective evidence for or against. Did the thought make the situation I'm in better or worse — is it helpful? Does it fall under any of my cognitive errors like over generalisation or magnification or dichotomous thinking? Would I be thinking such thoughts, say, if I was at home and not on this ride? What would I do or feel if I didn't think like this?

It is a little cumbersome but the real impetus is that if false ideas are unchallenged they tend to take root. I'm still getting up at ridiculous times in the morning because of the illogical preoccupation that I'm going to hold people up. Because of this new way of looking at my thoughts, I'm starting to be able to go back to sleep again but a simple matter like that is taking weeks to sort out.

With all this effort on long distance psychotherapy and the drugs, I'm told that there is a good chance that I might get over things in about a month or two. Apparently people with panic attacks take about 10 to 15 sessions of psychotherapy to get back to normal function. It's expected to be a rocky road with ups and downs. Well, this should be interesting. I take the Prozac and another sleeping tablet and get to bed.

When I come down to breakfast it's still dark. Ma had told us yesterday that the road from Luzhou to Chengdu is going to be hard going. Once again we are not allowed to take the expressways. Likely 30 – 40 km/h average speeds, so expect about eight hours in the saddle. He wants to get an early start because he has been chatting with the locals and there is a rumour that some of the roads have been closed for maintenance work.

To my surprise James and Cynthia are already at breakfast, and Mike is at another table tucking grimly into his plate of noodles. I join him and once again I'm craving for a proper cup of coffee but it is the usual watered tea. We both know it isn't going to be nice riding today, but that's the nature of bike trips. There are good days and bad days. Today is going to be one of the not-so-good ones. It isn't so much about the mileage, the main thing is the air. It stings the eyes, and sometimes I feel the grit in my teeth after going through the bad bits. With one of the world's largest cities as our next stop in Chengdu we aren't too hopeful about things getting better.

"How you feeling?" Mike asks me.

"Pretty placid. I think it's the Prozac. Still getting up before the alarm clock but it seems to be getting easier to get back to sleep. How about you?"

"This country is just magnificent. I was thinking in Yunnan

how much the riding really reminds me of Norway. And the history here is just so rich I really wish we could take a longer time. But these cities …"

"Yeah," I agree, "it's the damn air."

"Everyone's just wants to push forward, I don't think they're counting the cost," Mike goes on, "we haven't seen blue sky for almost a week now. The place feels like one big construction site."

While we were in Yunnan there was this daily rhythm. The timeless beauty of the countryside alternating with the grit and grime of the cities as we pulled in at the end of the day. Here in the flatlands of Sichuan there is no such cadence. It's just hard breathing all day long. Here in Sichuan there is a different kind of paradox.

In the car I would hear Ma go on about Zhuge Liang and Li Bai and Sun Tze and all that ancient wisdom. Long forgotten proverbs that had been drilled into me by Grandma and then my Chinese schoolteachers over the years. To hear all of it again coming from a native who really does believe is powerful stuff. It's difficult to define what being Chinese is but from what I understand from these Ancients it is about living in harmony – with yourself, your environment and with those around you, to find a way of life that perpetuates this mutuality.

In contrast, outside the car we see overbuilt cities, polluted waters, mountains being carved up or hollowed through for highways. Everyone in a mad rush, straining ahead as though making up for lost time. With the longest continuous history in the world I'm having trouble accepting that this is the best they can come up with for the future. Maybe this history isn't as continuous as I think it is after all; maybe there's been some major disruption I don't understand. We aren't starting our day with happy thoughts.

"Well," says Mike grimly after his second helping, "I will catch you ... someplace else." He goes up to his room to get his kit down, I join Cynthia and James.

This will be my last morning with them for some time. They're going to catch the flight to Beijing and from there back to Copenhagen. We will not be seeing them again until we arrive in Denmark by land. Without my bike I'm not entirely sure how I'll get there, but we'll make a beeline to their home by the beach in Hundige. I have it all fixed in the GPS.

It will be green then; two months from now it'd be nearly the summer solstice. We'll have long days and sea air and that wonderful beach by the back of their house. That's what I'm looking forward to the most: somewhere that's clean and green and water that's just water.

After the lectures yesterday James and Cynthia had breast cancer patients to interview at the Medical School in Luzhou, thanks to Rebecca's encouraging them to come forward. I'm very pleasantly surprised to learn that a half dozen or so Chinese cancer patients had been willing to come to share their stories.

As I join their table I have the impression that the interviews have had an unexpected effect on James and Cynthia. The last time we had met was at the welcome dinner two days earlier. They look like they've aged since.

"This is important work, Phil. We have got to make sure we get this published," Cyn says when I sit down to another cup of weak tea. She's usually excited about her work but there's something else now.

"Um, yes it is," I reply, "anything interesting happen yesterday at the interviews?"

"There are so many areas we can explore," Cyn goes on, "there was this lady that had to come from just 60 km outside of Luzhou for her chemotherapy. That meant her husband skipping a day's work to take care of the children, then walking to the bus station and a train here, getting home the same way. It took her three hours to get here and three hours to get back, even if she felt the side effects of chemo. She said it was the hardest thing she had ever done. How many times would she have to make that journey?"

"Chemo? Once every three weeks or so, can be up to six or 10 months, depending," I reply. Somehow the tea isn't so important anymore; Cyn has been affected by this.

"Six *months*?! So she would have to make these six-hour journeys each time?"

I nod and look at my tea.

"Then there was another lady who said that she knew she needed an operation and the only way she could afford it was to borrow money from her son, but she knew her son was already stretched with the grandkid's education."

"Hang on," I interrupt, "I thought that healthcare here was really heavily subsidised? That's what we were told."

"It is, and the prices are way below what we would pay in Singapore. By the way, how can that be? Are they getting the same kind of chemo or something less?"

"From what I can see in the hospitals and their clinical data, I think they get very up-to-date treatment."

"Well, apparently they have to make some sort of payment to the surgeon to get a bed in hospital," James says.

Ah, right. I had heard about that. In the past, surgeons often controlled the beds in their wards and if certain operations did not want to wait long, an unofficial payment would often grease things along.

"So she paid?" I ask. James shakes his head. He's trying to hide it but I can see he's finding this part difficult.

"No," says Cyn, "she said it didn't hurt. To prove it she lifted up her blouse … in front of us and the other patients in the room …"

Oh God. You effing idiot, Philip. You didn't warn her. They aren't clinicians, they're anthropologists.

"I think she had a cancer that had some sort of fungal infection. It looked like she had some sort of mushroom coming out of her chest, out through the skin. Could that be possible?" Cyn asks.

"Er, no Cyn, I'm really sorry … that's probably inoperable advanced breast cancer." I stare at my tea.

"So what to be done for her?" asks James.

"Probably chemo and maybe radiotherapy later, but if it's spread elsewhere — lung, liver or bones — there's a lot less we can do."

Silence. This is a pretty crappy way to start the day. Where's a bottle of 1573 when you can really use it?

"Did you ask what she felt about her condition now?" I ask them.

"She said it still didn't hurt. She was quite accepting of whatever comes. She said that even if she dies at least her grandchildren would live on."

It's a fleeting glimpse of just how big the problem is. There is the matter of public education. Women should know that it's not the painful breast lump that's dangerous, most of those are harmless. The non-painful lumps kill. Then there are the physical barriers: How do you provide transport? Social care for the children? Husband's time away from work? She was just 60 km from a cancer centre. How can you prepare for cancer care in China when it's a *hundred* million women at risk?

Soon Ma comes around and says it's time to go. I give Cyn and James a hug.

"Next time we meet it'll be at your home. Hardly seems possible now," I tell them.

"Have a good journey," says Cyn, "we have to come back and learn some more. We have to get this published. This is important."

"Right."

Outside, the sun is just coming up. Mike's putting the last of his items on to the Beemer and sorting his GPS. I tell him about what James and Cyn had gone through.

"You didn't warn them?" he asks.

"Nope. Slipped my mind entirely. Feel lousy about that."

"Maybe just as well. Good for them to see."

"Still feel lousy. I think it's affected them." I help him get the rest of the things secured and he gets on the bike and checks the comms set.

"Not quite all fun and games, is it, this ride?" I ask on the comms set as I head for Ma's Cruiser.

"Nope," Mike answers, "not fun and games at all."

Eleven
NOT THE PLACE SHE LEFT

IN THE END MA'S worries are unfounded and we approach Chengdu in good time. I am quite pleased with that because there are things to see and do here. When planning this ride we had trouble trying to get a collaborator from Chengdu on board. There is a big university here and a very good medical school but unfortunately nothing came of it. Without any medical component we only have one day for this megacity before we have to be off again.

That is a real pity. Grandma was from around here where her father worked for the Singer company, then one of the world's largest manufacturers of sewing machines. I remember the yellowed black-and-white photographs of the city, the curved Chinese roofs and wide empty streets with trishaw pullers and hardly any cars. It'll be nice to see the city for myself.

Our grandparents never talked about what made them uproot everything and come to Singapore to start a family. Knowing what Singapore was like in the 1930s, it must have been a terrible risk. Both Grandpa and Grandma were well-educated: he was an engineer and she a graduate teacher. I realised later on that they were almost unique among Chinese immigrants at the time in their fluency in English, which was always spoken with a slight American accent.

What always intrigued me was why they always hankered to come home to China — Grandma could literally break into verse about the beauty of Sichuan — but neither of them ever did. It was only later that I realised why no matter how rosy his recollections, Grandpa would always look a little wistful and conclude, "This is our home now." It was almost as though he had never intended to stay in Singapore. That he had meant to make his fortune and take it back with him like so many do nowadays, but events overtook him and he died without ever making the return journey. I will never know whether he thought his big gamble had paid off.

It's about just after lunch when we turn off the country roads and onto the ring road that surrounds Chengdu. The first sign that we are about to encounter something special is the change in the roads. Before long we're ambling along a six-lane expressway on the flat bottom of a vast basin with almost no trees or buildings in sight. The place is a lattice of roads, flyovers, street lamps, road signs and traffic signals, the lot. It's an asphalt and concrete framework of a city before the city shows up. Incredibly, what we are about to enter is still growing.

In the Cruiser Pierce and I are helping Ma with the GPS

as he tries to find the way through all these new roads. According to his basemap, this road doesn't exist, on the GPS screen all we can see is beige emptiness all around. I think it's Mike on his bike behind us who first sees it, coming out through the midday haze. The intercom crackles:

"Guys, will you look at that thing …"

We look up. Straight ahead of us there is this rectangular blob. A grey haze isolates it from its surroundings and it stands alone in the featureless landscape. Nothing too elaborate, just a rectangular monolith surrounded by flat ground. Pierce thinks it's a large aircraft hangar. There's no airport on the map but he wouldn't put it past the Chinese to have built one in the last few months. As we get closer we gain a sense of perspective. There is a convoy of tour buses next to the thing and they looked positively Lilliputian. We're still miles away.

Welcome to the world's largest building. I'm not kidding. This thing is 500 m by 400 m and goes up 100 m. Nothing even comes close, well, nothing except the actual Boeing hangar in Seattle and a large greenhouse in the Netherlands. For its 18 million square feet of floor space, it's more than a building, it's an assertion. One look and the message is received loud and clear: Chengdu has arrived. I'm even more impressed with Irene: it's where we're spending the night.

When we get to the hotel lobby we find that the inside is just as opulent as the exterior is functional. Marble as far as the eye can see in all directions, including upwards, with a ceiling that seems to be covered with crystal glass. It's the only hotel I've ever been in with a scale map of the lobby.

That must be useful for the numerous travelling parties that I imagine are still lost and waiting to be found. What we have no trouble finding is Boss. He's standing in the lobby with his suitcase and camera equipment, beaming at finally joining the party to Sweden.

Going to the room means using a golf buggy on an inner perimeter track to the correct lift lobby. That's required for every guest in this thousand-room hotel, so you can imagine the number of buggies. On the inside of the track, unbelievably, is a beach. A beach *in* a building. With fake sand and waves and sun from the biggest LCD screen I have ever seen. It may be grey and smoggy outside but on the inside it's a balmy, clear blue day by the beach, with the sun setting on the horizon. As I stand at the reception desk I think I feel fake wind. I'm sure that if that LCD screen was on the outside of the building, it can be seen from space. Think of the practical applications.

Next to the beach is a surf pool surrounded by a grandstand. The bellboy tells us this thing can create an artificial wave and people then sit in the grandstand and watch the surfers. Next to that is the longest water slide I have ever seen, part of a full theme park, with that beach and surf pool, on the *inside* of the building. It must be quite something when someone uses any of it. For the moment the whole place is empty. The bellboy tells us that the sun never sets here, and that the fifth IMAX cinema has just opened and we can call to make reservations. I thank him and wonder what an IMAX cinema is. Bet you it's big.

Since we've made such good time Irene's arranged for a late second lunch and wander about at Jinli Old Street and

I tag along. The drive to the city centre confirms what I had anticipated. Chengdu is the most impressive built-up city I have ever seen. Unlike many of the gridlocked Chinese cities we have come through with streets that seemed surprised by the traffic volume, this city is properly sorted out.

Broad, perfectly surfaced expressways feed straight to trunk roads that lead directly to the heart of the city. On either side, skyscrapers and gleaming shopping malls with just the same kind of billboards you would see back home in Singapore: Mango, Burberrys, Ralph Lauren and other things I don't remember because a gigantic Diane Kruger stares out of it and straight at me, arms outstretched and lips ever so slightly parted. My mind sort of empties whenever she does that.

On the streets are city people with city cars. They're in designer suits, toting leather accessories and wearing out crocodile skin shoes. They don't seem to be in a particular rush, just very comfortably enjoying life in the city: nattering on hand phones, doing selfies, window shopping. Some people have this absurd idea of China as a waking giant. Get with the programme, people. He's got dressed, powdered his mocha, put on his Fitbit and is striding into next Wednesday. There is no way to fight the impression that he's left us all far behind. And that's coming from a Singaporean.

After wandering around for a bit we settle in a quiet teashop with black marble finishing. In the middle is this gentle fountain bubbling away quietly with koi swimming around. We sit in recessed booths by the fountain on white sofa seats with thin woollen blankets to take away some of the evening chill.

A very pleasant waitress takes our order and asks where we're from and if it's our first time here. Again that Sichuan accent. I reply that it's my first time here but I have family that came from these parts. They left about eighty years ago. Did they ever return? No. "Ah well," she says, "this sure isn't the place they left, that's for certain."

The way she said it stirs a memory. Truth is, they didn't all stay away. At the end of the Second World War, Mao Zedong called the *nanqiao*, those who had emigrated from China to southeast Asia, to return to rebuild China from the ravages of that devastation. Especially those who had the useful professional skills.

While my grandfather had little faith in Communism, his younger sister and her husband did what they thought was their patriotic duty and gave up their lives in Singapore to return. As I remember, they were engineers as well. That may not have been as difficult a choice as it seems now. The end of the war also marked the beginning of the end of the British Empire. Just what that meant for Singapore, which was then part of Malaya, was anyone's guess.

It must have been a painful parting of ways. I heard that Grandpa was actually quite close to his younger sister, whom my dad always addressed affectionately as *siao auntie*, or little aunt. Strangely, through our growing years I don't think they mentioned her once. It was only in the late 1970s, after Mao's death and when China started opening up to the rest of the world, that she came back to our family's consciousness. Sadly, not in a good way.

Dad had come to China as part of one of the first international computer delegations in 1979. He made the effort to see his favourite aunt and her husband, I suppose it would have been around here. When he returned to Singapore after that visit, he would only tell their story after some strong drink. For a while their lives had been going according to plan, then came the Cultural Revolution when their own students in the university turned against them. I don't know if they were ever put in jail but they spent the rest of their working lives on a farm. There was a child that didn't survive. When Dad found them they were already past retirement age and living in very basic conditions in small lodgings over a shop house.

What really affected Dad was when the time came for him to leave. His uncle, whom he had not met since his teens, would not let him go. Or rather, would not let some of his things go, including his watch, a programmable pocket calculator and a Burberry coat and scarf. The old man felt that he was owed that much, seeing how he had missed out on the prosperity in Singapore. Dad conceded the items and unprotected from the cold, he froze through the rest of his trip. He could not deny his uncle, but he found the whole thing distasteful in the extreme, and described his uncle with one of his ugly words: clawing. He was glad that at least his parents would never get to see it.

Later, when ordinary Chinese citizens were allowed to travel, *siao auntie* made the trip to Singapore. I'm not sure if Dad had anything to do with it but she travelled without her husband. Dad could be pretty cold that way when he wanted to be. She spent a few days with us and other branches of the family, seeing some of the places she used to go and also to meet Grandpa for the last time. Of course, everything had changed in the space of over 30 years and in her grey Mao suit she seemed so out of place. What was it she had said about Singapore? It sure wasn't the place she had left, that's for certain.

Twelve
TURNING POINT

It is already dark when we get to Guangyuan. I know that this is a nice part of China with lots to see and do but it's been a long day and I'm glad to get to bed.

When I wake up it's still dark and again I have that feeling of apprehension. It's a little disappointing because it's been about a week since I've woken up this early and I thought I was through with that. Happily, I've learnt since to sit back and ask the questions. Why do I feel apprehensive? That's easy, I'm coming to the point where I will have to tell the minders to send the bike back from Kunming to Thailand. There is a chance of sending it up to join us again, but in conversations with Boss I think my mind's sort of made up. No point taking the risk of being unable to ride and having it stuck in the heart of China.

There are still a couple of hours to breakfast and today it's a short one to Hanzhong some 200 km away. The Wi-Fi is fine and I need to get in touch with our next set of collaborators: 10 days away in Almaty.

After sorting out what I can the sun's already coming up by the time I get to the WhatsApp messages. Soo Hwang, my old friend from Malaysia, is online. Soo is head of a cancer research institute in Kuala Lumpur and we've collaborated on numerous papers before. Soo's a good friend, quite simply brilliant and exceptionally clear-headed. I have a lot of time for Soo. This morning she says that she's starting her day catching up on some of the blog posts that I had sent out earlier.

Pretty rough, she says, *you must hang in there.*

Thanks, I reply, *but the difficult part is deciding in the next few days where to send the bike.*

What do you mean? asks Soo.

I explain. When I stopped riding in Kunming I had actually already decided to send the bike back. Trouble is that paperwork from the Chinese officials means that the bike can only leave the country at the same time as the rest of the convoy. At least that's what I was told. So it still sits in Kunming. In a sense it's leaving us time to decide what to do.

We could still get it brought up to us in time before we leave the country next week, or we could send it back as originally planned. If we send it back it's only going as far as Chiang Mai, where I can leave it with a friend. After that I need to figure out a way to get it to Singapore. I'm not even sure if I can ride it back from there after all the trouble I'm having just riding short distances.

Silence. I think for a moment that Soo has logged off and gone in to work, but she's still online.

Look. I know you're scared, Soo says.

Not really, not as long as I'm not on a bike, I reply.

Doesn't this fear make this Long Ride more about breast cancer than anything else you've done?

What do you mean? I ask.

What if a breast surgeon, capable and with his heart in the right place, has this catastrophic fear of failing at everything that he hopes to accomplish, but learns to face and manage his fear?

Oh God.

You're not suggesting ... I counter with Boss's perspective: This is not about bike riding, this is about breast cancer. The bike's secondary. *I'm* secondary.

Soo replies: *Isn't that what breast cancer patients face? Don't they feel they don't deserve this diagnosis? That it happens to other people? Don't they have the catastrophic realisation that life will not go on as planned? That treatment and its side effects can take away almost a year of their shortened lives, their careers put on hold or compromised entirely? That they will be a burden to their families and loved ones, they will need help?*

Look Soo, I reply, *you're going to make me take unnecessary risks. What if I send the bike deeper into China and then I find that I can't ride? What if something happens to Mike and the rack is being used up by my deadweight of a bike?*

That's a what if, says Soo. *What about their* real *fear? Of this kind of surgery, of chemotherapy and hair loss ... how their husbands will look at them, how they'll hold them, or whether they can even keep a husband, fear for their children who may not have a mother last their childhood?*

I suppose you could avoid facing the fear, Soo goes on. *So could they. All their fears would not have to be faced if they did not tell a doctor about their lump, or not go for screening, and just pretend it'll go away. Isn't earlier presentation and accepting effective treatment for breast cancer really all about facing fear?*

I'm buggered. I have no answer. She's right. It *is* about facing fear. After all that stuff about challenging cognitive errors and taking the pills and the rest of it, facing fear is what it is all about.

Soo goes on, quite unaware, I think, of the turmoil she's causing thousands of miles away:

What if at some point after this long ride you need to tell women to come forward for screening, or to see a doctor or tell their loved ones about a breast lump that they have found? Or to accept the treatment that you and your team are offering? You're going to have to tell all those women to face all those fears and to have courage. Before you tell anyone to have courage then, where should the bike be sent now?

This is not what I want. I'm not entirely sure if it's the right thing to do. I'm going to be a mess and need help. I'm going to be a nuisance and slow people down and put Mike on the road for longer than he has to be. This ride has a long way to go, and I'm about to make it a lot longer, but I am going to get the bike back. That is, if I can get some key people to go along with the idea.

I bring it up to Mike in Hanzhong at breakfast.

"Mike, I've had a word with Soo and Viola again. I think I want the bike back." I watch for his response, knowing that if he cans the idea it's a deal breaker. If anything should happen to him because of my riding I need to know he's completely on board.

"Ah, good," he smiles, tucking into a second bowl of tofu breakfast. "Completely your call, but I'm really glad to see the tablets are finally doing their work. It's starting to be a bit boring riding all by myself. Good to have the old Phil back. It'll be a real ride now."

"I should warn you, I don't think this thing has completely run its course yet," I point out, "relapses are expected in this sort of thing." Other people have their panic attacks sorted in the relative safety of a psychiatrist's office. I'm about to do it on the back of a fast-moving heavy motorbike surrounded by Chinese drivers.

"We'll take it one day as it comes," says Mike, "no pressure, just keep talking on the intercom and taking this one minute at a time. Best news I've had for ages."

One down. I walk over and tell Hung Tuan, the four by four group leader, and he nearly jumps out of his breakfast chair.

"That's great! This ride needs another biker! Now we can really get this show going! I'll fix up with Irene how to bring the bike to us, not to worry, leave that to us."

"Do you think this is the right decision?" I ask him.

"Oh, it's definitely the right decision," he smiles as he goes over to Irene's table, "but only you can make it a great one."

I decide not to tell Boss, even though I spot him coming down to breakfast just a few feet away. He'll find out soon enough. The thing about Boss is that what you say is not so important, it's what you get done. With that off my chest I return to join Mike.

"I wonder how long I've got before starting to ride again," I ask him.

Typical start to the riding day as Mike picks his way through traffic.

"Not to worry, if there's anybody who can make it happen it's Irene and Hung Tuan working together."

At the end of breakfast Hung Tuan comes over to Mike and me.

"OK, I've just had a word with Irene. She's going to get her people to bring the bike forward. It should be with us in Lanzhou."

That is about 1,000 km away, or three days. From Kunming they would have to get the bike on a proper vehicle and cover 3,000 km in three days. Pretty tall order. I'm getting a fresh perspective on just what resources Irene has to call on.

The road from Hanzhong to Xi'an starts out badly and ends even worse but with some real gems in between. Getting out of the city limits finds us on country roads surrounded by flat farmland and in a mild drizzle. This is hard going; the towns are close together here and each one is a mess of crowded, unmarked and often unsurfaced roads, with crawling traffic in between.

It's like riding through a 100-mile long worksite with dust and noise everywhere, piles of earth and granite, torn up tarmac, and all sorts of traffic, all thrown together in some mad melee. I'm really glad we have Ma to clear the traffic in front of Mike.

In the late morning, a wonderful transformation as the flatlands give way to rolling hills. When we pass in to a long tunnel through the mountain and out the other side we're immersed in a dazzlingly clear day.

It magically becomes riding in a postcard. Just like a typical day summer's day in the English countryside. There are running streams, patchwork fields separated by low hedges, wild sunflowers and gloriously luminous dashes of rapeseed.

The fabulous riding roads go on and on, with grazing fields on each side in different shades of green, and specks of sheep in the distance. The road runs like a black ribbon through this sun-kissed countryside, one gentle hill over another in a series of mild curves. Looking past Ma's shoulder from the rear seat I'm starting to think like a biker again: which gear, where the best line is for the corners.

By our side we have the mighty Wei He, whose flood plains formed the cradle of Chinese civilisation where it joins the Yellow River just east of Xi'an. There are hardly any buildings in the landscape, mainly crude brick walls with

Typical middle of the day through breathtaking countryside.

corrugated zinc roofing. It's hard to distinguish dwellings of farmer from those of livestock.

Before we get to Xi'an there is the Qinling mountain range to cross. This runs in an east-west direction just south of Xi'an. Soon the road takes us into a deep gorge that runs immediately along the steep banks of the Hei He. The Qinling mountains have some of the most majestic and sacred mountain peaks in all of China, immortalised by painting and poetry since the Tang Dynasty, but sadly all we see of it is a blurred landscape whizzing past.

Soon it's second-gear-only stuff as we leave the river further and further below us and ascend the steep sides of the gorge, into the low clouds. The air turns frigid and a light drizzle covers us. Everything is covered with shades of grey: the broadening river below, the vertical mountainsides vaulting a lead grey sky. It's like riding in a Chinese brush painting. Visibility drops to less than 100 m through one hairpin turn after another on rain-slicked roads. Mike's working hard now against the wind.

We reach the highest point in the road at just over 2,000 m. There is a coach park where locals can take the rest of the mountain by foot. We start our rapid descent down to Xi'an, which is a rude awakening back to the China of the 21st century. We're in gridlock even before we see the famed outer wall fortifications of one of the most historic cities in all of China. Unfortunately, this is also the beginning of a week in one of the most polluted valleys on earth.

The next day it's not a glorious start to our first day on the Silk Road. From here until Europe we will be heading westward on this most ancient of routes. It takes us over an hour just to get out of Xi'an. It's start-stop, first-gear-only, occasionally take to the sidewalk, air-cooled-engine-overheating kind of crawling traffic. I remember Dad saying that when he visited Beijing in the late 1970s, it was strange how quiet rush hour was: just the whish of a million bicycles. That's a world away from this mess.

We pull up for a petrol and pee break on the outskirts of Binxian by a small bus station. As Mike wanders off for the loo we stand about the opened back door of the Cruiser with the usual coffee and biscuits. There aren't too many people about but a few locals linger and we answer the usual questions about the red Beemer.

One local looks on with more than a passing interest. He looks to be in his early fifties, with a badly overgrown crew cut, tall and broad-shouldered. Dressed in jeans, collared shirt, a beat-up bomber jacket and cheerily puffing a hand-rolled cigarette, he looks like a truck driver on a break.

Typical end of the day as Mike picks his way through city traffic again, this time into Xi'an.

"Where you guys off to?" He's friendly enough but with a very heavy accent I can barely make out. We are well out of Sichuan now.

"Headed to Xinjiang, and then onward to Kazakhstan," I reply.

"Wow, crossing Xingjiang? That's a long holiday," he laughs.

Pierce's Chinese is a lot better than mine and he briefly explains what we're about.

When he hears about breast cancer the man's smile fixes for a moment, then fades. He puffs on his cigarette and looks thoughtful. We're still waiting for Mike and he accepts our offer of a coffee mix and some butter cookies.

"So you have breast cancer in Singapore as well?" he asks between puffs of blue smoke. There's something about the way he looks.

I explain that we have one of the highest rates of breast cancer anywhere in Asia, and how we've come to hear the experiences of other doctors in China.

"So you're doctors then?" he asks.

"Yes," Pierce replies. He points to me and then to Mike, who has just returned from the washroom, looking even paler than usual. The petrol stop washrooms in China can have that effect on the uninitiated.

"These two are breast cancer surgeons. From a university in Singapore."

We shake hands with him and share a quiet moment over the smokes and coffee. I can tell there's something he wants to bring up but he's not sure how. Soon the coffee is drunk and Ma starts to clear up. I think he knows we're behind schedule and need to make time. Our new friend can sense his chance slipping and decides to plunge in.

"My wife had breast cancer," he says abruptly. "She's gone now." He finishes his cigarette and grinds it into the gravel with his boot.

"I brought her to see the doctor in Binxian," he says with a grim smile. "That doctor said that it was probably nothing and gave her some antibiotics. It didn't help much."

There isn't any resentment, just a matter of fact. If anything, for the moment he seems lost in himself, like we aren't there.

"I'm very sorry. When did she pass away?" Pierce asks.

"Oh, it's about six years now. Not that long ago. Has it to

do with breastfeeding? Because she breastfed our youngest one for about two years."

"I don't know," I reply. Ma is cleaning up the cups and putting things away. We really need to move on.

"Right," the man says, returning to his coffee cup. "You have a nice journey. So you don't think it's the breastfeeding then?"

There is just no time. The schedule's a curse. It would happen time and again. It's not just the sights that we're missing. These are times when any decent person without a schedule like ours would take the time and just stay for a while. Isn't that supposed to be the highlight of a bike ride, to have time for the people you meet? This has never felt less like a bike ride. I don't suppose for a second that we can even attempt to cover his grief, but leaving so abruptly is so completely heartless.

They would stay with me for some time, these chance encounters with locals who have been affected by breast cancer. I really wish I could be of more use. Most of all I wish I had more answers. I don't know why their wives or sisters or mothers got cancer and why the medicines didn't work and why they had to die when it wasn't even painful.

Most often we would meet these locals at petrol stops. We have one of those practically every other day for a hundred days. With more of these chance encounters, I realise that we aren't after the same thing. These people aren't really interested in the causes of Asian breast cancer, or a strategy to reduce cancer mortality in Asia.

They're not looking for what gave her breast cancer, but why. Of all people, why *her*? Not an explanation for her illness, but a reason for their pain. Without that it's very hard to come to terms with the grief. And if there is no reasonable explanation, one is made up just so that they can deal with the pain. Something like breastfeeding, because anything is better than her going like that for no good reason at all.

Many times I can't provide the answers, but there are other ways to be a comfort. At interviews in the hospitals with James and Cynthia, or at the odd petrol kiosk, would be the first time any of these men had talked to anyone about breast cancer and how it affects them. Sometimes just listening is all we can do, but it helps.

Thirteen
THE RETURNING RIDER

When we pull into the Legend Hotel in Lanzhou I'm hoping to see the V-Strom but it's not to be. Irene explains that the couriers could not make the distance despite driving through the night and would take another day before we get the Suzuki. That would make it in Wuwei.

After that Mike and I both decide not to see much of Lanzhou. While in the earlier city of Pingliang, we had been told that there's been a bit of an environmental scandal here. In the month before, residents had complained of a strange chemical smell in the tap water. Investigations concluded the week before that a leak at a nearby petrochemical plant had led to industrial benzene in Lanzhou's water supply. The authorities say that this problem should be sorted out in a few days and suggests that people should resort to bottled water for the time being. One part of Lanzhou city had its water supply cut off altogether.

This predictably led to a shortage of bottled water, which flew off the market shelves last week. So at Pingliang we had stocked up on water as well as cup noodles for our meals. The government advisory does not seem to make much sense. If it's benzene poisoning I would have thought that it would persist in all parts of food preparation — you can't degrade benzene by boiling the vegetables. Local residents had also told us they were a little skeptical about how long the problem had been going on before people started to complain of the smell.

What seems a little unsettling is how little effect this has on the city. Industrial Plant Poisons City. I expect a more agitated response. Instead, life seems to be going on as usual, as though this is nothing more than a slight deviation from the norm.

This may be because there are other problems here. Coming into Lanzhou around sunset on a damp drizzly day, we find a city with this yellow-grey pall with patches of purple over it. Ma tells us that the main factors are the rapid rise in car traffic, and the persistence of coal as the main source of fuel for heating and electricity. He says that things are actually better now: more people have switched to gas, and electric scooters are all around us.

Unfortunately, Lanzhou sits in the plain of the Yellow River between two mountain ranges. The very air seems tepid and we can see huge chimneys belching out the stuff straight against the sides of high-rise residential blocks. The buildings themselves seem ill, stained grey and blotchy like smoker's lungs. Many glisten with the industrial muck that has condensed from the acidic air.

I think you have to be a really hardened city-dweller to tough it out here year on year. In 1999 *Time* magazine had called this place the most polluted city on earth and somehow I can't believe what Ma said about things getting better. It is the only place in the entire trip I can't wait to leave.

The next morning we cross a heavily silted river the colour of milk tea. That's the Yellow River, says Ma, China's Sorrow, for the damage caused whenever its banks have flooded over the hundreds of years people have lived here. Chinese leaders have been obsessed with trying to control this river through the centuries, and from the bridge we see one of the many dams that span its width. There are nearly twenty dams across the length of the Yellow River providing hydroelectric power and curtailing flooding.

Ma can remember a time when the river waters had actually turned red because of contamination from industrial wastewater. Presently, the problem is the difficulty in managing its waters with the increase in demand from irrigation of the farmlands. This had led to parts of the Yellow River simply disappearing. In the 1990s, for several years running the river failed to reach the sea altogether. Strictly speaking one of the longest rivers in the world had become a lake then.

Leaving Lanzhou and heading northwestwards we're happy to get to higher ground and leave some of that smog behind us. There is an appreciable drop in traffic volume although this is still classed as an A road and not an expressway. The condition is excellent and we make good time.

We are heading through the famous Hexi Corridor, part of the Northern Silk Road that links Xi'an (which has served as China's capital city for more dynasties than any other city) and the Yellow River basin to Central Asia and the West. As early as 1000 BC this route has been an artery for trade, knowledge and armies moving both ways. Many of the cities we're going to pass through started as oases in an otherwise near desert. It would end at Jiangyuguan, the westernmost extent of the Great Wall, where if all went well we would visit in about four days' time.

The congestion and muck for the last week make the present contrast in surroundings even more stunning. The air here is clean and visibility limitless. To the south we have a view of the mighty snow-capped Qilian Mountains, majestic in their scale and continuous as far as the eye can see to our left. To the north and just as impressive, the Bei Shan, or Northern Mountains, that separate the Ganxi from the Gobi desert and Mongolia. The twin mountain ranges would accompany us throughout the stretch in Xinjiang and we soon take their presence for granted, but on the first day of their appearance there are many stops for just appreciating their stunning beauty. China is a marvellous place, and I'm regretting that the bike didn't come back to me yesterday.

The road leads us between terraced hills on both sides, running by the side of one of the tributaries of the Yellow River. We pass through a number of tunnels that run straight through the middle of these mountains as we head west and gain altitude.

Through the last of these tunnels we have a view of the

valley below as the road starts to descend. It's a desert. On the right there is still a deep gorge where the river used to be, but there's no water. In contrast to the irrigated fields we have been coming through, here the banks look bone dry. Parched sand where nothing can grow, like a massive bowl of dust. I wonder if this is what I had read about the Yellow River being so overused for irrigation up river that deserts are now extending along its course. Ma isn't very sure, it could be.

The sudden appearance of the desert seems to stir something in his mind. Ma has heard about the decision to start riding again and is really for the idea. I don't think he feels he should offer his opinion on the matter, but he says, "This is as it should be."

He is concerned about where the riding is going to start. When I tell him most likely Wuwei, the very next city, he thinks it's a good idea. Most of the dangerous roads and horrible air is behind us. From here onward it's going to be highway riding across the vast expanse of Xingjiang, where there are few twisties and even less traffic. Just the right place to get back on the road again. Except …

"In Singapore do you ever have storms?" Ma asks.

"No, not really," says Pierce, "occasionally the place may flood if there is a torrential downpour. Usually during the monsoons towards the end of the year."

"Right … right … but that's just water. Do you ever have *sha chen bao*?"

That's a new one to me. Directly translated it means a storm built up by sand. It takes a minute for the penny to drop. Again Pierce gets it first.

"I think he means sandstorms," he says to me.

"Right! No sandstorms," I tell Ma. "No deserts for that matter."

"Right …" says Ma, relieved that he's managed to get to this obliquely, "in Xingjiang we don't have water so there's no flooding, but we do have sandstorms. They usually come around late spring, which is sort of, well, sort of like now. And how long before you get to Kazakhstan?"

"About 10 days," I reply.

"Well, 10 days in Xingjiang in late April. Very good chance you'll get to see a sandstorm."

"What's it like?" I ask. I have not been riding for over two weeks, have no idea how I'll take to riding again and this sounds a bit ominous.

"Oh, the worst one I was in lasted for almost a whole day and night. The sky turns red and soon the sun is blocked out. There's all sorts of things flying about and once even the rain wipers of the SUV I was driving were ripped out," he chuckles at the memory. "I don't think you or even Mike can ride in a sandstorm." He had his eyes on the road so I don't think he saw the effect of what he said had on Pierce and me, but he may have felt the silence that followed.

"Oh, but those are pretty rare. Usually there's just a lot of dust flying about and it passes in an hour or two. Should be quite a sight."

Right.

WHEN WE GET TO Wuwei once again it's just before sunset and Irene tells us that the bike hasn't got here yet. The movers are at Chengdu, where their plan is to drive through the night to be here by morning.

Next morning I'm up just after sunrise and there's a steady drizzle outside as I get dressed. It seems like ages since I last got the ride kit on. It's now 8 degrees and not the 40 degrees in Thailand. I re-pack the panniers for the second time and make sure the intercom's charged. Now there's nothing to do but wait for the bike.

I check out and get all the kit to the lobby and have a look at the car park outside. The concrete is slick with rain, I see all the four by fours lined up and the red Beemer, but still no Suzuki. Not much difference whether it comes today or the next, I suppose. I've lost about 3,000 km of riding spent in Ma's car and another 300 km wouldn't make much difference. Don't know if I'll be this calm tomorrow though. Inside for breakfast then, and wait. Right now all I want is another shot at this. I cannot believe that for all the planning and wishing and hoping all I'm going to manage is ride from Singapore to Thailand.

Yet at the same time I have to keep telling myself not to set targets. Just take things as they come, all part of the game of filtering thoughts and keeping the tension away.

Not much of an appetite and pretty soon I'm out at the lobby again waiting. The four by four crews are ready to leave, but decide to hang around and see me off. I have shared the reasons for my decision to ride again with some of them, but I can see some have their doubts. To occupy the time they start running their own vehicle checks. At least the rain's letting up.

At around 8:30 am, two very tired looking delivery men pull up into the car park in a white lorry with an open cargo bay. The bike's all strapped down and covered by several layers of tarp. As we pull the tarps down I realize that the Suzuki is on its main stand, supported by a very rigid rectangular metal frame that runs down the centre of the cargo bay. Irene explains that she figured the best people to transport something as important as this are glass windowpane movers. She really is the best. It's all hands on deck as the bike is man carried off the lorry and placed in the lot.

"OK," Mike says to me, "I'm going to check out. You run your checks and take your time. We've got a short day today." He's right — 250 km is like Singapore to Malacca — a distance I've done before without fully waking up.

I go into my routine. First take the seat off and re-connect the battery, then tyre pressures and surfaces, then chain lube and rear cassette, brake and clutch fluids, brake wear. Then the moment of truth. Get on, start the bike. She starts with hardly a turn of the motor and that wonderful V-twin sound.

A new beginning: the V-Strom being carried off the truck.

Lights are fine. I look over my shoulder and don't see Mike yet, so there's time for a spin around the block.

That's when the first hint of hesitation creeps in. *Look Phil, the fact is, there are movers right here in the hotel car park. If you have any kind of difficulty, it could easily go back the way it came on the same truck. It would look pretty bloody ridiculous, but you'll be safe.*

I'm conscious of the four by four crews watching. With the engine running I find what used to be motor memory is now taking a conscious effort. To gear in a bike it's left hand clutch in and drop to first gear on left foot lever. Natural as falling rain for a biker, but I need a conscious effort. I suppose it's just that I haven't been on a bike for over two weeks. Even at home in Singapore I ride more often than this.

OK, check the surface between here and the hotel entrance. It's wet concrete, and a ridiculous bit of marble just under the entrance to the lobby. One has little grip, the other no grip at all, so don't make any sudden moves. Then, as I wait at the hotel entrance for a break in the office hour traffic, I see roads slick with an oily film from the rain. Oh yes, and they drive on the wrong side of the road.

Going around a few blocks I realise that they sometimes drive on the right side of the road. In fact they drive pretty much anywhere there's a hole in the traffic, from any direction. I'm catching my breath too often and after a few minutes I have to pull over on the pavement to sort myself out. I'm not really having fun, it's wet and cold, and there's really a long way to go. About half a continent, and then all of Europe. I notice that the bike feels a little underpowered, and the voltmeter is reading a little lower than normal. I figure it's just the cold—it is 8 degrees according to the hotel thermometer—and being laid up for a fortnight.

Try this, I say to myself, *just look in the distance. Forget the road surface.* I take my eyes off the road and trust the Pirellis. A lot better. It's the start of the process of cognitive behavioural therapy (CBT) while riding. What's making me tense? Well, besides the road surface and the wet? That I seem to be moving very slowly and looking at the speedo rather than the surroundings. Tape up the speedo. *I'm sorry? That's probably illegal. Well, think of something so you can't see it.* I pull over again and position the tank bag forward on the tank. It blocks the view of the speedo altogether.

What else is bothering you? It feels like a really cold day. Is it really cold? Well, not really, this is a good riding jacket, and putting the insoles against the engine block warms me up quickly. OK, what else? I don't think the tyres will hold grip in this wet. Right then, start cornering. I circle a few blocks before heading back to the hotel, taking the right angle turns faster and faster each time. No trouble with the grip. Another cognitive error exposed.

And so it goes on. I remember what Soo Hwang had told me a few nights ago about how to get these errors sorted out as quickly as possible. She had all those questions go down to just four points:

Is it true?

Is it really true?

What thing would you do if it were not true?

Do that thing.

It's hard though, much harder than giving up. A lot like learning to ride all over again, but that was a lot less frightening. I remember an old army saying I used to hear from instructors before they got us to do something horribly dangerous: "You will now acquire courage." Where you got it from didn't concern them at all. Just get it, because now's the time for it. Can it be that all it takes to face my fear is just asking three questions?

An oil slick leading into a muddy puddle takes up the final turn before the hotel. I worry momentarily about what lies beneath. No, it's not true. This bike can take that, and so can you. Do that thing. Full bank into the car park, even over that marble bit in front of the lobby. I side stand the bike and join Mike by his Beemer. We do a comms check before I walk over to the movers who are standing with Irene. No need for further services, many thanks for all the effort in getting my bike back, we're good to go. Then I get the panniers on and we set off.

Mike's on new tyres he's just slipped on in Xi'an and before long his onboard computer is reading low tyre pressures so we stop for petrol and air before heading out of the city proper. It's still wet but I find if I just focus on Ma's lead vehicle, and not on road surfaces, I feel fine.

Soon the roads clear as we take a trunk road out of the city, lined by poplars on both sides with one lane going each way. The speed's come up and Mike's being encouraging on the intercom, riding in front and giving me details of what's ahead. His voice on the intercom is just the encouragement I need.

"It's good to have you back," Mike says as we take turns overtaking the slower movers. "Much better to have someone to talk to out here. Just remember one thing."

"What's that?"

"Fuck it. Just live in the moment," he says. Not a conventional part of cognitive modification, but useful for this first day.

Just then I come up on a bus on a clear stretch of straight road. I take a peek out and there's nothing in the oncoming lane, mirror's clear and a glance over the left shoulder clears the blind spot. Left signal, one last glance ahead and move out to overtake. Then it happens.

Everything dies: lights, engine, meters and display. I manage to get back in out of the overtaking lane and get on the intercom:

"Mike, Mike, in big trouble. Get the support vehicle back. I'm alright, but the bike's dead on the road."

I coast to a stop on the shoulder and try to figure out what's happened. This actually feels quite familiar because the precise thing has happened before when I first got the bike. The Suzuki is a bulletproof engine with an Achilles' heel, the stator. This is the bit of the electrical system that produces DC to keep the battery charged. In V-Stroms of my vintage that stator was known to give trouble, so I had the thing replaced with a stator I knew I could trust, from a Yamaha.

It should be good for another 40 – 60 thousand km, and yet here I am stuck on the side of the road in the heart of China. I had packed another stator but that is in the back of the Bumblebee since I really didn't think I would need it. Changing a stator by the side of the road is one of the things I went through with Ah Chye, but it's going to take me at least two hours, if I can remember how to do it at all. The dreadful thought crosses my mind that maybe I'm just not meant to get in on this ride, no matter what I decide. No amount of CBT dislodges that.

Soon Mike, Ma and Pierce are back with me and we find an entrance to a disused factory just a bit up the road where we can take the bike off the shoulder and start to do some work. I get the bike on the main stand and wonder if I could have seen it coming. On hindsight now I realise that when I started riding this morning the voltmeter reading was a little low, around 11.5 to 12.0 V, when the usual state is over 13.0 V. Also the engine did sound as though it was starting up more slowly than usual after we filled the petrol, although on first starting up after re-connecting the battery there was no trouble at all.

Ma gets out the coffee and biscuits and I take the bike seat off and have a look around. Fuses are intact. The stator lies next to the plastic fascia on the left side of the chassis under the seat and curiously this shows no sign of shorting. A fried stator and alternator coil usual leads to a subtle bit of charring on the side of the stator assembly. A voltmeter check on the battery shows that it's almost completely flat. That's when I see it.

In my haste to get on the road again I had re-connected the battery but failed to connect the stator cable to the battery leads. I see it lying free under the lead, not secured by the common screw. Things start to fall into place. Without the stator charging the battery it would work for a while before complete electrical failure occurs. To fix it, all I have to do is reconnect the wire properly and jump the battery. I really hope that's all there is. It would mean not having to lose the whole morning replacing the stator. All I need are the jump cables. Which are ... not with us. They're in the Bumblebee.

Hung Tuan shows up in his four by four and I explain the situation.

"So all you need are jump cables?" he sounds incredulous. "I have mine right here! Irene's already starting to call all over for possible bike mechanics!"

"Well if this doesn't work I really don't know what to do next," I tell him. I really want to get back into this ride now.

We move the bike next to his four by four, hook up the cables and turn the ignition. Once again that lovely sound of a happy V-twin. This time the voltmeter behaves: 13.6V. Everyone starts cheering. The relief comes over me like a warm wave. It is the first time in ages that something's gone right for me on this ride. I feel a weight lift and with shaking hands I silently put my tools away and put the seat back on. I think Hung Tuan notices it. He comes and speaks privately to me with a hand on my shoulder as I try to hold it together.

Moment of truth: Hung Tuan and his jump cables reviving the bike.

"That's the easiest roadside fix I've ever seen, man. You're going to be fine from here. You've had way more trouble than anyone deserves, but I tell you it's all clear from now."

As we get on the road again I'm finding myself hitting the higher speeds without any difficulty. The bike runs perfectly, as though trying to make up for lost time. Very soon we are away from the Wuwei city limits and in less than five minutes the irrigated fields run out and we're on the trunk roads again, surrounded by a flat dusty wasteland.

Our country road is right next to an empty expressway but bikes aren't allowed on. It's right there less than 100 m away but we have to put up with this broken asphalt. In some places the sand drifts get so deep that we pass heavy trucks marooned and waiting for a tow. Occasionally the road disappears entirely, with the next bit of surface just visible hundreds of metres away. The sun's up now and the going is hard, stand-on-the-foot-pegs second gear stuff.

It's hard dirty work but with every passing kilometre I feel more and more certain that everything will be alright now. Progress is slow and there's going to be hardship, and I'm talking to Mike a lot to keep filtering my thoughts, but this is where I'm supposed to be. It's hard to imagine I ever contemplated sending the bike back.

Up ahead our road joins an overhead bridge that crosses over the motorway and continues on the other side. From this high point we can see the landscape ahead. It's desert. Not just barren fields, but Peter O'Toole in flowing white robes, sand dunes and wild camels, wind-driven-ripples-in-the-sand kind of desert. We are in the middle of nowhere, even though that's officially a fortnight away. It's all overwhelmingly

Two bikes from Singapore, in the middle of the desert

surreal, I can't possibly be out here doing this. Mr Iau's younger kid with the slightly clumsy disposition is riding a bike in the middle of the desert. It's rider's high, pure and simple, and out it comes over the intercom:

"We're in the middle of the FUCKING desert!! Woohoooo!!"

On the other side of the intercom Mike is just laughing away. We haven't had much to laugh about for some time and it comes out unrestrained. It's one of those treasured moments, when all the trouble it's taken to get here is completely worth it. It's slow going for now, but we're going to be alright.

By the time we get to lunch it's about three in the afternoon and there are storm clouds ahead. The wind is picking up and there's a chill in the air. Things always seem more of a crisis when I'm hungry but we do seem to be in a bit of a pickle. It seems impossible to find any real food out here. What few villages we come across are curiously deserted. Eventually we come to a small cluster of buildings around a traffic junction. There is a village school with a basketball court and next to this a small home-based noodle shop with a glass door out front. Encouragingly, there are a few trucks parked along the curbside. Ma pulls over and we dismount.

Just beyond the glass enclosed front porch is a darkened room with a few truckers passed out and snoring quietly on some sofas in the corner. With the state of my clothes, including a left trouser leg which went knee deep in mud on the way here, I'm reluctant to step in. Out of the darkness the proprietor emerges, a pleasant Han Chinese woman only a little shorter than me in her late forties dressed in black jacket over a T-shirt and a pair of black jeans. She gives me a welcoming smile, takes one glance at the state of my clothes and asks, "Did you have a good swim?"

All I can manage is just a stupid grin. Ma places the orders and in a few minutes mother and daughter cook up one of the best meals I've had in China: a simple vegetable soup and sweet roasted pork with generous helpings of rice, washed down with Chinese tea. In a village that does not appear on any map or GPS in the middle of the desert about 90 km from Zhangye. I may have overdone things and fall asleep in the warmth of the front porch.

Before long Mike wakes me and tells me we better go, looks like the nice bit's over, the storm's catching up. On the way to the bikes I notice that the wind's picked up considerably and there's bits of sleet, intermingling with litter from the streets.

Heading up towards Zhangye the road improves and we come to a series of small rolling hills right outside the town. It's late evening now but with less than 30 km to go we should be all right getting to the hotel before nightfall. The winds have been intermittent since lunchtime, alternating between bright sunshine or a mild drizzle but no real rain. The dark clouds are still there though, looming in the horizon beyond the mountains.

The effect of the alternating weather on the desert is quite distracting. Despite being seemingly featureless at first glance I realise that up close the desert changes all the time. There is a constant play of light, wind and the constantly shifting sand. Increasingly I'm noticing these "dust devils" popping up all over on both sides of the road. I remember reading about these before and bring it up to Mike.

"Hey Mike, you notice the little bits of sand popping up everywhere? Like small mini-tornadoes?"

"Um? Where?"

"In the desert, both sides of the road, about 200 m out."

Mikes turns to look. "Ah, right. Yes, I saw some earlier but there seem to be more now," he replies.

"Well they're called *djinns*. I remember reading about them before. Many desert cultures think they're spirits. I guess from which we get the word *genie*, which is why every time Aladdin rubs the oil lamp there's this same swirl of sand before Robin Williams appears." I think that coffee after lunch is starting to kick in.

"What?"

Sometimes I do get the feeling that Mike is starting to regret his offer of having me talk about anything that comes to mind on the intercom as a means of real-time thought filtering. I've been talking a lot.

As we climb the next ridgeline the wind suddenly picks

up and it's a struggle to keep the bike in line. The wind is coming right to left and I'm being dragged to the centre of the road and listing considerably to correct. For the first time I see a dust devil actually crossing the road in front of me. Looking back I see another two more in the mirrors. They're about three metres tall and getting larger.

Then I see it, or rather I stop seeing them.

"Mike ..." I start. The mountains, which have been a constant companion for the entire day, have disappeared, blocked by something that can block out mountains.

"Yes I know ..." Mike replies, "What the hell's that?"

The sandstorm hits with a suddenness that takes my breath away. One moment a troublesome cross wind, the next I'm surrounded by swirling dirt and feel like I'm working underwater against a rushing cross current, except I'm on dry land. Every movement against the direction of the wind takes a full effort. Even though I'm barely moving now the wind noise in the helmet resembles 100 km/h down a highway. The sound of the sand particles hitting the helmet makes me hope there isn't anything bigger flying around in this muck. Whatever you do, leave your helmet on.

I'm down to first gear, not so much moving as trying not to fall over and looking for Ma's Cruiser, which seems to have also disappeared in the swirling dust. Thankfully, I can still see the Beemer behind me. About 200 m up the road I see Ma parked to the side with his distress lights on. Ma is running towards me, incredibly his hat staying on despite the high winds.

He shouts something I don't hear. There's the helmet, earplugs and then the wind noise.

He signals for me the lift up the visor and when I do, the wind noise is deafening despite the earplugs. Ever the professional tour guide, he feels an introduction to this new development in the weather is necessary.

"This is a sandstorm. Would you like to carry on or find shelter?"

Riding is impossible. He points to a shallow gully next to an archway which looks like an entrance to a plantation of some kind. We get the bikes over and put them in the direction of the wind on the main stand and all pile into Ma's car. Incredibly, he already has hot coffee and biscuits waiting.

After he hands us the beverages, he sits back in the driver's seat and radios Irene with this latest development. The four by fours have had no problems on the motorway and have already arrived at the hotel. Some have already headed out for dinner. Right. What we have to choose is a night in the back of the cramped Cruiser or chancing it and heading out in this weather, probably in the dark, as soon as the wind dies down. If it dies down.

After some of the initial shock subsides and buoyed with the new load of caffeine and carbohydrates, the storm does not look too bad. After about twenty minutes, we notice that the heavy sign under the archway isn't swinging about in the wind as wildly as before, even though the noise through a crack in the window is still impressive. The mountains are not yet visible but that could be because of the dying light, which will be a real problem soon. After another 30 minutes of each other in that cramped space we all decide that there is no way we're going to spend the night in the car. Like it or not we have to be on our way.

It's last light when we get the bikes back on the road again. The cross wind still bites and a light drizzle clouds up the visors. Within twenty minutes we're riding in darkness. As we approach the town, visibility becomes almost non-existent.

On the helmet visor is a semi-opaque mixture of dirt and light drizzle and trying to wipe that off with a glove that's covered in muck from earlier in the day has resulted in this grimy layer that's making everything murky. On top of that the traffic's built up and car drivers coming the other way are having the same problem with poor visibility and have left their high beams on. This scatters the light on our visors, so Zhangye is the only city I've ever ridden into without seeing it first. The good thing is that I can't fixate on road surfaces if I can't see them. All I can do is follow Ma's vehicle with its distress lights on.

Everything gets better once we arrive in the town proper. The wind dies down as soon as we enter a built up area. Now it's just the rain and when I raise the visor the fresh night air is a godsend. As we arrive at the hotel I find the last of the adrenaline drifting away and I'm suddenly very, very tired.

We turn the bikes into the secure parking area in the back and even getting off the bike takes real effort. It seems like ages since I last put up at a hotel. Then we take the luggage off and head to the lobby. After what we have just been through, the chandelier-lit lobby and its soft carpets seem like another world.

As we wait for our room keys we see the four by four crews just coming back from dinner through the revolving door entrance. Their spirits lift at seeing both riders standing in the lobby, even if one of them does look like he's been for a swim in a swamp.

"How was it?" asks Boss.

"Well," answers Mike, "I think our plans for Philip's flooding therapy have gone perfectly. We had electrical failure, off-road riding, rain and a sandstorm, all on his first day back."

Boss looks incredulous.

Mike turns to me with a big grin and adds, "But he's made it."

Yes, I suppose I have, but only thanks to Mike, Ma and Pierce. Tomorrow will be a new day, but today I've outlasted the circumstances simply by staying in the moment, talking things through and just not thinking of giving up. I am a rider who's returned to the Long Ride. I hug everybody. This includes a waiter at the coffee house, two doormen, the concierge, a complete stranger at the concierge's desk and the bellboy who hands us the keys to the room.

Fourteen
GOODBYE CHINA

THE NEXT MORNING I have this feeling that the last 24 hours didn't really happen. Then I see the bike gear hanging in the shower stall where I tried to get all the mud and dirt out before getting to bed last night. *Right then, so you appear to have managed quite well yesterday despite everything. Now just try and forget all of it and keep going.*

I go into a routine of keeping my mind in the moment. The best way I've found is to just concentrate on what needs to be done in five minute intervals, right from the start of the day. I find that if I can get my head around to doing this as soon as I start checking out of the hotel, then the day is going to go well.

Setting out, the first stop is at the petrol station. That's when I realise just how frustrating fueling up in China has been for Mike. Even in a proper petrol station in the middle of the city we are not allowed to fill our tanks at the pumps. Instead we have to park off to the side, fill kitchen kettles with the fuel from the pump and then transfer the fuel to the bike. Apparently this is because of the risk of motorcycles exploding. I mention to the service station crew that in all my travels I have never seen a single exploding bike, and ask them if they ever have. No, but them's the rules. It's very frustrating. My bike takes 18L each refill so on a 5L kettle it's a chore. Fully loading a BMW 1200GSA is 33L.

Today's ride is going to take us to the westernmost end of the Hexi corridor to Jiayuguan. The corridor itself runs in a northwesterly direction, a pass between two mountain ranges within which runs the northern route of the Silk Road. At Jiayuguan the corridor is at its narrowest, just over 10 km wide, the ideal site for the fortress that marks the westernmost extent of the Great Wall. Beyond that lies the boundless emptiness of Xingjiang and the start of the "–stans".

It seems inconceivable that we are about to come to the end of China. Sure there is still all of Xinjiang to get through, but to me although it is obviously a part of China, Xinjiang does not seem very Chinese. Certainly in times past Jiayuguan was considered the end of civilisation itself. Within the protection of the Great Wall was law and order and a thousand years of accumulated wisdom and culture, the greatest kingdom the world has ever seen. West of that was a place for warlords and lawlessness. A fate only fit for the barbarian and the banished.

In sheer contrast to Sichuan, Shaanxi and Gansu where thousands of years of vigorous Chinese civilisation have shouted at us at every turn, here towards Xingjiang nothing has really made a mark on the land. We have had weeks of endless terraced fields, run on thousand-year-old ancient trading roads, massive bridges and cities and flood works along the Yellow River, visited mind-boggling tombs and fortifications. Here it almost feels like the energy has just run out of the place. As the roads lead us out of Zhangye the landscape gets more and more barren and finally gives way to empty desert on both sides.

There is nothing on this road. This is a place where people travel through rather than stay. No road markings, there isn't even a turn in the road for miles. Just bare tarmac through a desert. Occasionally there are small mounds of earth that stand out in the featureless landscape. Later on I would learn that these were signal towers, providing an ancient alarm network to defenders should Jiayuguan come under attack. The overall feel is that we are in the outlands now. On a 10-km stretch that runs straight downhill we don't come across a single other vehicle going either way — even the air seems to stand still as the silence becomes a pressing presence all by itself. You can hear yourself a lot better out here, for better or for worse.

With increasing frequency we see small altars in any place where a god might consider a reasonable residence: by a bridge, the entrance of a cave with a slightly interesting rock formation, by the edge of a cliff with a bit of a view. And what the few towns that are out here seem to all have in common is one outstanding mosque or temple. I get a feeling that in times past just making it this far is enough to offer some gratitude to the powers that be.

The absence of any distractions doesn't help my mental state. The main problem is thought retention. As the day gets on I find myself remembering stuff that I would normally just let go. Like a slight wriggle that the rear wheel makes as it hits a patch of sand, or a gust of wind from an unexpected direction. The bike shrugs these things off in an instant, but instead of letting it go my mind keeps playing it back. I keep wondering when the next treacherous gust of wind is going to be, and from what direction. It's so completely ridiculous. How can you possibly worry about something that you cannot possibly predict?

As a distraction to my thought retention I try and look out for these religious relics. I wonder if some of them have been visited for the last century, or if the god truly has expired. Then purely by chance when I glance off road I notice a truck driver come out of one of these thousand-year-old watch towers, his trousers still about his knees and showing a pair of snow-white buttocks. Chinese practicality prevails no matter where. God or not, it's the only place to take a private crap in the desert.

Typical landscape in Xinjiang — nothing but perfect tarmac.

The next morning we're out in Xinjiang proper, beyond the boundaries of Imperial China. This does not feel like China at all. It does not feel like anything at all, just empty perfect asphalt as it leads to the far horizon, mile after mile after mile. Majestic snow-capped mountains surround us on the horizon in the distance. I now understand why Ma thinks that Xingjiang is a good place for a nervous rider to return to riding. There's nothing out here but road. We learn that in Xinjiang there's no restriction on biking on the expressways, for the simple reason that this is the only way across this vast expanse of nothing.

Mike's been a real help with his offer to leave the intercom open for me to say whatever comes to mind. I find that just rambling on helps to keep the breathing regular. What it does to Mike's state of mind I never quite find out. I think it's the most he has ever done for a friend, or at least for a mental patient.

By and large it is a one-sided conversation but he makes enough of the appropriate noises to suggest that he is paying some sort of attention. In the evenings towards the end of the day's ride when he knows that I'll be alright, he would always wonder aloud over the intercom how on earth one head can contain so much rubbish, then plug in his Guns N' Roses and lead the way into town.

The only distractions are the occasional road signs along the highway. They usually signal the exit ramps for the upcoming towns, which remind us how far we are from the established capitals of ancient China. Here things have a more ephemeral feel. Not for the first time I point out one of the town names on a passing road sign to Mike over the intercom:

"Now unless my written Chinese has really gone off the deep end, I understand we are three miles away from a turnoff to a town called Three Miles."

"What?" We are doing 120 km/h down a featureless straight highway and it's possible the wind noise is interfering with the comms.

"I said we're three miles away from Three Miles," I repeat.

I hear Mike switch off the intercom. There are limits.

So we pass the town of Three Miles, and then an equally fleeting road stop called Two Trees, where we stop for a dodgy ham lunch and a short game of pavement basketball with some kids. Come to think of it, I think it's street basketball. No one ever comes by here and there are court markings painted on the asphalt. After that we head out for another town called Eight Miles before heading back onto the expressway. I guess we're eight miles from something but for the life of me I can't see what. There's nothing out here. Come to think of it there weren't any trees in Two Trees.

In terms of the older habitations here the Han Chinese do not seem to have left much of a mark, although Ma tells me that the number of Han Chinese immigrating to Xinjiang increases every year. That's not to say that they haven't made their mark in other ways. Here in Xingjiang, the lasting impression is that of paradox: massive investment in infrastructure in an almost completely barren place. We may be surrounded by endless swathes of desert but there is more than what meets the eye.

We ride past vast oil fields with their innumerable pumpjacks incessantly rocking away in a rhythm all their own. Huge wind and solar farms and their high-tension cables are a constant sight along the entire length of this highway. Just outside Wuwei, in the city of Yumen is the largest wind farm in the world. It produces a staggering 6,000 MW, five times more than the largest wind farm in the US, and unbelievably, it's still growing. In fact, they are still growing it when we ride past. Massive 50-m-long trucks run in convoys of four with police escort, each one transporting just one single windmill blade.

Just as impressive are the trains. Their tracks would occasionally run next to the expressways and would haul 50 or 60 cargo cars, which is pretty much when I lose count. One of the world's longest railway lines runs through Xinjiang. It starts at Yiwu in Eastern China and runs all the way to Madrid in Spain. Over 12,000 km long, it's the rail version of the Silk Road.

As we descend the edge of a massive dust basin I notice

a black line on the horizon that I initially think is a very long raised highway. This is a little curious because there is no such road on the map, although it would not surprise me that the Chinese have built one since the map was printed three years ago. It isn't until I point it out to Mike over the intercom and we both have a closer look that we see the black line move. It isn't a road the length of the horizon, but one long train.

I had read about a real effort to make Xinjiang more Chinese and we see signs of that. Most of the merchants in the newer shopping complexes seem to be typical Han Chinese. We would see Uighur merchants in the older villages running the usual mom-and-pop shops, but the newer shopping arcades in Hami and Tulufan are manned mainly by Han Chinese.

I suppose some local resentment is expected. In the month before we started on our ride there was a knife terrorist attack at the Kunming Railway Station that had been attributed to Xingjiang separatists. It left over 30 dead but I don't think the Chinese will be leaving.

If it seems that the Uighurs have been living here through the centuries and not left any lasting mark, all that is to change as we near Tulufan. The city lies at the bottom of the Tulufan Depression, the second lowest exposed point in the earth's surface at 150 m below sea level.

After crossing a series of dramatic sandstone ridges, the road heads continuously downward for about 40 km. I notice the occasional row of low mounds in the desert to the right, on a long plain that leads gradually upwards to the Tian Shan mountains. They're placed in almost completely straight rows and stand about 2 m in height and 100 – 400 m apart. At first I think they are a more modest version of the watchtowers we had seen in Gansu but they're placed too close together.

We take the exit off highway and after a sharp right hairpin the descent to Tulufan starts in earnest. We can see the entire depression before us. To the right are the Flaming Mountains, an imposing vertical wall of red sandstone with its gorges and gullies brought to relief by the setting sun. To the left our road twists between another majestic series of sandstone hills before the final approach to Tulufan.

Around the next bend everything changes. There is a burst of green as the Flaming Mountains are replaced inexplicably by row upon row of verdant vineyards. After hundreds of kilometres of barren landscape we are surrounded by a luxuriant leafy green that seems to cover the desert as far as the eye can see. The effect leaves us quite speechless and we forget ourselves, put the bikes in neutral and just coast downhill. The vines are grown either in rows or draped across arches that provide a cooling shade in the middle of the desert. Between the vineyards in mud-bricked trellised

The miracle of Tulufan: vineyards in the desert

huts the size of shipping containers are where the grapes are dried to the sweetest raisins in China. An oasis.

Then I remember. Most of the towns that we had passed in Xinjiang started life as oases on the Silk Road and Tulufan is the most celebrated. This is our introduction to their famous karez wells.

These wells have ensured Tulufan's year-round water supply for over 2,000 years. An incredible feat, considering that it is one of the driest places in all of China, with less than an inch of rainfall a year.

The system consists of vertically dug wells which link an underground series of canals that draw ground water from the Tian Shan and Flaming mountains, making use of gravity to run the water into the Tulufan depression. Remarkably, there are over a thousand of these vertical shafts and 5,000 km of underground canals, most of which dug by hand, and some run 100 m below the desert. When the water arrives in the Tulufan's irrigated fields it's still fresh and cold. The straight lines of mud mounds that we had seen on the way here were none other than a line of these wells.

THE HUO ZHOU HOTEL in Tulufan is located in the centre of town and is the largest building around. Next to it is a rather tired looking fairground with some rides and a Ferris wheel that has seen better days.

Ma comes over to help Mike and I with the bags and asks what's on the schedule for the next few days. Well, we're only here for the night. Next day it's 150 km to Ürümqi where we have a meeting at the Xinjiang Medical University in the afternoon. Should be all right—it's a highway the whole way. After that it's a long ride to Korgas and the China-Kazakh border. Ma looks a little doubtful. He's heard from some locals that a major sandstorm might be headed our way, but we won't be sure until tomorrow.

When morning comes I am awakened by the sound of branches scraping on my second floor window. I don't hear the wind; most of the rooms here seem hermetically sealed from the environment. Taking the kit down to the dining room I see worried faces all around. The hotel staff explains that the highway's closed because of a major sandstorm. No one seems too bothered; it looks as though this is something they're used to around here. There aren't that many guests but what few there are mill around the reception counter, calling secretaries to convey apologies and making alternative travel arrangements. Then they move to the lobby, light their cigarettes and wait for developments.

Irene explains that Ma's taken the Cruiser to check the highway conditions and will call back if and when it clears. He's since told her that they've blocked cars from getting on to the highway, although the situation might still change. He's parked himself on the on-ramp and will be the first to know if anything happens. That means we might not be able to make our Ürümqi appointment if it doesn't clear by late morning.

Looking outside, things have certainly deteriorated from yesterday evening. I have got used to dust-coloured buildings, cars and trees, but this is a dust-coloured sky. Everything is a dull beige as the sun makes a feeble attempt to get through. The wind isn't too bad and it's quite pleasant to walk out in the cool. It seems hard to believe that a mere 20 km away the authorities have prohibited use of the highway. Then a sudden gust of wind and sand comes up that makes it less unreasonable. I notice the Ferris Wheel in the fairground turn gently in the wind like a child's windmill. I would not like to go riding in this weather, and certainly not at highway speeds. Mike looks like he's thinking about it, though.

"It's doable you know," he said. "It's only dust and it's only 150 km. We could give it a try."

At 12:00 pm there is still no word from Ma. We need to decide soon whether to stay or move out. I don't like the idea of missing a promised appointment but the wind is now stronger and the streets are nearly empty. The only way to get there is to use the highway. Visibility has dropped considerably and we can barely make out the Ferris wheel. The idea of riding really doesn't appeal.

Mike suggests that we wait at the highway entrance in case there's a change later in the day. It would be good to cover that 150 km to Ürümqi today and get closer to the border with Kazakhstan, even if we don't make the meeting. If not, it will be over 900 km the next day. The Chinese authorities being what they are, we have to arrive at the border on the promised dates.

I think it's madness to even try. What if the storm gets worse and not better? We would then be stuck out at the highway entrance, unable to move either way. Whatever happens I feel that the last thing Mike needs is to look out for me. And I don't have any confidence of riding in this muck. I decide to throw in the towel and put the bike on the back of the Bumblebee. As

Mike helps with getting it strapped down, I suggest again to him that we both sit this one out. Few sandstorms last a whole day and we could push on tomorrow.

"Nah, not to worry. We'll just go to the on-ramp of the highway and if they say we can go, we'll go. If not, we just head back here. Nothing to lose. I don't like not making that appointment."

The four by fours get together and Irene radios Ma, who is still waiting at the highway entrance, to expect us in a few minutes. He points out that coming out is really not necessary; he can call us if the situation changes, but Irene says we're coming anyway.

As we head out through town, the wind gets progressively stronger. The quiet town that we had ridden into yesterday is not recognisable now. The wind is whipping every piece of loose litter and debris into shrapnel. Up in the lead vehicle with me, Pierce points out that this isn't just a sandstorm. It's different from when we were caught out in open country. In the city it should be called what it is. You could call it a shop sign-storm, or a pail-storm, and passing a few metres behind Mike just now is an awning-storm.

When we get to the on-ramp of the highway our little convoy is broken up by stuck traffic. We manage to get through with Mike but the rest of the convoy is separated. Mike is really exposed out here in the cross wind that comes right down the highway but as long as he isn't moving he seems stable enough. I don't think it will be easy for him to dismount in this wind though. I notice that he has to keep his head down and away from the wind.

What is more disconcerting is the way the traffic is moving

in all directions. It's a mixture of cars, trucks and tankers, all making their individual decisions whether to wait it out or to head back to town as the weather deteriorates. Visibility in the blinding dust is such that no one can see the directional signs, much less the road markings, and the traffic policemen are fully occupied in just keeping people off the highway rather than directing traffic. I don't blame them; it looks hard enough just staying upright in this wind.

In the distance we see Ma's familiar Land Cruiser and Pierce and I leave the lead vehicle to join him. Just getting out is an effort and I have to keep my foot on the door to heave it open. Walking against the wind to Ma's cruiser I wish I had brought my helmet with me. There is so much dust and sand just blasting about and I am having trouble keeping on my feet. Ma must have seen me in difficulty; before long I'm grabbed by the shoulders and chucked in the rear seat. Incredibly, he still has his hat on.

When he has an idea of where everyone is, he settles back in the driver's seat and asks if I want a coffee and cake. I say no, but could we please decide whether or not waiting here is worthwhile? Are these traffic policemen people to be negotiated with? Ma points to the highway entrance about 50 m ahead. It's closed in a very non-negotiable way.

A line of police cars has formed a barricade across the entrance ramp and despite the queue of cars and trucks waiting, no one was being allowed through. Just beyond the cars are the gantries proper with their covered booths. All around us are 30 or 40 vehicles hanging about, drivers in their seats. I guess that means there may be a chance that they might still get through. So here we sit. Except Mike, who is still on the Beemer looking for some truck siding to put between himself and the wind.

After a few minutes waiting we see what must be a policemen's conference coming to its conclusion. Out of one of the covered gantry booths a dozen or so uniformed policemen emerge and start to make their way down through the crowd of vehicles. Their message passes between the cars faster than they do: Weather reports say the sandstorm has closed the highway to Ürümqi, probably till the next day. The gantries are to stay closed all night. Well that's that, I think, so much for Ürümqi. It would be the only appointment that we didn't make for the entire Long Ride, but hardly within our control.

Pierce gets out of the Cruiser and passes the word to Mike to inform him we're heading back to the hotel. He gets back and all the waiting vehicles start moving at once; Ma starts to turn the Cruiser around. Pierce keeps an eye on Mike to make sure he follows us through the melee. As we start down the off-ramp there is a gut-wrenching cry from Pierce:

"Fuckfuckfuckfuck oh FUCK!"

I snap my head around. Mike has his bike across the middle of the main off-ramp, head facing away from the down wind, when a van and a truck come down the ramp right at him, running abreast. With his head turned away from the wind he can't have seen, much less reacted with the speed they are doing. In between the truck and the van is a small interval the precise length of a BMW GSA, through which Mike passes unscathed. I'm not sure if he even realises what a near thing it was.

It's the closest I have ever been to seeing anyone get killed and strangely enough, it was my life that flashed before my eyes. As we drive back to the hotel I wonder to Pierce about this. He says that it's easy enough to explain: If anything happens to Mike, Mette would have me cut up into small pieces. Whatever is left, Viola would finish off.

BY EVENING THE WIND settles considerably and the skies clear. Sunsets in Tulufan are golden when there isn't a sandstorm. We take the chance to leave the hotel and see some of the city. The main street runs right across the entrance to the hotel. It seems so incongruous that in the middle of the desert the streets would be lined with rows of luxuriant trees on each side.

After the anxieties of the day we seem to have chosen the time of our stroll perfectly, when the city finishes its toil and starts to play. The winds have waned with the setting sun. Hand-holding couples are in a world of their own, taking in the fresh air. Merchants shutter up their shops and head home to dinner. There's something therapeutic about watching kids play football in the park.

At the next junction we find a street lined with eateries on both sides. The pavements run under archways that are richly covered with vines. The patchwork of golden and green is irresistibly inviting and we decide we've just arrived at the best part of Tulufan. Mike and I decide for sweet pork and noodles in this shop run by a Han Chinese woman just setting out her tables for el fresco dining.

It's a family business, with the husband and wife doing the cooking and serving while Grandma takes care of this lovely cherubic looking toddler. Business is picking up quickly and soon Grandma is recruited to take care of the patrons, so I offer to hold the kid. Sitting there with the baby in one arm and sipping tea the grandma has given me as babysitting fees, it's the last touch I need to feel perfectly at home. Home, in this place I've never been. It's hard to believe that in two days I'll be out of China. I'm going to miss this so much.

NEXT MORNING THE SANDSTORM has passed and we start out under clear blue skies. Today is going to be hard. To make up for the lost riding day, we have to cover 900-odd km from Tulufan to the border town of Korgas, where we will cross the border into Kazakhstan the day after. It is critical that we cross the border on the arranged dates.

I know that with my travelling speed I'll probably keep us on the road for a good 10 to 12 hours. There is also the chance of some really cold weather as we cross the Tian Shan mountains before arriving at Korgas. That will probably slow us down further. That means getting into Korgas after dark. I decide to take to the car again. We leave the Suzuki on the Bumblebee and have Mike tear through that distance like I know he can without me holding him back.

What follows is a truly special piece of riding. Mike manages to keep his speed up to 140 – 150 km/h most of the way despite the temperature changes. When we leave Tulufan it is 19 degrees as the sun comes up but as we ascend the mountains around Ürümqi, the temperatures plummet to just below freezing. The expressway turns into dense, fast-moving traffic towards the city. Chinese drivers don't seem to have the habit of clearing the snow off their cars before starting out, leaving great chunks of ice on the highway which Mike has to avoid.

What makes up for everything is just how beautiful this part of China is. It is almost as though she's saved her best for last. After days of desert desolation, here is something really special. As we pass Ürümqi towards Kuytun, the mountains loom large to our left, with a background of the clearest, bluest sky we have seen in weeks. The desert gives way to green alpine forest; it feels like we're in the Alps, and not just four hours away from the Tulufan Basin. This is the lingering memory of riding in China: there is just so much natural beauty within such short travelling times.

The effort does take its toll though. Even with its oversized fuel tank, the Beemer can't make the entire leg without a refill. When we find a petrol station along the highway at Kuytun we pull up near the back of the office, away from the pumps. It's a drill we have got used to, to find the kettles to top up the bike.

When we get to him we find that we almost have to peel Mike off the bike. He's even paler than usual and as Pierce and I help him get off he mumbles something about the trick to staying warm being just rigorous wriggling of the toes. They are the only parts of him that aren't frozen stiff. Ma suggests that he'll be easier to peel off if we stuff him with hot coffee from the thermos first.

As we walk over to the petrol pumps, the problems begin. The attendants are giving the usual wave-off. At first we think it's the whole business about re-fueling with kettles again, until they make it quite clear that we're not allowed to take any gas at all. When we ask for the reason — the Beemer is by now running on fumes and will not make the next town — they direct us to the manager's office.

It takes some direct intervention and some terse messages faxing between Ma and Irane before we finally do get our petrol. Apparently the police had prohibited stations from topping up bikes because of the security risk of using them as bike bombs. Sadly, we were to learn later that the precautions were not misplaced. About a week after we left, Uighur separatists drove two cars through a crowd of people in a market street in Ürümqi, and then started throwing petrol bombs. Over thirty people were killed and many more injured.

That's all in the future and nothing to do with us. For the moment we're just glad that we have Ma. It is a fitting end to four weeks with a driver and guide who has become a friend who has made all the difference in how I have experienced China. Without his local knowledge, his navigational and driving skills, but most of all the personal pride he feels towards the things and places he's shown us, we would have had a mere riding holiday. Instead I have gained a profound sense of wonder of this place. It's not all good of course, but Ma let us see both good and bad.

On this last full day of travelling together he's more expressive than usual. He still wishes that we had more time, there is so much more of this country that he wants to show us. There is the southern route through Tibet towards Lhasa that he's certain would cure me of my fear of heights. It's a rideable road all the way up to the Everest Base Camp. Then there is also the central route through the great grasslands to Ulaanbaatar.

An achingly beautiful desolation surrounds us on our last day in China.

He says that Mongolia is a place that is changing so rapidly that we would miss all of that living history unless we go soon. Then the driving routes north of Beijing towards Harbin and then on to Vladivostok, where the roads are improving every year. "You've only seen the smallest sample of what there is, you've got to come back again."

The smallest sample. That seems completely impossible. We have travelled for four weeks heading in the same general direction and not crossed a single border. It feels like we've crossed an entire continent and not a country. And here he is telling us that we've rushed it, and that we are cheating ourselves if we do not come back.

All around us the scenery is being just as persuasive. The last 200 km of Chinese road just past Yining is one of the most magnificent in the whole country. This comes as a surprise, no one's mentioned it in any of their blogs. I guess it's because among transcontinental overlanders only a few would come through China for the cost, and fewer would take this route.

Mike has slowed down and is taking in the sunshine.

It's just four in the afternoon and we know that thanks to his berserk riding in the morning we will make the time. All around us it's alpine forests, snow-covered peaks in the near distance and this unbelievably clear blue sky.

As we crest a small hill, with no warning at all, taking up the entire view right in front of us is Sayram Lake. We are over 2,000 m above sea level now, and the lake is still partly frozen. In the foreground is water of the deepest blue with the wind buffeting up white crested waves. About a kilometre offshore the ice sheet stretches out to the snow-covered mountains and glaciers in the far banks of the lake, along the entire horizon. The banks are already thawed out and covered with spring grass. We can see scattered yurts on the hillsides and shepherds tending their herds.

No words are needed. We just stop and get out. This place alone is reason enough for me to come back. I'm already plotting it in my head: Maybe in the reverse direction the next time, out of Kazakhstan. Pierce is already planning what cameras and other equipment to bring to record what can be seen over a few days of hiking. Most of all we just stand there, agog.

Even Ma steps out and for the first time I see him remove his sunglasses. He stands on the edge of the lake and takes it all in. The look in his eyes says it all: This is *my* country. *This* is where I come from. I fucking *live* here.

"I promise, Ma *shifu*, I'm going to come back here," I say to him. I shake his hand warmly and thank him for making all the difference.

"Yes, but next time, take your time," he says, "there's so much more to see." Then he wipes his eyes and we get back to the Cruiser.

China's parting shot: the magnificent Sayram Lake.

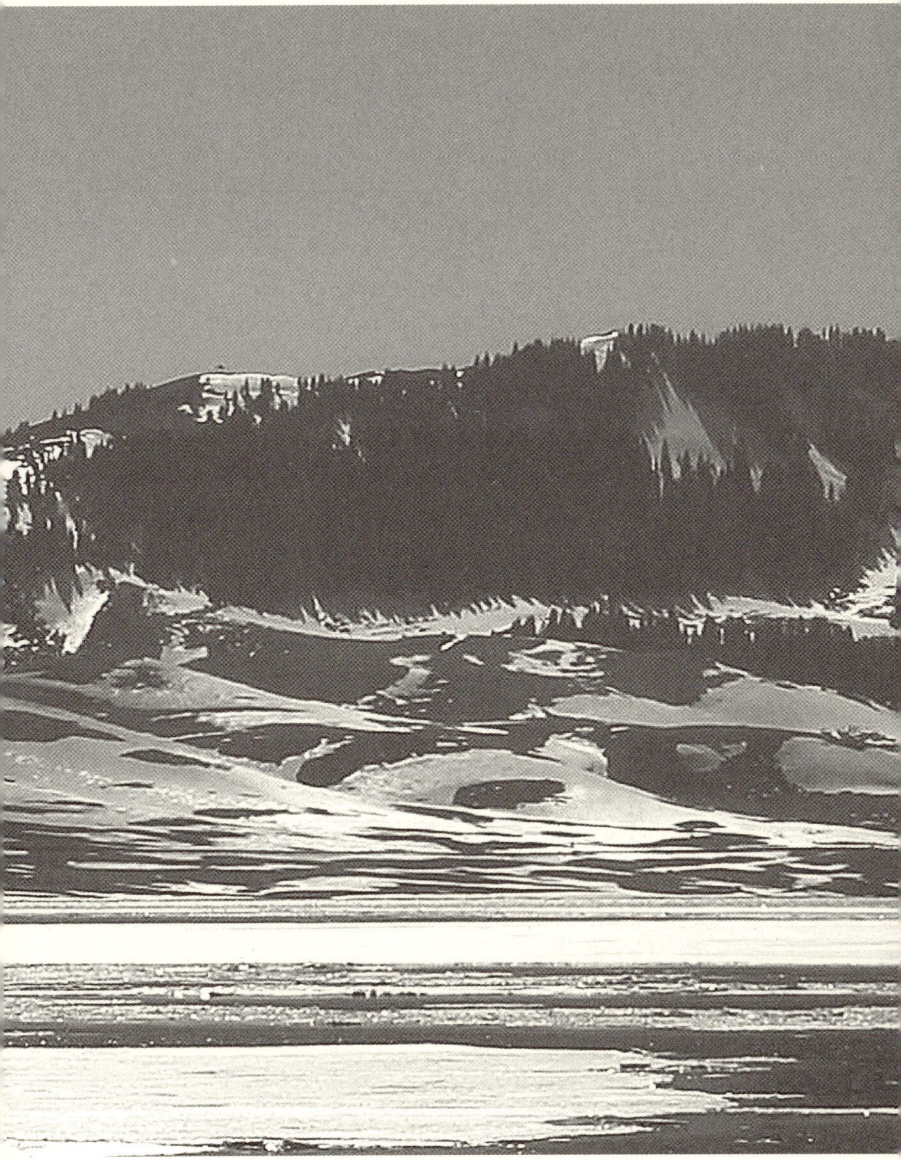

Fifteen
SAVED BY BLACK HORSE

I HAVE BEEN ANTICIPATING coming to Kazakhstan ever since Boss introduced us to their junior health minister in Singapore over one of his dinners. I was expecting some stereotypical Soviet-era official resembling Leonid Brezhnev. To my surprise I found that he could have passed for my younger brother. In his early forties, he seemed completely Chinese but for his Russian accent.

I have my re-acquaintance with Kazakhs at the border crossing. Like their junior minister they look more Chinese than one might expect with their dark hair, full faces and low nose bridges, but Caucasian about their rounder eyes, thicker eyebrows and of course in their Russian. Perhaps as a result of all that time in rural China, Kazakhs seem positively cosmopolitan, the women exotically attractive.

Soon I start to worry about how long this border crossing is going to take. There is another 140 km before getting to Almaty and after taking five hours at the China side, night riding seems certain if we are to make our major cancer congress in Almaty day after tomorrow.

As soon as we clear the Kazakh side Mike and I sit on the curb by the bikes and wait for the rest of the crew. A white van pulls up to us and out comes a very attractive woman in a leather jacket who introduces herself as Nazgul. She has been sent with a news team and a camera crew. I suppose she's the anchorwoman, she's certainly appealing enough.

The television interviews at the border take three hours, with another two hours spent over a sumptuous official lunch at a nearly village, chaired by the local health secretary. By the time we can actually start biking to Almaty it's nearly five in the afternoon.

Thankfully the roads leading away from the border are nearly empty. In fact, the same can be said about the entire countryside around us. In sheer contrast with China where even in the desert you can see signs of modernisation, here it's mile after mile of perfect nothing. It's all covered with this wonderfully pristine verdant grassland. As we approach one of the few villages I catch the sight of an unsaddled horse grazing peacefully. Time stands still here and is in no hurry to get going again. The perfect opposite of practically everywhere in China.

Kazakhstan is the size of western Europe, with the population just slightly over half that of Malaysia. Uniquely, most of the people live in cities rather than in rural areas. What this means is that there are great swaths of just ... space.

Making our way from the border to Almaty

And we are seeing that in every direction.

The roads near the border have been potholed and worn down by heavy vehicles but as we get further into the country the surface is almost perfect. It winds its way through one grassy valley after another in the golden sunset. When we crest the hills we can see ominous storm clouds and flashes of lightning in the distance. It seems that we are going to get into Almaty not only in the dark but also in the wet.

As the buildings start to get further and further apart, I'm not sure if we are losing light because of nightfall or because of the encroaching storm. The hills have a curious effect on the wind. At times it's a straight headwind as the road passes between two parallel spines of mountains. In the deepest parts of the valley the air is completely still. As we mount the next ridgeline the wind would then shift again. It's all I can do to try and keep up the speed and stop the bike from tipping over one direction or the other as the wind shifts.

Looking into the mirror I see the frustrating sight of Mikael Hartman behind me, oblivious to the challenges of the strong crosswinds. He languorously stretches out a leg. In fact, I think he's actually steering with only one hand. The other hand is holding a half-eaten Mars bar. He can clearly see the difficulty I am having and has this wicked grin on his face.

"Do you know why BMW adventure bikes cost so much more than some Suzukis?" he asks. "It's because every bike has been tested in a wind tunnel, with their hard panniers which come as standard. I'm so happy at just how stable this bike feels." Over the intercom I think I hear the sound of chewing.

"Yeah right. OK." I reply. I'm a little preoccupied about staying upright.

"In fact, would I be wrong to say that your Suzuki might be the only V-Strom to be tested in a wind tunnel?" he asks with his mouth full.

"I seriously doubt this bike knows what a wind tunnel is," I reply.

"That's what I mean. I think your Suzuki is having its first wind tunnel right here in Kazakhstan … whereas my bike has been meticulously tested by Bavarian wind tunnels. By the way this Mars bar is fantastic in this sunset."

The wind starts to pick up rapidly. "Yeah right. OK." I'm wondering why despite a strong headwind the bike sometimes feels like it's tipping over sideways. Could it be catching my hard panniers?

"No," Mike answers, "it's more likely because you've got too much of a side profile, not much ground clearance. This is in contrast with this BMW, which has a high enough clearance to let enough air get through between the wheels," Mike says. "The sort of thing German designers would take into account."

"You mean after considerable testing in a wind tunnel?" I ask.

"Exactly," said Mike, "it may cost a little more but every cent is worth it." He had finished the candy and was stuffing the wrapper in his jacket.

Nothing changes a rider's frame of mind more rapidly than bad weather. About 80 km out of Almaty we ride into the storm. The cold and wet turns our scenic ride instantly into a grim reeling in of the miles.

I find that the only way I can keep upright in this crosswind is to ride at a 20-degree list to the right. Loose dust and gravel seem determined to take me to the other side of the road. Looking in the mirrors I can see that even the German juggernaut was having trouble in the high wind.

"How you doing, Mike?" I ask over the intercom. "I'm having trouble holding the line in this wind."

"Just keep going," says Mike grimly. There is nothing for it. Nowhere to stop, all around us is just dark countryside and hardly another car on the road. In the distance the mountains are just distinguishable from the night sky as a slightly duller shade of dark grey. Flashes of lightning in the near distance.

We descend into another valley along a length of low hills on each side. As we clear the hills we once again ascend on a low ridgeline with dark steppe country on both sides. As we crest the ridgeline I notice something I never thought I would ever see again.

"Er, Mike ..." is all I manage to get out.

"Yes, I know," he says, "here we go again."

In a few seconds it's clear this sandstorm means business. It's like riding into an invisible wall. Unlike the situation in Xinjiang we are on our own now, and the storm seems particularly vindictive. Visibility goes from lousy to non-existent. We stop the bikes on the shoulder and kill the engines to save the air filters. Even with the engines off the bikes continue to twitch beneath us. Trying to get a leg off the bike means dropping it, and it'll be nearly impossible to lift it in this wind.

"Better see if you can get Pierce or the Boss on the radio," I shout to Mike over the intercom, "hopefully they're not out of range yet. Keep your helmet on."

"OK, I'll sign off now and try and reach either of them."

I hear him switch his intercom to the radio and try to take stock of the situation. The good thing is that like Ma had recommended, we have the bikes in the direction of the wind. Actually, that's pretty much the only good thing. With the wind like this neither of us can get off our bikes. OK, we might have to spend the night like this. With the wind noise we would probably not get any sleep. It's starting to rain now and hypothermia might be an issue.

The winds are much stronger and growing by the minute. A golf ball-sized rock flies straight at me, bounces off the edge of the windscreen and whizzes past. *OK, keep crouched down behind the windscreen and leave the helmet on.* The rear view mirrors hum in the wind. I look back to check if Mike is all right but all I can see is him shouting at the intercom in his helmet. There is no cover anywhere around, not that we can see very far. There was a café about 20 km the way back. There aren't any vehicles on this road either. Not that we could actually communicate to anyone we manage to stop anyway. It is impossible to ride in this weather. What is ahead in the direction of Almaty is unknown. We are in a bit of trouble.

After a few long minutes Mike comes over the intercom again. He can't contact Boss but has managed to get Pierce in the film crew's van and they are coming back for us. Apparently they had hit the sandstorm about 20 km ahead and had been expecting our call. Before long the van arrives and with the help of the film crew we manage to get the bikes on their main stands. We all clamber into the van to consider our options. With their local phone network we manage to reach Boss. He has already reached the hotel in Almaty. His suggestion is to leave the bikes there and come into the city by van, the hotel here is really great. We can come out and get the bikes when the storm passes, or at first light the next day.

"Well, bollocks to that idea," says Mike.

I agree. "No, we're not doing that. We stay with the bikes. What are the other options?"

The camera crew is local and has no English. We communicate through Nazgul, our anchorwoman. No one knows how long sandstorms like this last in this part of Kazakhstan. Some could last all night, others might pass after a few hours. What they do make clear is that they want to get home. They have been on their feet since yesterday, so asking them to spend the night out on this dark road is not an option.

Mike mentions that we did pass a lit cottage about 6 km back, with two trucks parked out front. I have a vague recollection, not sure if I can find it again. If we can make it there we could ask for shelter for the night. We manage to persuade the van crew to at least follow us back there. If that doesn't work we could at least leave the bikes there and take the van back into Almaty. That'll be better than leaving the bikes at the side of the road.

It hardly seems possible but the winds are even stronger now. With considerable effort I get on the bike and turn it around. We haven't started moving yet but the howl of the wind despite the earplugs and the full-face helmet is deafening. The only way I can tell I've turned the engine over is by the instruments. I can't hear it at all, and the engine was already trembling in the wind before I hit the ignition switch. Just getting the Beemer off the main stand has tipped it in the high wind and I see Pierce and Mike struggle to get it pointed the right way again. I'm not sure where the cottage is, I plan to follow Mike in the dark. It seems crazy to ride when we can barely stand astride the machines.

What follows is a very long 6 km. Thankfully the rain has subsided a little but there is still all this stuff flying about. Mike goes ahead first and beyond 50 m, all I can see are his tail lights. We are heading back the way we came, fighting a very awkward tail wind, although the trailing van does offer some protection. The wind seems to be carrying most of the countryside with it and I'm getting broadsided with little bits of everything that pings cheerfully off the fairing and windscreen.

Finally, we see the front porch lights of the cottage about 50 m off the road to the right. It's in a gully that's surrounded by hills on three sides. In the darkness all we can see is a murky outline of a single-storied cottage with a darkened front porch, two heavy trucks and a bus parked in the front. As we pull the bikes in, our headlights pick out a water tank to the left and in the darkness behind the cottage what seems to be an abandoned cowshed. The warm glow of unshaded light bulbs spills out of the clear windows to the gravelled driveway. We park the bikes between the cottage and the water tank, out of sight of the road, then with the panniers off we head across the porch and through the front door.

If poor weather and impending darkness had got us down on a bike, nothing lifts our spirits faster than stepping out of the cold and into the warmth of the cottage. It's a simple place, the front door taking us straight into what looks like a home kitchen with a few tables and chairs thrown in to accommodate passing truckers. There are two groups of them, sipping their coffees and cigarettes and hardly raising an eyebrow at the sight of the new arrivals.

Nazgul has already negotiated a simple back room for us and dinner is being thrown into pots on a coal fire stove. There is the rich aroma of mutton stew on the boil, the homely comfort of woollen carpets that drape the floors and sofas, and a heady mixture of working clothes, cigarette smoke and vodka in the air. Most of all, it is out of the cold and the wind. We can hear the rain coming down now in earnest on the roof and windows, and it's really nice to be indoors.

Mike and I insist that our rescuers stay and have dinner on us; they are all a little sheepish but the truth of it is that they have saved us. Without their coming back for us we probably would be sleeping out in the rough.

Tea is served as soon as we're seated and it's nothing like the nuanced subtleties of the traditional Chinese brew. Here it's strong, milky, out of a tin teapot with a floral pattern, and into large hand-sized porcelain bowls. This comes with home-made bread and then the main course of *lagman*, which is like a wet pasta with lamb and peppers and onions and this wonderfully sweet gravy. After the trials of the last few hours, we wolf down the food and Nazgul says something to the proprietor that I gather just means, keep the food coming.

What really does break the ice is this clear liquid that enables me to pick up the Russian and even the local Kazakh dialects with ease. Nazgul calls it *Qara Jilqi*, or black horse, and it's wonderful. Very useful for toasts, and Kazakhs like to toast with their meals. Goes down very nicely, with a warm assurance that it will do what's needed.

With my improved linguistic abilities I understand that the camera crew actually consists of two directors — Shokan and Rawan — who will prepare the Russian and Kazakh telecasts of our arrival for the national news stations tomorrow. The camera crew of Arsen, Oscar, Dachan and Jixen has been on their feet all of last night and the whole day today filming the preparations of the medical congress and then waiting for us to cross the border. They are tired to get home, but the *Qara Jilqi* is helping.

As we get started on the second bottle I wonder why I've never seen Kazakh vodka at the duty free shopping outlets before. It builds understanding across linguistic barriers,

Qara Jilqi — the fastest way to make new friends

complements traditional foods, makes friends from total strangers, and puts the warmth back in your bones.

After dinner we are the only guests left in that small cottage. Now that she has a moment to herself we are introduced to the proprietor, a middle-aged woman helped by her teenage son, Hossan, who is clearing up the kitchen and putting things away. In a few minutes the eatery looks like a home kitchen again. Just before leaving Nazgul asks Hossan to keep an eye on our bikes, which are visible just outside the side window. Hossan gives us thick carpets, which convert the benches we had dinner on into our beds, and thick blankets for the night. I have the best sleep in weeks.

THE NEXT MORNING IT'S first light when I awake to the sound of a passing lorry shifting gears on the downhill outside the cottage. It's completely silent except for the sound of Mike's breathing on the bench across the table, and the lorry's engine note seems to linger in the air. Despite the frugal arrangements it is difficult to leave the comfort of a woollen carpet and blanket sandwich. I feel completely rested as I get up on my haunches on the bench and look around.

Hossan sleeps on one side of the kitchen. He's pulled two tables together and put his own carpet on them to bed down for the night with his head inches away from the windowpane. From where he sleeps he would have seen and heard anyone come near our bikes just outside the window.

As the sun comes through the pale blue cotton curtains I see the room in a new light. In the stillness of the morning it feels much more like a home now than a place of business. Each of the window ledges have rows of small flowerpots and polished copper lamps without their wicks, placed simply because they make the place look nicer. In the corner next to my bench is a small pile of children's wooden building blocks neatly put away, next to a small, weathered lean-to blackboard and a box of chalks. Over Mike's bench hangs a print of Bruegel's *Peasant Wedding*. The very same print used to hang over my brother's bed when we were growing up.

I put my boots on and step out the front door to the porch. The air is perfectly still with the last of the rain clouds clearing, leaving a barely perceptible drizzle and what promises to be a wonderfully bright morning ahead. The landscape that had seemed so threatening the night before is now the very picture of rural tranquility, fresh green grassland dotted with bright pink flowers and dew glistening in the morning sun, as far as the eye can see.

When I turn back into the cottage, Mike is just getting himself together.

"Sleep well?" I ask.

"Oh yes, that was some good vodka. What time is it?"

"7:10. I think that's breakfast on the table," I said. Two bowls of clear meatball soup have magically appeared, with more home-made bread. Hossan has already cleared his bed and is busily making the place ready for another day's business. I guess the breakfast crowd will be showing up before long. We offer to pay for the night but he refuses anything. When his mother arrives she indicates that Nazgul had already settled everything the night before. So the best night's sleep on the Long Ride is on the house.

It's a crisp, bright 13 degrees when we get on the bikes. The whole countryside seems completely still. The Suzuki is still dripping with morning dew and eagerly starts up with the first turn of the starter motor, moisture vaporising from the engine block in a fine white mist as the V-twin warms up happily. As we head away from the cottage we have a feeling that this is going to be a good day.

Rural Kazakhstan is a wonderfully refreshing change after a month of China madness. Heading towards Almaty it feels as though we've not only crossed from one country to the next, but into some earlier century. The villages we pass have more in common with that Bruegel painting than China, less than 100 km away. Life is slow and old here, with none of the glaring newness we have gotten used to. There are still horse-drawn carts. Houses here look centuries old — thick mud walls and thatch roofs the norm — with mature gardens and large shady trees, overgrown rose bushes and coarse wooden garden furniture. No one has a fence and no one seems to be in a hurry.

Most of all, there are so few people. At one of the villages just before Almaty I think it must be a market day, with stalls set up on either side of the road through the village. We slow down for locals who cross the road as though cars never come this way. I glance at the dashboard clock: It really ought to be rush hour now.

Teenagers carrying books to school are dressed in jeans and neat shirts and blouses, without the headphones or tablets or designer clothing that have become their universal uniform elsewhere. In China, there would have been the yammering of electronic gadgets and mobile phones. Here there isn't a single battery-powered anything in sight and people shuffle along quietly about their business. Thick planks held up by stout wooden benches make up the stalls selling roses, lettuce, pears and some of the most beautiful apples I have ever seen. I'm looking for my personal bottle of *Qara Jilqi* but this is nowhere to be found. Just behind the row of stalls a horse grazes lazily in someone's garden. This is a kind of place where you can open your kitchen window in the morning and find a horse grazing in your front yard.

As we near Almaty things start to look distinctly European. There are proper barriers and dividers on the roads, cat's eyes and skid-proof road markings, and international standard road signs. It's the first time I've seen any of these since leaving Malaysia. The biggest change is the petrol stations. We pull into a proper Shell station with a small supermarket stocked with the familiar dozen kinds of soft drinks and candy. Payment is by Visa, and there's Enya music in the background. Staff in familiar yellow-and-red uniforms push us in Russian if we want to buy a membership card for a discount. There isn't a hint of a kettle anywhere.

We are guided to the Rixos hotel by Mike's GPS, where the cancer congress is starting tomorrow. It's hard to get used to just how un-Chinese Almaty is. The people are dressed in spring fashion, and as we approach the city centre, many look like they've stepped out of a Cosmo magazine. The cars are mostly European makes, for some inexplicable reason with a disproportionate number of Audi 100s. There is even the occasional big bike, and I think I might have caught the characteristic uneven rumble of a Harley V-twin. We're just 150 km from the Chinese border, yet there isn't a single Chinaman but me. Not even a single Chinese character on any of the road signs or shops.

It's when we get to the lobby of the palatial Rixos hotel that I realise we have well and truly left China behind. The place is full of pharma-rep types putting up stalls for the cancer conference. As usual there are some pre-congress workshops running in the side rooms.

Outside one of the rooms, the pharma sponsors have put out the very epitome of European refinement and decadence: It's about a metre tall and in three layers, that luxuriant dark liquid forming a solid circular sheet as it cascades down to this warm gooey foot-deep pleasure pool in the bottom bowl. It smells heavenly and I stand there in my grubby, dirt-covered bike kit, completely mesmerised. I think this is the biggest mistake of Jiayuguan. It wasn't just barbarians out there to the west, in Xingjiang and beyond. And if the Chinese hadn't closed their minds and their borders, they might well have discovered chocolate fondue.

OVER THE NEXT FEW days Mike and I will have to part company. After the ride had already got underway, Boss managed to get one of the largest cancer centres in Uzbekistan interested in our cause. Unfortunately, the dates they want to meet clash with the dates of the cancer congress here in Almaty. I suspect that the Kazakhs may have even changed the date of their national annual cancer congress for us. The breast cancer team from NUH is coming up and we are doing one whole day on multidisciplinary care for breast cancer. With all the ground work done I've done, leaving is out of the question. So Mike is to ride ahead with the Boss to Tashkent with my Suzuki on the rack, and I would catch up by flight after the congress. As Pierce is a late addition to the team, he'll need a few days to get his Uzbek visa cleared in Almaty as well, so we'll be flying out together.

After the best breakfast in months, I have the shock of familiar faces waiting for me in the hotel lobby. My breast cancer colleagues from Singapore have taken time off work to come up and give lectures on their respective specialties in surgery, medical oncology, radiology, radiation oncology and breast cancer nursing. These are people I have worked with every day for years and it's been only two months since we last met, but now they seem to be from some place so long ago and far away.

I can tell they're a little uncertain about me. Part of it is the time away I suppose — that, and the facial hair. Early in the ride Mike had suggested that in true Nordic tradition we should remain unshaven while we're on this quest of ours. What he could not have anticipated was that while he is shaping up nicely into a tallish version of Björn Borg, I'm morphing uncertainly into a tallish version of Mr Miyagi.

Conversation with the gang is a little difficult at first. Being on the road for so long means orbiting in a whole other reality. I've been working with an entirely different set of priorities they could not possibly relate to. It's hard to find something to say. *Hello people, you wouldn't happen to have any soap powder, would you?* No. *How about Life on the Road lesson #26: To prevent severe chaffing from long hours on the bike seat, remember army foot powder – it's not just for your feet.* Er, no. *Hi guys, have you tried cognitive behavioural therapy? It can change your life!* No, definitely not.

In the end, it's all a little unnecessary. It's just a meeting of good friends and in the initial apprehension there is also genuine concern. I figure they've read the blogs and are grateful that their friend and colleague isn't a stammering, quivering wreck. So am I. Then Serene, our breast care nurse, hands me a box of my favourite pastries from home and gives me a long hug. That says all I need to know. It's time to get to work.

OVER THE NEXT TWO days I learn many things about breast cancer care in Kazakhstan. It's a lesson in contrasts. Kazakhstan is about the size of western Europe, and there are vast differences in the availability and quality of cancer screening. They feel that the main challenge to providing screening services is the problem of physical distance. They're quite taken aback when they hear that with the screening services available in a place as small as Singapore, women still don't come forward in greater numbers.

When I point out that we think it has to do with cultural factors, my Kazakh colleagues find this difficult to accept. There are very successful screening programmes for other female conditions in Asia such as cervical cancer, and breast cancer should not be any different. We concede that it may be factors unique to southeast Asia and not in the central Asian regions.

In the afternoon I meet Nina Ambramovic in the lobby of the hotel over tea. Getting to know Nina was one of the extreme kismet events during the preparation for the Ride. She was introduced to me by her boss, Antonio Corbi, through a chance meeting some two years ago. What Antonio said sums up Nina's capabilities perfectly: In Almaty, anything you need, she can get done.

Since then her involvement with our cause has been nothing short of extraordinary. She helped us with the route planning, getting visas, and putting us in touch with the right people for the cancer congress. When some of the connections started to falter, as is the nature of these new distant relations, she was the one that got them going again. Back then they seemed to have nothing to gain from two mad surgeons riding through. There was a good chance we might not even make it this far.

Nina helped us overcome all that. Having someone with the influence and the contacts on the ground had been the decider for taking the route through Kazakhstan. Even now she's in the process of getting the plane tickets for Pierce and I so that we can catch up with the long ride in Tashkent the following week.

It's good meeting her at last. Nina looks just as I imagined her. In her early forties, cheerful and reassuring, and very quick. The kind with an eye for the details. I immediately get the impression that while Antonio may have been the head of the organisation, I'm meeting the neck.

Over tea I discover that she is Russian-born but had moved here as a child and for all intents and purposes considers herself a Kazakh. Right from the start of our meeting she is a perfect mixture of fixer and friend. She wants to know how else she can help, and in a few short phone calls arranges transport for Pierce and I to the airport tomorrow afternoon. She is also very keen to catch up on our experiences on the Ride and how the cancer congress has gone. She is especially interested in the morning's discussion about how to get women to come forward for screening. Aside from the problems of access to care and cultural factors, Nina has her own take on this.

"Women are afraid," she says plainly.

"Yes, that I can understand," I reply. I remember the look of women at my Results Clinic. "The treatment's more than removing an organ. Often women feel that it's removing or mutilating something a lot more intimate than that."

"No, it's not that they're afraid of," she says, "I mean there is that, but there's more."

"You mean the chemotherapy, and the loss of hair, the way they look?"

"No, no. I mean that's also important," she says, "but there's something more. Woman are afraid that their husbands won't love them anymore."

I say nothing, but must look surprised, because the next thing she says:

"Don't look like you don't know this. Take yourself. How would you look at your wife if she had breast cancer? Or needed that operation," she jerked a line across the front of the right side of her chest with her finger, "would you view it the same as any other cancer?"

"Well ..." I'm a little unsure about this. I've never thought of that before. I make sure Viola goes for her regular mammograms, but we've not really talked about what to do if it actually picked something up.

"Most men don't," says Nina.

"Well, I'd like to think that Viola knows that I'll stand with her regardless of what happens," I reply. It sounds weak, but like I said, I'm unsure.

"It's not a matter of standing by," Nina smiles, "it's a matter of loving her the same way. Losing that is what women are most afraid of. In fact, I think that if they can be assured that they would not lose that love, that closeness, many more would come forward."

Maybe we're not only sending the wrong message, we're also sending it to the wrong target group. Breast cancer awareness could target men with the tagline, "Just tell her you'll love her anyway". Maybe men should invite their women to breast cancer screening.

"Seems maybe a little too intimate for a public health message?" I ask Nina.

She gives me a puzzled look over her teacup. "What do you think breast cancer is?"

Sixteen
NOT-SO-GOLDEN ROAD TO SAMARKAND

THE CHANGE IN PLANS at Almaty allow me to stay in the city for an additional two days after the congress under Nazgul's hospitality, and help Pierce to sort out his visas. Most of all, it's time away from the ride and time to rest without having to think about any conference preparations or miles to make up for. In short, it's a mental break, something I've been needing for ages.

When we eventually leave, the plane journey from Almaty to Tashkent in Uzbekistan takes less than two hours but it's another world. The European feel of Almaty evaporates in a blinding flash of light and heat as soon as the plane door opens. This is desert country. It may be late afternoon but still 38 degrees in the shade. It's dusty, dry, very quiet and … beige. As Pierce and I sit in an un-air conditioned beige Fiat

127 through a beige dust-covered countryside into the city, I notice that there are also far fewer cars on the road. Maybe it's just too crazy to be out in this heat.

When we arrive at the palatial Lotte Hotel I see my bike out front for the first time in five days. She looks grubbier than usual. Then I remember that the last time we were together it was just out of a sandstorm. I'll have to check the tyre pressures, chain, fluids and wiring before starting out tomorrow — not much time now at sunset.

I really can't wait to get going again. Tomorrow we ride into Samarkand. Samarkand! We'll tread in the footsteps of Omar Khayyam and Ulugh Beg. Who were they and what had they accomplished? Only contributions to work in algebra, trigonometry, and advances in astronomy that surpassed Copernicus. They were true polymaths, and what appeals to me more than all this is some of their most haunting poetry. Even when translated from the original Persian, the poignancy of Quatrain 51 of Omar Khayyam's *Rubáiyát* remains:

The Moving Finger writes; and having writ
Moves on; nor all thy Piety nor Wit
Shall lure it back to cancel half a line,
Nor all thy tears cancel a word of it

In my vivid childhood imaginations I heard those words ringing through some faraway fairy tale land of desert sands and starry skies, minarets and caravans, cross-legged old men wondering about their role in this "chequer-board of nights and days". I can't even remember when I had first read of

Samarkand, but it is the stuff that stirs up the primordial need to go wandering. Was it pictures of the blue-domed Registan Square that stared back from the glossy pages of some old *National Geographic*? Parents who want to keep their children from dreaming of far-flung places and fixed on the straight and narrow should never give them access to Nat Geo.

Who among us hasn't finished leafing through any edition without wondering, *when will it be my turn to go?* Not just the Silk Road, mind you. It's sowed the seeds of transecting Africa across the equator, doing that ride from Alaska to Ushuaia, pushing through on the Road of Bones to Magadan. I'm pretty sure I won't make the others on that list, but no matter! Tomorrow I ride to Samarkand! Tomorrow night I'll have my starlit skies and while I may not be part of a caravan, a bike's not a bad way to get there.

I'm awake at sunrise, this time not with any feeling of dread but just excited anticipation. The hotel is completely silent. I bring everything out to the bike and run the usual checks. Except for being dirtier than usual the Suzuki seems none the worse for wear. Feeling energetic, I take the tank off, rinse off the air filter under a garden tap and K&N fluid and put it all back together.

I'm eager to get going again before the day really starts to heat up. Right now the city seems quiet and the riding conditions ideal before the rush hour. There is no trace of the cramping anxiety of Thailand anymore though. I feel good. I want to get on because today can only get better.

Over breakfast Mike and Boss exchange glances. Philip's starting to spout poetry, should they worry? They must think the medications have finally kicked in, but it's really something else. The point is, no more formal meetings until Denmark. We are riding for ourselves now. Flecker's ode to all wanderers, set against the backdrop of the city gates as caravans leave for Samarkand, just as we are doing, comes to mind:

> *We are the Pilgrims, master, we shall go*
> *Always a little farther; it may be*
> *Beyond the last blue mountain barred with snow*
> *Across that angry or that glimmering sea*
> *...*
> *Sweet to ride forth at evening from the wells*
> *When shadows pass gigantic on the sand*
> *And softly in the silence beat the bells*
> *Along the Golden Road to Samarkand!*

We've come a long way already and seen some things beyond my wildest imaginations, but always under a sort of cloud. It might be the pressure of deadlines and people to meet and deals to sort out but now all that is over and done with. It's the second part of our ride now, where we'll be riding pretty much for ourselves. From now on it's just seeing what the road brings.

As we leave the hotel parking lot a whole convoy of police cars are waiting to escort us out of the city. I figure that Mike and Boss must have seriously impressed some very important people in their two days here. Our exit from Tashkent is celebrity style, with policemen on their loudspeakers clearing the road ahead of us with choice language. A bit uncomfortable going through red lights and having already very courteous drivers make way for us, but I guess it's just their way here.

Soon the police escort leaves us and we come to what seems like an intercity highway. This is where the riding gets a little interesting. It's about 300 km to Samarkand and the first bit is nothing like what I expected from all that Nat Geo. The majestic tree-lined broad thoroughfares of the city are replaced by a four-lane highway. Faster traffic consists of newer low-end Chevrolets and older indestructible Fiats, while the slower lane is occupied by pickups, beat up Fiats on their last legs, and the occasional horse cart. The road surface deteriorates and there are runs of road where the tarmac has been worn away, exposing the loose granite chipping underneath. The choice is either to trust the big bike to eat these up, or weave in and out of the traffic. Here Mike and the Beemer have no trouble at all but the firmer suspension on the Suzuki is killing my kidneys and I have to slow down.

What is remarkable is how these newer low-end saloons manage this road without any noticeable drop in speed. In fact, I notice they don't really slow down when coming up in my mirrors either. I'm playing cat-and-mouse with the arse sniffers and the slower traffic, weaving between the lanes and trying not to slow Mike down too much.

Every time one of these newer saloons hits a particularly deep pothole there's a sickening crunch of tortured plastic as the hubcaps take a hit on the edge of tarmac. About 50 m ahead of me I see a plastic hubcap come clean off, arc gracefully through the air and land just behind me. No one bats an eyelid and we just keep going. The older Fiats do not have any of these plastic niceties; occasionally a door lurches open on hitting a pothole and the driver nonchalantly reaches over and shuts it without slowing down at all.

As we approach Samarkand it starts to look more like the Nat Geo pictures. Samarkand is a city set on a hill — the traffic thins, and the barren desert turns into arable grassland, dotted with shepherds and their huge flocks of sheep. In the distance we see the first signs of the fabled city, traces of worn-down fortifications playing hide-and-seek with the surrounding hills.

We're chatting excitedly on the intercom when suddenly Mike, who has been graciously letting me set a pace my kidneys and elbows can tolerate, charges ahead full throttle. What looks like pure unburnt petrol spews out of his exhaust. The big BMW sounds like a Fiat with a holed silencer.

"I've got a big problem, Phil. Anything less than full throttle and the engine dies. I don't think my left piston is firing. Can't slow down for you."

"Right, you go ahead, we're nearly there and I'll use the signposts. What seems to be the problem?"

"No idea, but it sounds pretty horrible. I'm burning up petrol fast." He's already disappearing beyond intercom range.

There's nothing for it. I can see he's stalled a few times already and re-started the bike on the move. As long as he keeps moving we can sort it in the city. At least I hope we can.

When I get to the Grand Samarkand Hotel, Mike's already looking over the Beemer in the front of the hotel. It seems he's only just managed it. In the 40 km or so since the trouble started he has practically emptied his petrol tank, a process that usually takes almost 600 km to do. It really is raw petrol coming through his pipe.

The engine sounds and smells like it's flooded, and won't run for more than a few seconds unless the throttle's wide open. We're in Samarkand for only one full day so we're in urgent need for a quick fix, or it'll be the Beemer's turn on the back of the Bumblebee.

There are still a few hours of daylight left and with help from the Grand Samarkand we get a list of where a bike mechanic might be found. This surprises me; I don't think I saw a single bike in Tashkent or on the way here, but we're desperate now. Hung Tuan narrows the concierge's suggestions and we get directions to our best bet: a reputable car mechanic not far away. It's the best we can do, at least there'll be the necessary tools. We have the Beemer strapped on to the back of the Bumblebee.

When we get there my heart sinks. It's a garage at the back lot of a Ford and Chevrolet car rental. The place is well stocked and full of activity, but there isn't a single bike in sight. It looks like a well-run garage business, with cars up on hydraulic jacks, engine blocks with their top ends off, and a row of wheel balancers. There's a whole section of the yard that's devoted to hammering out dents and changing panels. The point is, not a single bike. The dozen or so mechanics don't even come in to work on a bike, as they do the world over. Not a good start.

A stocky senior mechanic comes out of his office and gives the BMW a good look over. In fact, as we take the bike off the rack and wheel it into one of the service bays, work stops as everyone gives it a good once over. I'm certain they've never seen a bike quite this big, shaft driven and more horses in the engine than anything else here.

Stocky isn't much of a talker. Just a heavily-built man in his early forties with grease-covered Chevrolet overalls. He looks like he was born in a garage, with a pair of huge hands, dirty rag jammed in this trouser belt and a cigarette hanging on his lips, the next one lodged over his right ear.

With the hotel guide as translator we run through what we think might be the problem. We had taken low-grade fuel for the first time on this ride earlier this morning; that may be the cause of the trouble. It might have fouled up the spark plugs so we bleed out all the petrol, add fuel additives and fill up the gas tank, before cleaning out the plugs.

Still no luck. That's pretty much the end of the easy options. Everything else is going to need taking apart the fuel injectors. That means taking the tank off and getting to the mad tangle of cables and circuit boards between the pistons. The nightmare of BMW owners is not how well it runs, which is perfect, but what happens when it stops running. Roadside fixes are beyond most mechanics outside of a registered BMW workshop.

While Stocky tries to figure out what goes where, Mike and Pierce get online to ask other BMW owners for an opinion. Like I've said, it's the default adventure bike for people who can afford it, and there's no shortage of online help.

The possibilities all sound dreadfully complicated, ranging from worn piston rings, jammed fuel intakes, clogged fuel lines, fried computer chip, shorted circuit breakers. Recommendations on what to do are more consistent: Unless you're used to removing that fuel tank and tinkering with What Lies Beneath, don't do it. Get it to the nearest BMW workshop. Where is that? Ankara. Ankara? The one in

Turkey? Yes, that's the one. Good man there who's serviced at least a dozen stricken Beemer-riding overlanders, honest and a good pair of hands. Ah, good. We look at the map. That's 4,000 km away. In between is the rest of Uzbekistan, all of Turkmenistan and Iran and two thirds of Turkey.

In the dying light, Hung Tuan comes over with a few cold bottles of Coke and we sit down and consider our options. There aren't many. The travel arrangements are such that we need to cross the borders as a single convoy. Get the bike back on the rack where it stays as we make the distance to Turkey, then head straight for Ankara.

While we're considering our limited options Stocky's finished looking over the bike engine. I can tell he's never seen anything like it before today, but an engine is an engine and it must have been some time since one failed to leave this garage in at least some sort of running order. He's been tinkering on his own and I notice that he's already figured out how to get the piston heads off and checked the valves.

He comes over and offers each of us a cigarette, the universal sign of the start of a working conference. He gives us another option through the interpreter: "Leave it with me tonight. See what I can do. Enjoy Samarkand tomorrow morning, but come over again after lunchtime and see what I've managed. If it works, at least you can still ride out. If not, well, I hope your truck's strong enough to take it to Ankara."

Mike decides to leave it behind. Maybe it's something straightforward that we've missed. No one mentions the bike until tomorrow evening.

We spend the next morning at the majestic Registan Square among some of the most impressive Islamic architecture anywhere, now restored to its full glory. It's all breathtakingly beautiful, the azure tiles give the impression that these madrassahs have descended from the heavens. Unfortunately, Mike and I are viewing all of it under a cloud of uncertainty. Not having him around until Turkey will be a big disappointment.

Our visits to the must-see sights done and dusted, we head out to the mechanics again to see how the Beemer is getting on. Mike had given Stocky some leeway to get the bike moving again. We figure that even a half-functioning bike would be enough for him to keep up with me – I'm certainly not hitting breakneck speeds, and just hobbling along would be better than having the bike at the back of the truck.

When we get to the shop I see the fuel tank is still on the Beemer and prepare myself for disappointment. It means that Stocky has not tackled the fuel pump at the bottom of all that wiring and circuitry. That would have needed the tank off. Still he has done some tinkering and wants us to start it up and give it a try

We wheel the bike out to the courtyard and turn over the engine. It starts first time but is still burning rich; pure petrol continues to come out of the exhaust and unless we are running 5,000 rpm the engine floods and dies. Mike makes the final decision. He can't ride like this. We'll get it on the back of the Bumblebee and head back to the hotel.

At sunset we find ourselves in the inner courtyard of the Grand Samarkand Hotel, shaded from the heat on all sides by four stories of hotel rooms. On the left is the dining area, and up a spiral staircase there is the most pleasant of wood panelled balconies, with a bar with a few discrete beer taps. Here, Mike and I settle down for a bit of a chat. The day was drawing to a close, and as the room lights come on, we can see the first stars come through our little tent of sky.

I really am sorry things have turned out this way. Mike had, in his quiet way, seen me through the worst of the darkest moments of sheer panic on the road. Every morning I have to face the mental struggle of just getting onto the bike and starting the engine, and it was Mike's presence that convinced me I could meet the day. He had slowed down, ridden longer than he had to, kept the intercom open and not once complained about all the grief I have caused him. This isn't fair.

"Ah, well," he says, "you'll have to manage on your own for the next bit."

"I really am sorry for this, Mike."

"Well, at least we now know that you made the right decision about not sending the bike back from Kunming," he said.

"What do you mean?"

"If you had sent the bike back, there would be no bike to ride now. The Long Ride would be over. It would have been this ridiculous picture of two bikers riding in the cab of a pickup. That would have been a disaster."

That's just how Mike would have seen it. We have a cold, quiet beer under the stars and call it a night.

THE NEXT DAY IT'S just over 250 km through the desert to get to Bukhara. The road is very much like the not-so-fabled one into Samarkand. Pot-holed, washboarded and rutted, but thankfully almost entirely free of traffic. I'm doing some decent speeds on my own, but at the cost of wrists, testicles and kidneys. I can't really tell how fast I'm going because the dials are just a jarring blur as the front end takes one series of ruts after another. I deeply regret not getting softer suspension. I had figured that almost all of the journey was going to be long miles on surfaced roads, but had underestimated how wide the definition of "surfaced" could be.

The bike is taking a beating. Broken bits of road throw up a continuous staccato of gravel on the bash plate and fairing. The additional brake light that I had fitted has fallen off, presumably just shaken to death. All that's left are the ends of two mounting screws and frayed connecting wires trailing in my wake.

I suppose I could take my time but I really don't want to stay out here in this heat. It's 41 degrees by 11:00 am, and not a spot of shade in sight through the desert. It isn't the sort of desert I had seen in books either, more like rocky wasteland with the occasional half-hearted bush. I spot the odd herd of wild camels in the distance.

There is another reason why I want to get a move on. There's no one to talk to out here, no distractions. With his helmet off in the support vehicle, there is no Mike on the intercom. I'm alone with my thoughts in the helmet for the first time in weeks. I'm not quite comfortable with this as yet. I keep remembering the one consistent thing I had read about panic attacks: Relapses can be expected and I should take care not to set expectations too high. What if I find that I can't keep going out here in the desert?

By sheer practice, I get into my mental routines. Mike and Pierce would tell me later they can tell when this happens. Apparently I sort of look blank, there but not really there. While nothing much seems to be happening on the outside, inside my head there is some real exertion. Most of all, I need to take down a lifelong trait of setting targets. I have to keep telling myself that the idea is not to make Bukhara by a certain time, just get through the next 10 minutes. If I manage that, I switch down to fourth gear and cruise a little slower for five minutes, and then pick things up again for another 10. As things settle, I move it up to 20 minute intervals.

To keep the tension from escalating I have to keep taking these small bites, and to keep myself in the moment. It's all I can do to stop fixating on the clock in the middle of the instrument panel, and keep my eyes on the road. The tentacled beast isn't through with me yet. I yearn desperately for some kind of distraction, anything except being out here on my own with nothing else to think about.

The thing about panic attacks is that the mounting fear

shuts out everything else. It's almost impossible to divert your mental gaze to something else when there is this snarling, visceral menace just beyond the horizon of conscious thought. It's very difficult to find any kind of distracting train of thought and worse of all out here in the desert there isn't a thi—then I hear it.

In the middle of the desert on the Silk Road, I hear the unmistakable sound of a Weber carburetor. Now to the non-petrolheads out there, this is a little hard to explain. It's clearly a guy thing, and guys of a certain age. It's the primal call that makes boys of a previous generation hang up posters of Alfa Romeos and Ferraris on their room walls, with or without Christie Brinkley draped across the bonnet. The car's the thing. It's why they beg their dads to let them tweak the tuning on the family car. Why the first Italian I ever learned was Pininfarina and Bertone. Let's just say it's what a proper sports car should sound like.

Nowadays with fuel injectors to give cleaner emissions and greater economy, the sound of a Weber is all but gone. Some fine-tuning of exhaust manifolds have tried to imitate it, but it's not the same thing. I have a younger colleague in private practice with possibly too much spending money who says he bought a Porsche 911 because when he first sat in it he loved the stylish clock in the middle of the dash. The effing *clock* for cryin' out loud. I was surprised that he knew the engine wasn't in the front. I think it's true to say that my generation of kid is going extinct as well.

Now coming up in the mirrors I can see where that wonderful sound is coming from. It's one of the surreal moments in the ride. Christie isn't coming up in the red

Ferrari 308; the only thing back there is a beat-up beige Lada 1600. It's riding out the ruts in this road with stubborn determination — the driver has one hand pulling on his door window to keep it from slipping entirely and irretrievably into the door. Then I remember. The Lada 1600 is essentially a Fiat 128 that they've kept building out here like some kind of automotive coelacanth. They still have their Webers out here.

It was how Dad and I used to spend Sunday afternoons. We had a Bertone X1/9 then and it was the car I grew up on when I started driving. An avid car tinkerer his whole adult life, Dad said that knowing how to take care of your own wheels was what Real Men do. He had also seen my first year medical school grades and suggested that learning an honest trade might not be such a bad idea. Just in case, you understand.

So he and I would try and take the X1/9 apart after church on Sundays. Like some ride into the unknown, the key was knowing when to turn back. Attempt too little and I didn't learn all that much. Go too far and we soon realised that putting an engine back in the dark was just not funny.

It was where I learned about "redundancy engineering". Car engineers, especially Italians, always give you more parts than you really need. The proof was that after Dad and I had put things back together after tuning the carbs or changing engine oil or bleeding the hydraulics or tensioning the belts, there were always a few bits and bobs left over. These would go into the designated recycled peanut butter jar and placed on the shelf in the storeroom. There were a few cars over the years (Lancia Montecarlo, Mercedes W123 series, Alfa Romeo 121, Volvo P1800 and one unfortunate Lancia Fulvia Coupé) and it was crucial that the right bits went into the right jar. As far as I know we never took any bits out of any bottle to find their rightful place, and the cars still ran pretty much as they should, although considerably lighter.

The only time when Dad insisted that there was going to be absolutely no redundancy was when he taught me how to change the pads on the disc brakes in the Lancia. We started a little late that day and when it was done it was already dark. As far as we could tell there weren't any redundantly engineered retaining pins or return springs anywhere on that semi-lit garage floor. He must have been extremely pleased about that, because he was quite happy for me to use that lovely car to classes the next day, which was unusual. He offered to take a taxi to work. It was, according to Dad, what a Real Man would do.

After three hours of punishing riding we make good time and just before lunch I pull into a slightly dodgy petrol station, the only one for miles. Despite the language barrier I want to be real sure that this is legit petrol of the proper octane grading. Like what Mike said, the Suzuki is carrying the show now.

After filling up I look around the station with my cold Coke in hand and there it is: another beat-up Lada 1600, with the front bonnet open to cool the engine before taking in radiator water. As I stroll over, I see a familiar scene from Sunday afternoons decades past staring back at me: the characteristic transverse layout of a 128 engine, pushing the front wheel drive below. There are the familiar rubber hoses that always leaked, the radiator that you could hear rusting away on a quiet night and the odd-sized battery. Here in

Mike about to take his turn on the V-Strom after taking Uzbek petrol. Note the Lada cooling off in the background.

the dry desert air there's hardly a touch of rust at all. In tropical, humid Singapore that would by definition make it not a Fiat.

Right on top of the engine block is the air filter, and I know removing that single winged nut would reveal a box filter. I remember that from the afternoon Dad had replaced it with a ring paper K&N filter that improved the X1/9's acceleration considerably. Under that would be the Weber. It's so easy to find in this Lada compared to the X1/9, where the small space available in the mid engine configuration had forced the engineers to put the carbs in at a bit of a tilt. The X1/9 used the same engine, but with its tiny bonnet opening it was an effort trying to even find the mixture and idle screws, much less adjusting them. After considerable hunting Dad had found a 12-inch slotted screwdriver from Jalan Besar that could do the job perfectly. It was a prized possession, but it wouldn't have been necessary here. With the wide bonnet and spacious engine bay it's all so easy to get to.

There's no one about and I have no idea whose car this is. Then I see a middle-aged man with a moustache having a quiet smoke in the office, sensibly in the shade and far enough from the pumps. We make eye contact through the opened door and with sign language I ask if I can have a look around his car. He tilts his head. Please yourself.

Inside, the Lada is pure Fiat. Grubby plastic seat covers, hard black plastic dash, near horizontal two-spoked steering wheel, fake walnut veneer. I have never seen a Fiat with door windows that fit their frames and it seems this is true for Ladas as well. In the footwell's tiny pedals, the one for the clutch you can't completely depress because the left wheel arch gets in your way. Ah, the joys of Italian design. What was the old saying? "Buy Fiat: We give you engine, gearbox and suspension. The rest we throw in for free."

The owner walks over with the universal pleasure of any car owner pleasantly surprised that someone is taking an interest in his wheels. He leans over and points to the temperature gauge. Overheating. Losing water. Ah yes, that old dodgy radiator and hose, usually it's the retaining loop screws that rust away and leak. We go round to the engine and look in. I point at that bit of radiator hose that is probably the trouble, but it's too much of a leap across the language barrier.

As I look at the tuning screws on the side of the Weber, just about as far away from a Sunday afternoon in Singapore I could possibly be, Dad's mantra on tuning Webers comes back. *Mixture first, and then idle. Not the other way around, idiot.* He had a way of teaching that helped you remember. Later on in the Lancia there were two Weber carbs, not one, and we had to not only tune them, but synch them as well. Now there are kits and strobe lights and the rest of it, Dad had said. Then with a gaze into a half distance and a drag from his Dunhill, he said, but Real Men do it by ear. That required a bit of sacrifice on my part.

My new stethoscope, with the diaphragm pulled out, was the perfect tool to hear the jets at idling. I am certain that I was the only third-year medical student walking the wards whose Littmann stethoscope, stem shortened for greater acuity, was used to hear mid-diastolic murmurs, carotid bruits and downdraft carburetors. What was it Dad had said when we got it just right? Three of the sweetest sounds ever made by man: the Preservation Hall slide trombone, Bing Crosby in mid-octave, and a well-tuned Weber carb.

Soon I'm back on the road again. As I go down this Uzbek meat grinder, I realise that all three were from a world that was already fading when I was growing up. The Weber went the way of the dinosaur when fuel injectors came into all cars. Soon you needed a computer and an engineering degree to even know what the engine was doing, much less try and tinker with things. A good ear and Real Men are as far removed from the process as I am from Sunday afternoons with my Dad now.

I like to think that those afternoons have served their purpose. It was more than getting your hands dirty, taking care of your own kit, sweating through the process of cleaning things out and taking ownership for what happened next. I think it was Dad trying to give his son a chance at developing some qualities he might appreciate.

As the years went on we never had that closeness again. I graduated, moved out, got married and had kids. After Dad sprained his back trying to get into the Lancia, he switched it to a Mercedes C180, a car that practically fixes itself. And the last car he had was a Jaguar XJ6 that only a select few were allowed to touch. They all had engineering degrees and computers. I had to have a bath before I was even allowed to sit in that.

Still later, Dad moved to a flat to get about more easily and got married again. A lot of stuff from the old house was thrown out or given away to make room for the new. We still talked, but it was about grown-up things now. Off and on the occasion would call for cigars and single malts, and by the way could you get another bottle from the cupboard? There are few things in this world better than cigars and a newly-opened Glenlivet. And knowing that in one corner of that whiskey cupboard, completely out of place, were three peanut butter jars full of washers, rusting coil springs and the odd rubber bung. They were labeled X1/9, Montecarlo and 121.

The road gets busier and better surfaced — we are coming into Bukhara. Through a series of roundabouts we head into the centre of town. The heat is oppressive now, and there's hardly anyone on the streets. Bukhara is not a modern metropolis. It's an ancient city in the desert. The streets are lined with low, tough-looking little houses of brick and concrete, built and lived in by tough-looking people. The last few kilometres the road gives up entirely and I'm riding on fine sand until the hotel entrance. When I get to the hotel lobby Mike comes up with an iced tea for me and asks if I was all right on my own. Odd question — for some reason I did not feel alone at all.

THERE ARE ROUGHLY TWO square kilometres in the old centre of Bukhara that works like a time machine. While Samarkand may have its Registan and its incomparable architecture, here the experience is more immersive.

Bukhara hasn't been too bothered about the tourists. In fact it feels like it's been going about its business unperturbed through the centuries. Rather than the usual arrangement of having the place plundered by giant tour buses in even bigger bus parks, here the original plan of the working city has been largely retained. The streets are filled with people and Ladas going about their work, and brisk business is carried out mainly in the bazaars that dot the ancient streets. Large parts of the old town are accessible only through narrow alleyways that run between the high mud brick walls that separate ancient enclaves.

Bukhara had a major role in that Great Game that played out here over much of the 19th century, and perhaps things haven't changed that much in that department either. The Great Game refers to a period of strategic contests between the Russian and British empires for about a hundred years, starting from the early 1800s. The chessboard was central Asia, which Britain wanted to preserve as a buffer between the Russians and India, the jewel of its crown. The phrase itself was coined by a certain Arthur Conolly who, in a wicked twist of fate, would play out his final role in Bukhara as a needlessly sacrificed pawn.

There is enough to see and do here. The bazaars are what Boss and some of the four by four crews have come all this way for. There are bargains to be had in silverware, jewellery and most of all, carpets.

I'm more interested in the bazaars themselves. These are typically single storied and found at the junction of ancient streets. They have a perfect balance of stone-walled sides that let in just the right amount of light while shading away the heat. Narrow pillars hold up domed roofs perforated at the top to let more light in and the warm air out. Inside, rows of shops line a regular grid of walking lanes. The simple arrangement works remarkably well: It's over 40 degrees outside but comfortably cool for shoppers inside.

Entering a bazaar is like strolling into an illustrated volume of *A Thousand and One Nights*. There are hat merchants, dates from Xinjiang, salt merchants from Turkey. One shop sells only silver spoons, another makes a roaring trade selling raw sugar. Everywhere, the carpets. I'm having my Aladdin moment. Or maybe I'm just happy at the absence of a Starbucks.

Some of the larger bazaars have an attached *caravanserai*, sort of a lay-by stop on this most ancient of highways. These have an arched entrance tall enough for a camel to come through and then a small shaded courtyard with a well or water troughs for the animals, surrounded by shops and stalls and the occasional hostel for overnight stays. In the days of Timur, these would be guarded by his troops and served not only as a place of rest and replenishment but safety from banditry.

London has its Tower, Edinburgh its Castle, Angkor its Wat, and Bukhara has its Ark. In fact it's had its Ark here on and off for some time since AD 500, one fort built upon another in a cycle of destruction and rebuilding that seems typical of life on this chessboard. The one that now stands

Mike going native and haggling for spoons— we're bikers and can't buy anything big.

is modern, largely reconstructed after the Soviet aerial bombardment in 1920. Besides serving as fortified defence it has over its long and varied history housed local rulers, viziers, their administrators and harems. And prisoners.

From the outside it looks like a typical tourist magnet. It stands in its own square, lined on three sides by two-laned roads. The 20-m-tall parapets, now partially complete again, slope outwards to a paved skirting about 200 m wide. On its western side is the 18th-century ramped entrance. As Mike and I stroll across the pavestones we see the group tours and busloads of schoolchildren making their way up the ramp with their coloured flags, led by guides wearing portable megaphone speakers blaring away. Mike and I cross the

Discussing the finer points of rugby with a new friend in Bukhara

square to the base of the ramp. Well about here is where it must have happened I guess, all those years ago: the end of the Great Game for Arthur Conolly.

It was Charles Stoddart who first arrived in 1838 to try and arrange an alliance between the local ruler Nasrullah Khan and the British East India Company. I suppose as an emissary of an empire on which the sun never sets, with its infamous lack of transcultural sensitivities, Stoddart cannot be entirely faulted for what happened next. Apparently, he so offended the Khan that the latter left their first meeting without a word in return to Stoddart's salute.

One faux pas after another followed and soon Nasrullah had Stoddart in the infamous Bug Pit in the Ark. Now this we got a chance to see ourselves, complete with two very emaciated-looking mannequins within. It's a black hole within the dark foundations of the fort, about 3 m in radius and 3 m deep, with a metal grill from which a pulley would bring food and water to the prisoners. And every night a new helping of live bugs and scorpions. Stoddart survived this hellhole for a year. The Emir in his magnanimity offered him relief out of the Pit to house arrest if he converted to Islam, which Stoddart did eventually.

Help did not come for years. The British Empire was fully invested on multiple fronts, against Qing China in the First Opium War, and propping up an unlikely puppet ruler in Afghanistan. All as part of the Great Game.

In 1841 Conolly is sent to the region to take up where Stoddart left off. When he arrives at Bukhara he is initially well treated but this turns a little less warm when the Emir discovers that no letter has come from Queen Victoria, whom he considers an equal. At first, it's just a bit of diplomatic awkwardness. Then when a British holding force is slaughtered by Pashtuns, Nasrullah, emboldened by this and the lack of any reprisals for his treatment of a British emissary, throws both Stoddart and Conolly into the Pit. After six months of unspeakable horrors the two decrepit British soldiers are brought out of the Ark and asked to dig their own graves. Colonel Stoddart spends his last words cursing the Emir as a tyrant. Conolly is offered his life if he should convert to Islam. He refuses, and both men are beheaded.

Their deaths went largely unavenged by an Empire that was over-extended elsewhere. Britain abstained from further excursions into this region, which would increasingly fall under Russian and then Soviet influence until the fall of the Soviet Union in 1991. *That would explain the Ladas*, I thought. And why anyone speaking Russian can get by anywhere around the "–stans".

Well here endeth the lesson. Leave these people alone. They are among the kindest, most generous, painfully hospitable people to sojourners, but they reserve a particular savagery for potential occupiers. Time and again the great powers would get their nose bloodied by these seemingly primitive people. You'd think they would wise up by now, after all those years of horror and bloodshed and needless waste.

Or maybe not. Less than five years ago, they sent an army surgeon with once again more curiosity than good sense to man a NATO combat surgical hospital not 900 km south of where I am now. That's less than a day's ride on a good day.

By the parapets of the Ark, where Stoddart and Conolly met their ends

Back then I spent four months working in a fortified area the size of four football fields. The work was occasionally hectic, but in quiet moments I would sit on the parapets and look to the mountains to the north, wishing for the day when I could see these people outside of the walls.

A third of my patients were civilians, many were children, covered in shrapnel or with bits missing. And I was told to always keep them, even my Pashtun interpreter, on my left when first meeting them. Why? Because you're right-handed, and that's where your sidearm is. I remember what Hayat, my interpreter, had said when I asked him what he thought of the future. Well, the Americans have all the watches, he said, but we Afghans have the time.

Now, by the pond in the Lyabi-Hauz square, it all seems like a world away. Bukhara has always been famous for its fountains and ponds and in the cool of the evening, families come out and gather around these natural meeting places. Square wooden tables are laid out and young men crouch over their games of backgammon and carom, inviting us over for a game or a round of sweet tea. We're benefiting from their long-standing traditions of letting the visiting traveller, whether he arrives by caravan or motorcycle, feel perfectly welcome in their lives.

After numerous cups of sweet tea, Mike and I take our turns in getting our first haircuts in months. A little two-year-old Uzbek girl called Sharifah can't take her eyes off us. She hangs around shyly at the entrance of the barbershop, refusing to come any closer. Her father, having brought her out to enjoy the bright lights of the cafés around the water, coaxes her to shake hands but it's no use. We're just too strange. We don't have their language, but we can still sit by the water together and just enjoy their company.

Pierce finally breaks the ice with a big glossy print of a picture he's taken of her, developed in the photo shop down the alley. Her eyes light up as bright as the stars above when she sees her own image in print for the first time. Her father can't believe the generosity of these wonderful strangers. And neither can we.

Seventeen
FATHER'S DAY IN IRAN

Now crossing the border from Turkmenistan into Iran we take the wonderful Gaudan highway. It takes six hours to clear Iranian customs. This is despite having our Iranian minder meet us in the border complex. It seems he hasn't quite followed through with the paperwork. He's surprised that we want to enter and leave Iran from different borders. The man is a little vague about lots of things. The four by four crew realises that he is the person they'll be depending on to get us through Iran, and this isn't a good start. By the end of six hours and several revised updates from him as we wait for the paperwork to get sorted, they already have a nickname for him: U-Turn.

After spending the night at Bojnurd we head to Gorgan, where U-Turn has arranged for some hiking near Ziarat,

The wonderful winding through Golestan National Park, in Iran of all places. Who knew?

just south of the main town. The ride out puts to rest all preconceptions I have about Iran. This isn't a country of just deserts, nuclear reactors and reactionaries. Among all the countries I've ridden through, Iran gets just about the worst international press. Just goes to show what international press knows.

As I ride through the temperate forests of the Golestan National Park on a perfect black ribbon of road that cuts through the green mountainsides, I soon have an acute case of scenery overload. Each turn of the road, every ridgeline I ride over leads to another postcard landscape of pristine mountains, covered with every shade of green and the spray of colours from the summer blooms. The further on I go, the more-than-familiar feeling: I want to take longer and stay here. There are Persian leopards and wild boar in those trees whizzing past.

As we leave the mountains through a series of descending ridges towards Gorgan, the traffic starts to build up. Looking to the north on some of the higher ridges I can see the Caspian Sea. It's the first bit of blue water since Thailand. The riding is perfect, with the mountains to the left and the coastal plain to the right, all the way to the sea.

It's hard not to notice that Iranians have a thing about Peugeots. They're everywhere and they're all white. I put it down to one of the mysteries of Central Asia. Why Audis in Kazakhstan, Ladas in Uzbekistan and Peugeots in Iran?

The Iranians are friendly people who never let something like lane discipline get in the way of making someone feel welcome. Thanks to the international press this is something I haven't expected either. In truth, as a result of their natural curiosity and hospitality, they keep drifting across lanes, giving me a both thumbs up (while driving), holding up kids so they can see the bike (while driving again). They do get uncomfortably close in Iran with their wing mirrors though. Contrary to what I had heard before, I see that a lot of the drivers are women. They tend to stay to their lanes.

When I pull into town I can't decide if Gorgan is a small city or a large village. There are enough cars, people and conveniences to make it a city, but they can still leave their vehicles on the side of any road and go get a packet of something at the roadside stalls. Complete strangers still wave as I go by and have chats at traffic junctions. And in the distance, the lush green hills suggest that the Gorganians seem to have the best of both worlds.

A single street takes me out of Gorgan southwards to Zialat and it's choked with traffic both ways. What should be a four-lane trunk road has turned into one long six-row car park with a mad Chinaman weaving on a big bike between the cars. I've lost Mike and Pierce and their white Peugeot in this sea of white Peugeots. *Somewhere behind me,* I think. Going up the next hill on the right side I see the reason for the jam.

It's a fairground with a small Ferris wheel, dodgem cars, some shooting galleries and an overfilled car park with families heading home in the evening light. Most of them have parked on the side of the road, village style, and are now making village-style U-turns across four lanes to try and head back to Gorgan. There are a few overwhelmed traffic policemen trying to get some order in the gridlock but they don't look too hopeful.

At least they've got reinforcements. In my rear mirror I see a flash of blue lights. I'm completely stuck but somehow the traffic behind me clears — must be something about what the cops are shouting in Farsi over their loudspeakers. Soon they are right behind me and start blipping their siren and with unmistakable sign language indicate I am to pull over. I glance over my shoulder. Pull over where? We're stuck in traffic. They somehow squeeze in to my left and have me wedged in between the parked cars at the side of the road. Four cops spill out, one of them holding this really clean AK-47 with the stock folded and no strap. He points it at the bike.

The one in charge is this stocky, hirsute fellow in his thirties with a bushy moustache. We'll call him Bill. He's in plainclothes but wears one of those police singlets with yellow reflectors over them and starts shouting at me in Farsi. At first, I'm not quite focusing on what he's saying, I'm fixated on the AK. I flip up the helmet visor up to show that I'm clearly a foreigner and leave my hands on the handlebar facing upwards. It's clear I'm cooperating and not going to make a run for it. We've gathered a fast growing crowd of bystanders from the fairground. Some have English and through them I offer to show Bill my papers and passport. I ask why I've been pulled over. Motorcycle illegal, Bill says. But I have papers from your customs authority and interior ministry, I reply. Motorcycle illegal, you bring bike there! Mad pointing across the street, machine gun. It's not illegal, I have papers – he's holding on to my passport now. You give me keys, Bill signals. Ah no, not going to happen, if you're a policeman you know you're going to have to break the rules and take it without my permission. Deadlock.

Jam starts building up behind us and soon we are drawing more attention than whatever the fairground has going. A younger light-haired uniformed police officer from the other side of the road squeezes through the crowd and in much better English asks me politely to please bring my bike over the other side of the street for his manager to clear, it shouldn't take long. I figure this is my best chance of a fair hearing and half-ride, half-crab-walk the bike through the traffic, over the divider to the other side.

With Bill leading me I'm soon in an improvised car pound off the side of the street. I wait on the bike and soon the manager shows up. He has a lot of gold trimmings on his shoulder epaulettes, gives me and the V-Strom one look, gives Bill another look and gives me back my papers. "Go," he says. That look said it all: Foreigner, not worth the grief.

I get back on my side of the road again and re-join the jam, wondering where Pierce and Mike are. Things start to thin out as it ascends up a small hill, but half a kilometre later it's jammed solid again by a road block checking all the cars for something. This time things are a little different.

It's soldiers in battle order, not uniformed police, and the roadblock's well placed, on the top of a hill on a straight stretch of road. Everybody's armed, with a sand-bagged position in the middle of the road. I have a hunch something's about to happen so I flip the helmet again, showing that the bike and me cannot possibly be local. True enough, three young soldiers come through on foot between the queuing cars right at me. Here we go again.

These have been less well briefed. After we make some attempt at understanding each other one of them doesn't ask for the key, he takes it from the ignition. Then he tells me to move my bike up to the roadblock. I tell him I can't, it's uphill, Dick. Doesn't understand, drawing a crowd again. You give me back my keys so I can start the bike so I can go uphill, Einstein. Then a police car pulls up and incredibly, Bill steps out and tells me to go with him. The earlier time was just an adminstrative clarification. This time it might be a little different. I saw the look that first manager had given him. Bill had lost face. He was pissed with me to start with, and he could have his way with me now. Did he get that soldier to take my keys away on this uphill so I couldn't possibly move without abandoning the bike? I look back and note that I'm out of sight of that first station, but with a relief I also notice Mike and Pierce coming up to me between the jammed cars.

"Please," says the young officer with the blond hair, "follow me to see my other manager."

"What about my bike?" I ask. "If you let me have my keys, I can follow you."

"No need to ride, leave the bike here. My men will watch for you." He turns to Mike, "Let me have your passports." Two soldiers stand of each side of the bike.

Mike and I decide we have no choice. He is obviously an officer of the law doing his duty. We tell Pierce to hang around here with the bike. He's carrying a comms set with the rest of the convoy that might be just too difficult to explain to these people. Mike and I are led up the street for about 50 m or so into a small single-storied light green building surrounded by high fences with rolled-out barbed wire on all sides. It has a small garden with soldiers and their AKs hanging about.

We're led through the front door to a narrow L-shaped corridor into a room where there is a middle-aged man in plainclothes sitting behind a desk facing the entrance. Bill stands in front of him, apparently briefing him on the situation, then leaves as we come in. Blondie places our passports on his desk and motions us to a small black sofa, back to the wall. The man in charge looks at us for a moment, then glances through the documents on his desk. He doesn't say a word. I get the impression he's waiting for something.

Mike sits next to me and whispers, "What the hell is going on?"

"No idea," I say. "There's a possibility that bikes may not be allowed in this country."

"Well, they let us through their customs, didn't they?" At that same moment, we both remember just how good U-Turn is at getting official paperwork sorted out, and really start to worry.

"I am starting to have this idea that the different agencies don't quite talk to each other. The first stop was by police. These look like soldiers," I tell Mike.

We sit silently. The man behind the table sips his tea, lights a cigarette, flips through our documents again and makes occasional glances at us. Figuring that anything we do or say can be construed as some form of suspicious behaviour, we just sit there. I have no idea what the threshold for "loitering with suspicious intent" is in Iran, and don't want to find out. Then suddenly, Bill makes a reappearance.

From where we're sitting, we can just see a few feet down the corridor and we see Bill dragging someone presumably taken off the street and manhandled into the next room. Then we hear someone being slapped about, and furniture being thrown. There are cries of protest at first, then beater obviously convinces beatee that this just makes things worse, and it's just the sound of a comprehensive, un-interrupted thrashing.

Mike and I look at each other. Are we really in for it, or is this some sort of "good cop, bad cop" routine? Mike shrugs. He's got his poker face on. What happens next, happens next. I look at the man behind the desk and he's staring intently at us. Bill drags the unfortunate out of the next room to another part of the building. The man behind the desk speaks in accented English.

"Welcome to Iran. I hope you enjoy your stay. This is one of the prettiest parts of the country."

Wordlessly, we get our documents back and fight the urge to dash out of the building. We thank him and apologise for any inconvenience we might have caused. "No problem," he says, "I apologise if my men may have caused you any delay. Please have a nice stay." He hands me the bike keys.

Back at my bike one of the soldiers is actually on the seat. I give him a smile and he smiles back and lets me have the bike.

When we get to the hotel in Zialat we find that Pierce has already called ahead and told U-Turn about our troubles. He's still out looking for us but now that we're back, we can call off the search. Boss is especially relieved to see us. For some reason he keeps asking whether or not we have any trouble sitting down after our encounter with the Iranian police.

WE LEAVE ZIARAT FOR Chalus along the coast. I'm slowly getting back to the routine of big bike touring. The roads here are almost empty except for the odd truck and underpowered white Peugeot 405. The V-twin's broad power band means there's no trouble staying in fourth, keeping over 4,000 rpm, checking blind spots and easy overtakes. It's one of the happier places in the world to be riding a V-Strom.

Below me the hardy no nonsense V-twin keeps doing what it says on the box: trouble-free touring. Carry everything you need in the panniers, find a point on the horizon, press the ignition and just go. That warm, fuzzy feeling of being in a Zen-like happy state with my bike is starting to come back. With roads like these it seems completely unthinkable that this might be a privilege for us few and that bikes are illegal out here.

In what seems like no time at all, we reach the outskirts of Sari. Here the arid coastal road gives way intermittently to managed pine forests. It's a nice place and Pierce reaches me on the intercom for a break. It's glaringly hot and dry out here, but the breeze from the hillsides is cool and welcoming. In a roadside teahouse we lounge on thick carpets in the shade just off the side of the road. The standard refreshment is black tea, served in a small glass cup not with the usual sugar sachets but in a sort of crystalline gob, stuck with some syrup to little plastic toothpicks. You stick it in the hot tea and it dissolves. Quite marvellous.

A hookah is offered and I can see a few dreamy-eyed truck drivers in a shady corner about to pass out. I consider this for a moment. I had read about what strange stuff you can inhale out here in the boonies in Iran, and decide that I feel good enough, thanks very much.

What follows next makes me suspect it's not just sugar I've added to my tea. A Kawasaki ZX 10 wheelies down the road like a roadrunner cartoon, so fast that the scream from its exhausts seems to come after it's half way past us. This is followed by a parade of who's who in the world of psychotically fast super sports bikes: a Gixer 750 in blue and white dress, a red Ducati 916, a Yamaha R1 and a Honda Fireblade. Following on slightly behind is the more respectable CB1000, a Bandit 1000 and the Honda CB750.

One of the riders sees the Beemer on the back of the Bumblebee and pretty soon we are the toast of the local superbike club. So much for bikes being illegal. We don't understand much of what's being spoken but there is a universal brotherhood of bikers and pretty soon we're buying each other tea, trading stories in sign language about the personalised changes on our bikes, and taking endless selfies.

Our new friends stand out from the rural people we've been riding past. There are Rolex watches, Ray Ban shades, very carefully tendered goatees, and some truly sick riding leathers. As for their bikes, the custom paint jobs and spotless finishing show no expense has been spared. For me, that CB750 is the standout. These bikes haven't been made for over 10 years but this one looks like it's just left the factory. The only thing that's missing from our meeting are biking babes. You know, the kind with the knee-high boots and that tattoo on the behind that's visible through the midriff showing leather gear. That would have been asking for too much out here in Iran.

Instead it seems to be an all-male thing, doing what bikers do when left to their bikes. We're listening to the sweet sound of four exhausts in the CB750 — carbureted, mind you — that resting rattle of the dry clutch on the Ducati, that whine of the Akrapovic pipes on the Gixer. There is some general horsing around and pretty soon car drivers and their families are stopping by and joining in. I like it that Iranian fathers don't keep their young sons and daughters from bikes and bikers, the way they sometimes do at home like it's some dangerous infectious disease. I mean, I'll admit, to some of us it does seem like an incurable disease but it's nice to see engineering perfection appreciated for what it is. It supports a view I have that there is a universal appeal to a thing well-made and maintained, no matter what it is.

We seem to have started an impromptu party. Fathers are putting their children on bikes for selfies. The teahouse is working hard to keep up with the orders. I try to pay for our teas but the owner refuses to take the money. For drawing a crowd like this, yours are on the house.

They ask us where we're from and what we're about and

we manage to get some of this across. It's hard to describe breast cancer in sign language without raising some eyebrows. Some of them do speak English and we discover that they are lawyers, accountants, engineers and the like. Bikes in Iran are expensive. Some of their custom paint jobs would not look out of place at a Sturgis rally.

That's when I learn something about my V-Strom. Remember how I said it's possible to reach some sort of mystical connection between rider and ride? Well, let's just say that these qualities are not immediately apparent. In this pantheon of what I think are the most-loved bikes in all of Iran, the one ride that is getting all the attention and adulation is … the broken down Beemer on the Bumblebee.

With its transverse twin, final shaft drive and distinctive telelever front suspension, this is the bike from the gods that started adventure touring. Our new friends know all about this, but this is the first time they've seen one in the flesh. Most of all, it's all about that blue and white propeller logo on the side fairing. I think I see someone taking a selfie kissing it.

Now don't get me wrong, it's a great bike, but let's not forget what it's doing: looking for a mechanic in Turkey. What about my trusty machine? Waiting over there like a faithful friend in the shade? Waiting to start on the first press of the starter, more reliable than Tonto? I mean, come on. I think it's the lawyer Beemer kisser who eventually comes up to me:

"So ... my friend ... where your bike?" he asks.

Finally! I point nonchalantly to the shady bit to one side of the front porch. There she is, with my helmet crooked over one of the side mirrors, all ready for its turn in the limelight.

The lawyer looks, blinks, and waves his friends over. Excited voices in Farsi. Soon there are a dozen Iranians all over the bike. Sounds like some debate about which Suzuki model it is. Obviously it's not as well known as the other models in their group, or the one that's hitched on to the back of the yellow truck. Someone says 650. It's a common enough mistake. I point out the error.

"Actually," I begin, "it's the DL1000, also called the V-Strom. You can tell by the twin pipes. The 650 looks the same but only has ..."

"Wow. What is range?" someone asks.

"Range? Oh, on your roads I can get up to 500 km," I reply.

"Five hundred kilometres? Cannot be! You mean five hundred metres, yes?"

"Er ... what?"

They pick up the helmet, ignoring the bike. Excitedly, they look carefully at the intercom system fitted within the helmet's inner lining.

"This intercom. You can hear phone?"

"Er ... right ... the intercom. Yes, I can hear the phone ... Bluetooth."

"Oh ..." they echo together, "Bluetooth ..."

Soon it's time to part company. Handshakes all around and a group photo to remember this most happy of chance meetings. Taken in front of, you guessed it, the stricken Beemer. I ask where they're heading. Zanjan. Oh, I say, maybe we'll ride together? They look at my V-Strom again. My friend, says the lawyer, not on that. We go fast.

Right.

They do mention that the road up to Zanjan from the coast is one of the best riding roads in the country. We decide to take them up on this and change our itinerary accordingly. The next day, instead of heading inland from Chalus to catch the highway to Zanjan, we stay on the coast, heading inland only at Rasht.

Thanks to the tip from our new friends we discover one of Iran's best-kept secrets. The road up the mountains towards Rudbar is one of the prettiest I've ever been on. It winds through the valley of the Sefid River, climbing green hillsides in ever tightening hairpin turns that flatten out at the top of the ridgeline before easing out in the next valley.

If the word gets out that there are roads like this in Iran, there would be a lot more sportsbikes out here all the time. But the word's not out and it's completely empty here for a hundred miles. We have the place all to ourselves. As we ride up over 2,000 m, the air is cleared of all the brown and dust of the deserts. The setting sun gives an emerald green to the grass-covered mountains. It looks like a giant blanket of green moss on a background of perfect blue sky. Here, in Iran! We can see the glistening of brooks and streams between the trees. To the left we see the Sefid Rud dam and its rows of wind farms on the deep azure of the lake, like seagulls cresting the waves. After weeks of dust and sand, this seems too good to be true, that riding roads as perfect as this just can't last for long.

It's not just the dropping temperature that is giving me the chills. For the first time I realise that we are coming to the end of something. It's all about to change completely. There's only Turkey left after Iran and then it will be, inconceivably, Europe. We're about to run out of Asia.

THE NEXT DAY IT's Father's Day in Iran. According to our guide it's a big thing here, and in the eateries in Zanjan we see specials for family lunches and dinners to celebrate the event. I'm not sure if it falls on the same date, but back home it's the one time a year when Viola would tolerate my one cigar and whiskey on the front porch in memory of Dad. According to U-Turn, that's what all the signs are saying: "Father's Day today, we remember fathers."

We're going to Tabriz today, a distance of some 300 km. There are two ways to get there. One is to take the national highway, with higher speeds but that's boringly straight. The other is to take the W38 trunk road through Miyaneh and

Baston Abad, which runs in the same direction but, according to our new biker friends yesterday, is a much more scenic route. And there's supposed to be the remains of a bridge in Miyaneh, built before the time of the Crusades.

I think it's true to say that I've got the riding bug back. I'm looking forward to each day on the saddle now, and keeping the cognitive errors at bay seems to come more easily. The feeling of dread, over amplification of small errors and self-recriminations all seem to have receded, at least for now.

I know that a lot of it has to do with getting help. To me, this comes in the form of my psychiatrist friends on Wi-Fi after a day's riding. More personal perspectives come from other colleagues who have had similar problems before. They all warn of the waxing that comes after the waning and that it might be wise to use this relative period of quietness to get some perspective on why it should happen to me. When

Riders' heaven in Iran: endless empty roads, the mountains in the distance and a big happy bike below.

I mentioned to one of them that it's Father's Day today out here in Iran, he said, "Now that's something to think about."

Right from the moment I approach the junction at the on-ramp for the highway I know we're making the right choice. Iranian drivers aren't more dangerous than drivers anywhere else, but they do have unique views on personal space. We clear the Zanjan city limits on this unmarked three-lane-wide expressway with five lanes of crawling traffic. Iranian drivers in Peugeots try and get my attention by coming as close as their wing mirrors nudging on my right knee, just a sort of good-morning-how-are-we-today kind of poke. This is usually accompanied by a broad smile and introduction to all the other family members in the car. When I don't panic through this jostling for lane space, I know that I'm well on the mend.

Soon I peel off to the country roads and find myself on perfect tarmac winding through the countryside. I have the entire road to myself through the Sendan Dagh mountain range. It's 23 degrees out with bright sunshine. If I stand on the footpegs out of the cover of the V-Strom's windscreen, it's like stepping in front of a cooling fan. To the right is a stunning view of irrigated fields with arable grasslands and grazing herds in the distance. The far horizon is a rolling scroll of hills and their layered contours. Shades of red and brown and every hue in between blended together in wavy brush strokes like some massive watercolour. And all around is that sky, as blue as can be.

That's the difference between biking and sitting in a car. I'm in the elements on the bike and they affect me with an immediacy that's missing when shielded by windscreens and windows. What happens around me soon happens inside me in very short order. In a place as stunning as this, I'm feeling sublimely blessed. It's quite wonderful how timeless all this is. Some of the earliest traces of civilisation come from around here. In fact, the Garden of Eden is thought by some to be located near Tabriz, our destination for the day.

Below me the V-twin chugs away happily, taking the gentle curves and passing traffic easily with no brakes or gear shifts. It's one of the rare moments during this frantic schedule of ours that I wish the miles would pass more slowly. I really don't mind staying on a bike out here. It's like riding in a postcard. Closer to the right there's a sheer drop as the Shahr Chay river cuts its way through the rocks in a steep ravine, intertwining with our road under a series of bridges. Further in the distance to the left I see the national highway, straight as an arrow with multiple lanes of faster moving traffic. Strange thing, to want to be in a rush through all this. With Mike and Pierce in the support car out of sight somewhere behind me, I seem to have the whole place to myself. There are some who like travelling these massive miles alone but I'm not one of them. In my helmet and all to myself, I wish that I could show this to someone, to have this as something to talk about for days to come.

Right then, who would I show this to? There would be the biking gang; Ros and Yu Seung who turned back at Chiang Mai would be kicking themselves if they knew what was out here had they kept going. Without having a mad boss like ours that would mean quitting jobs and putting everything on hold just to come see this. Then again that's a lot easier said than done. The thought makes me feel doubly blessed, that I can be out here and still have a job to go back to.

More than anyone I wish that I could show this to my children. As the road intertwines with the river between tall cliffsides on both sides, it abruptly opens out around a blind corner and the vast valley lies before me. *Look at this place*, I find myself shouting to no one in my helmet, but really to James, Jean and Jon.

Hang on, better concentrate on this windy bit. A series of quick S-bends and through a tunnel that opens up onto another bridge with the river gleaming far below. Drop to third, bank left, then right with the throttle constant and use the camber. Watch the apex, listen for 5,000 rpm, back to fourth as the road crests over a ridgeline. Below and to the right the river runs past verdant fields and a shepherd waters his flock by the far bank.

No, really people, look at this marvellous place! Come and feel this! The world is just full of these places and waiting! It has taken nearly two months on the road to get here, and there have been some dark times, but I have also been helped by the most generous people who have wanted so little in return.

I don't think we've actually paid for any of the roadside teas yet. People see you're passing through from some faraway place and have this idea that it's their privilege to give refreshment to the sojourner. In the middle of nowhere yesterday and out of gas, just shy of Zanjan, a complete stranger had disconnected his fuel line from his beaten-up pickup's carb and milked me two litres of gas to get me to the next petrol station, refusing any sort of payment. There is no likelihood that I will ever meet him in this life again, but somehow he gave me the feeling that just being able to help a stranger is reward enough.

What would James and Jean and Jon do if they ever discover this kind of wonder? Would they take the effort to come and see for themselves? Would they take two years to prepare and three months to go wandering? Would I encourage them? Or would I say that it's some sort of passing madness and could you please go back to studying or building a CV or whatever, just get the thought out of your head?

It's Father's Day out here in Iran today, we remember fathers. What should a father say? What would a son think of his father if he followed his advice, years later, when the chance had already passed and the less trodden road was untaken? As fathers we look out for their best, it's what fathers do. What would be the best for them if they wanted to put life on hold and come out here?

It's Father's Day out here in Iran today, we remember fathers. I wonder how Dad would feel if he were still alive, about his son on this mad ride. Not for the first time I remember that I haven't been the easiest son to sort out. In truth, things would have been a lot easier between us had he been a conventional father, if there is such a thing. As things turned out he left us very much to our own devices, as long as we realised that choices have their consequences. And when things hit the fan he would consider bailing us out as "an amusing option".

So there was the time when my brother Richard thought it might be fun to go climb this mountain in Malaysia during the college holidays. When Dad asked about the details the replies were all a little vague, but Dad let it play out. When Richard came out of the jungle two weeks and seven river crossings later he had lost about 10 kilos and gained some strange jungle rash. As soon as he got home and cleaned up he slept for a full day. What clothes he brought back were so rancid we just threw them away. There was no reproach. The point is that Richard had sorted himself out and finished what he set out to do.

Then there was the time in medical school when I decided to get a biking licence. Dad said that he wasn't so keen on the idea. My uncle Moses, a forensic pathologist, had regaled him for years about how riding a motorcycle was the surest way to wind up on his table. There was the one time, Mo had said, when the biker was hit by a lorry in front of the hospital, flew across two lanes of traffic and actually wound up very dead and just about still in one piece in the pathology department car park. Someone still felt the need to call an ambulance, which travelled 10 m to the unloading bay, fill up the necessary paperwork and deliver what was left to his table.

Dad's view about biking was not based on heresay though; he felt he was being fair. When he was a young man he wasn't allowed to get a bike licence after his parents heard about a good friend who had killed himself on a Norton Commando on that nasty curve at Fort Canning Road. But, I countered, his parents let him fly fighter planes, and surely that had to be a lot more dangerous. That's when Dad made a bit of a slip. Well, actually they didn't really let him do that either; he just went and did it.

As soon as he said it, he knew he had to concede that there had been precedence, so I went ahead and got the bike licence. This was on the condition that if anything happened to me he would convert my room into his personal study. He always thought that the sunlight in the morning came through my windows just right.

As I say, not quite a conventional upbringing. The idea was to get us to a place where we had thought enough for ourselves so that we could decide what we wanted to do. Not to listen to what others were doing, or worse still, do what someone else thought was best for us. Once we figured out what we wanted, the next thing is to never let our employers know that we would do it for free.

Then there was the time when I said that I would do a year of trauma surgery in Johannesburg. Things had changed by then: this was not so much "asking for permission" as "keeping him in the loop of things". They had changed in other ways as well. I was married with three young children. I had a very satisfying and absorbing career as an academic breast cancer surgeon, with a very real chance of being in a very lucrative private practice. There was a clear run to the finishing post—Johannesburg was not really necessary.

Some of my friends had their doubts as well. There had to be some reason for this constant need to over-achieve. Could it be that I keep pushing because I need some kind of approval? The downside of letting us find our own way is that Dad never quite let on if he thought I was doing well enough. He was very sparing with his praise. In his view, it was immaterial. It's what I thought of what I've done that's the thing. Could it be that the unmet need for parental approval was what kept my screws on so tight that I came apart within one week of starting on this trip? I have learned that one of the risk factors for anxiety attacks is carrying too much, or caring too much about the outcomes.

When I first told him about Joburg, Dad's first reaction was mixed, although as usual he tried not to show it. I had been regularly keeping him in the loop of how life was going mainly over weekend dinners and often this would come down to just how badly severely injured patients were being treated by non-trauma surgeons, myself included. The thing about trauma surgery is that a lot of it is time related: the faster you can decide and the faster you can move, the better the outcome. Unfortunately, surgical speed depends largely on surgical experience, and in Singapore we were not getting the experience.

Joburg was at the other extreme: 4,000 murders per year, compared to Singapore's 16 with roughly the same population. More than half the trauma patients I would be elbow deep in would be HIV-positive. So after I told him about my plans to work there for a year, there was this barely perceptible flicker of a raised eyebrow. When he politely asked for the details, I remember they were pretty vague as well.

When I came back after spending 10 months in Johannesburg we went down as a family to the Banana Leaf Apollo for the fish head curry. I had to be real careful not to mention the 40 gunshot wounds I had seen in the course of the Christmas weekend, but truth was, they were not completely out of my mind yet. There was more in what was unsaid and I saw that flicker again. He didn't ask me to chuck it and come back and be a wealthy and healthy breast cancer surgeon. Instead, he said to "keep my head down". Never forget to duck.

It was the last thing he ever said to me. When Viola called me a few weeks later to tell me Dad had died suddenly of a heart attack at home I was already back in Africa, giving a lecture in Witwatersrand Medical School's postgraduate surgical programme. We don't put the phones to silent in the trauma unit for any reason. The next few minutes were awkward to all concerned – they had to empty the hall because the lecturer was just standing there at the podium, phone to his ear.

I remember my Armenian colleague Serguei Darchiev saying something about getting drunk and letting someone else make the arrangments to get me home. Then he drove me back to my rented lodgings and I just sat there. It was around sunset when some of the nurses and residents drove by with the plane tickets. They asked if I was alright and I shook my head. Not being alright was the only thing that I was certain of. Then we just sat by the garden and watched the African sun go down, the first without Dad.

AHEAD IS THE CITY of Miyaneh and we stop at a local chai shop next to its ancient bridge built in the Sassanid period in the third century. It is the end to a truly magical day. We lounge on thick carpets with the cooling breeze coming up from the river and the sweet scent coming from the *shishas*. The sun is low now, setting the ancient buttresses to sharp relief. The central span of this famous bridge is missing after it was blown up in the 1920s during the civil war. No matter, what remains is just as majestic in this evening light.

The end of Father's Day today in Iran. Dad's never been here before, but he would have loved to be. He would have appreciated this madness, not because it was seeing his dreams fulfilled, but mine.

THERE ISN'T ENOUGH TIME to see all that's available in Tabriz so we go for the essentials. Although we have passed some very impressive bazaars on the way here in Samarkand and Bukhara, we have been consistently advised by the locals to spare ourselves until we got to this place. The Tabriz Bazaar is the largest covered market in the world, all 47 acres of it. And Mike Hartman is on the hunt for carpets.

When we take the hotel bus to town the next day we find that this great market is paradoxically difficult to find. It's been here for the last 400 years or so and was one of the greatest commercial centres on the Silk Road. It's survived Tamerlane, the Ottomans, the Russians and several earthquakes. Whether it will survive the battle with the surrounding city is difficult to say. Modern streets and shop fronts surround the bazaar. The entrance we've been advised to take is no more than a few marble steps up between a tailor and a *kebab* shop, next to a modest mosque with a silver dome. We've also been advised to mark this place well. It's almost impossible to find the same way out.

Step up the marble steps and it's a time machine. The bazaar surrounds us with smells and sights from another time. It is several miles of covered corridors lined with latticed alleyways of bare brick. On both sides, shops line the corridors with their wares, careful not to overstep the limits of their property or encroach on the walking space.

Our entrance places us in a world of shoes. After a few turns it's all cutlery, then schoolbags and children's clothes, then what appears to be every spice, tea and dried fruit ever harvested. It's lovely to see that this isn't just a place for tourists; housewives with their distracted children in tow haggle for the best deals. It's part of the normal life of the city, has been for centuries. A few corridors later we come to more traditional crafts: carpets, woollen shawls, *shishas* and this marvellous shop with an octogenarian with a skull cap who is selling sugar by the pound block, or the two-pound cylinder. He's using a medieval block cutter that really does look from the days of Timur. One turn away, and we are inexplicably in the kaleidoscopic world of Tupperware.

Even more impressive than the merchandise is the building itself. At ground level it all seems a little random but for a sense of order I only have to look up. Each corridor is covered with intricately vaulted domed ceilings of bare dark brick, with a small orifice at the apex to let out the warm air. Incredibly the whole building, and this is one single, achingly large structure, appears to be naturally ventilated.

At the junctions of the major corridors there are much larger domed atria with the most intricate mosaic tiling and brickwork, again with that stoma at the top to let out air and let in light. Here some of the shops move more high-end goods, with soft lighting and clear glass shop fronts framed with cast iron trellis. Some have two or three levels of merchandise.

I realise that like many of the remarkable buildings in this land of the Islamic Renaissance, there is a subtle, almost vital design. Not soulless, utilitarian, drawn in by rulers and set square boxes, but living spaces. In many ways it's like a huge, breathing lung. The geometry makes the most of the space given to squeeze in just the right proportion of shops and shoppers. Like a lung it is in its essence a platform for exchange. It's a marvellous place.

The Tabriz Bazaar, a veritable Aladdin's cave of treasures

Mike, however, is on a mission to get his carpets.

"Right," I say, "anything in mind?"

"Nope."

"OK, know anything about carpets?"

Purses lips. "Not a thing, but I know what I like when I see it."

"Ah right, that's good," Pierce says. "Any idea how much to pay for what you like when you see it?"

"Nope."

"Right then," says Pierce, "this should be fun. Mind if we tag along, we won't interfere in any way. Promise."

We wander off to Mozzafarieh, a centuries-old carpet bazaar to one side of the main bazaar. There's not much of a crowd here and there is an air of reverence as a more select clientele run their eyes and fingers through the exquisite collections in the shops and walkways.

The three of us don't know much about carpets, but that doesn't stop us from feeling the magic about this place. The carpets here are works of art. An endless variety of colour, intricacy and design. They have an odd effect on our completely untrained eyes: If you look at one long enough, you'll want that one too, no matter what the price is. Fact is, the air of veneration may have something to do with three lambs being led to slaughter.

In the end we are drawn to the familiar. As we pass one of the shops there is the completely incongruous sound of Queen's English. We walk in and meet Houseffi. He's taken over his father's shop after coming back with a history degree from Cambridge. It doesn't have much to do with selling carpets, but he has learned to put foreigners at ease with English tea, butter cookies and a running commentary of Persian carpets as his wares are placed before us by his assistants.

In the end Mike settles on two large and one smaller prayer carpet, which Houseffi says he can ship to Stockholm, not to worry. Money changes hands. Not knowing how much these things ought to cost I'm unsure if he's got a good rate or not, but Houseffi does treat us to lunch, tea, and a night out. When we take a last stroll through the bazaar the next day his shop is still closed at lunchtime.

Eighteen
KILLER SHEEP, FALSE GODS AND TRUE GODS

WE'RE ABOUT TO PASS out on the curb in the shadeless no man's land between Iran and Turkey waiting for the minders to clear the paperwork. We've travelled some 200 km from Tabriz to the border just before lunchtime. Our first view of Turkey is two barred gates before us with miles of barbed wire fencing on either side. I can see it's hill country beyond the gates, with barren rocky hillsides and the occasional scrub of bush. Most of the hilltops are bunkered with red Turkish flags everywhere, including carved into some of the hillsides. Behind us is another set of barred gates separating us from Iran.

Mike passes me a cup of coffee and sits down. He's keen to get across as soon as possible. In many ways getting into Turkey is very much like getting back to the civilised world known as the European Union. Geographically speaking,

Europe starts on crossing the Bosphorus some time next week, but to us, it's where we can get the Beemer fixed and Mike on the road again. Arrangements have already been made for a mechanic to pick the bike up across the border at Doğubayazıt where Mike and Pierce will follow it to the nearest BMW mechanic in Ankara. At this rate that might mean an overnight drive.

"I must say," Mike starts as he sips his second cup of coffee, "that Iran has been the nicest surprise of this entire trip."

I agree. Iran doesn't get good press. If we only listened to network news we would think that the place was full of flag-burning, nuclear arms-building, Salman Rushdie-hating, high-pitch wailing, covered women living in a barren desert. This last week has put that all to rest. They've been the friendliest of people living in the most scenic of countries. We've taken the shortest possible land route through Iran because of our time constraints, which is along the Caspian Sea coast, but not a single day has gone by where we did not wish we could stay longer.

"The problem in travelling through these countries is not the people," Mike continues, staring at the customs building in the compound ahead of us, "but the customs officials. It's come to my attention that customs officials and policemen from different countries have more in common with each other than with the people they represent."

"Yes, actually I think you may have something there," I reply sleepily, flapping the headscarf to keep the flies off the coffee.

"I know. Look. Thai villager outside Surat Thani, Iranian

man outside Gonbad. Anything in common? Not much. Thai policeman at roadblock outside Surat Thani and Iranian policeman at roadblock outside Gonbad? Could be close cousins."

"Yes ... you could actually put all the policemen and customs officials in a single country ... they would all get along."

"Exactly," says Mike, still staring at the customs building. We spend the next two hours deciding just what to call the country.

The sun's blazing from above but the four by four crews are old hands at this. They're all out of their vehicles and finding what shade can be found, some have already dozed off, other using hats to keep away the flies. Hung Tuan's clearing the customs with U-Turn.

It does feel a little melancholy here though. I can't help noticing that on the Turkish side all the flags are flying half-mast. It's a country in mourning following its worst ever mining disaster in Soma last week. Some 300 lives were lost, the tragedy compounding what is already one of the worst mining safety records anywhere. It must be the grimmest measure of industrial safety: the number of miner deaths per million tonnes of coal taken out of the ground. Turkey has seven times more fatalities than China.

It's more than just sadness though. There's anger in the cities. Apparently, the opposition party had raised concerns about the safety of the Soma mines only last month, their voices having fallen on deaf ears. Now there are demonstrations in Ankara and Istanbul, and calls for the president to step down. He's had to duck into shops and alleyways in order to escape

Mike loading the bike for an overnight van ride to Ankara

a beating by demonstrators. I don't think there'll be a change though. From what I've heard from the locals Mr Erdoğan has survived far more than this.

It's a theme that will run throughout our visit of Turkey. This is a country that seems to have had more than its share of conflicts. It may be over an idea, a religion, an empire, or just a nice view, but nothing seems to have come easy for Turkey. The relics of these struggles make Turkey one of the most culturally enriching places to ride through. Just beyond the border flags is the majestic snow-peaked Mount Ararat. Someone's said that he has found traces of a boat-shaped rock formation on the mountainside there. Possibly Noah's Ark, some claim. Bet there are people here who would fight for that idea as well.

When we finally clear the customs U-Turn discovers that he has inadvertently entered Turkey with us and now makes his way back across no-man's land to Iran. At least for our convoy it was his last U-Turn, and we go straight on without him.

It's about four in the afternoon when we finally clear customs and head on this smooth tarmac towards Doğubayazıt, where we will be spending the night. At least most of us will anyway. Turkey will mark another change in the travelling arrangements. In Iran we needed to travel with a guide but we're in Europe now. Mike will make the dash with Pierce and the mechanic tonight, the four by four will start their restaurant tours with Boss, and I will be pretty much on my own until Mike's bike is fixed.

With no strict schedule to follow and no four by four convoy to keep up with, I've decided to take things slower. When planning the itinerary I had put relatively short legs on this part of the journey. This is one of the most beautiful biking countries and I am going to enjoy it.

About 25 km outside of Doğubayazıt the tarmac deteriorates with road works and it's a bumpy ride into town. Soon the tarmac disappears entirely and we're on what is essentially a four-lane dirt track. I'm in a steady stream of thick dust and dirt thrown up by the trucks and cars heading into town. The only way to get air fit to breathe is to keep the speed up and pass these trucks quickly, but it's one of those teeth-chattering, kidney-grinding rides.

Thankfully before long there's the familiar sight of a Shell petrol station just about 100 m off the road to the right. Haven't seen one of those in a long time. It's good to get out of the dust. After filling up and paying for the petrol I catch a glance of my reflection in the pane glass windows. I'm supposed to be a fashionable dark grey in this riding kit, but it's all khaki now. So's the rest of the bike.

Ah well, nothing for it, better get moving. Just need to

turn on the GPS … hang on … all I'm seeing instead of the GPS receiver is its base plate with the plastic chipped off the upper edge. Must have been dislodged together with the teeth fillings on that road on the way here. I look up at the road. It's dense with dust from the passing trucks. No chance of finding anything in that lot. Can only go forward and try to find the hotel once I get into Doğubayazıt.

Turns out I needn't have worried. There's nothing much to Doğubayazıt, just a main street with side lanes that lead out at right angles. It seems to be the archetype of border towns. Like all other towns in central Asia, there are the usual *kebab* joints. In addition to this, Doğubayazıt seems to be trying to cater to all of Europe's backpackers who want one last taste of home before crossing the border into Iran. There are Irish pubs, Italian cafés, and even a Swiss restaurant in the shape of an alpine lodge. Completely out of place is a rooftop Reggae bar. I'm seeing beer advertisements for the first time in three countries.

More importantly, I've spotted the rest of the convoy. The yellow Bumblebee is holding up a very patient bunch of local motorists while trying to negotiate some of the narrower unpaved side streets, the big Beemer precariously hanging out the back. Soon we find our way to the large parking lot, where there is a large white van with a mechanic sitting on the edge of the rear loading bay. We start loading the Beemer into the white van and strapping it down.

It's last light when the van's finally loaded. Mike's eager to get a move on.

"Right," he says, "it's some 1,200 km to Ankara so I figure if we drive all night we can probably get there late tomorrow.

It'll be the day after before we can get working on the bike, no idea how long it's going to take but should not be more than three days. That means we'll probably meet up in Istanbul. If things go better than planned, I'll see you in Cappadocia." Mike has already loaded his kit into the cab.

"OK, we're in Europe now so I guess we can keep in touch on Wi-Fi," Pierce says before joining him.

Pierce has already decided to follow Mike instead of me through the rest of Turkey. He can't film without a support vehicle anyway.

Mike looks me over, dust and all. "Think you'll be alright?"

"Not a problem. We're not in a rush anymore and I'm feeling fine," I reply.

"OK," says Mike, getting into the passenger seat. He looks down to me through the door window, "You know, next time we go on one of these intercontinental rides we should try to actually ride together. See you in a few days." Then they disappear in a cloud of dust for their drive through the night.

THE NEXT MORNING AFTER a short visit to Doğubayazıt's one saving grace, the Ishak Pasha Palace, I begin my solo ride. From Doğubayazıt to Van the road leads through a series of gradual ascents up the Caldiran Ovasi range of mountains, with peaks of over 2,000 m. The air cools rapidly and I'm glad I've spent proper money on the riding kit. I'm warm and snug inside but temperatures must be falling more quickly than I thought.

I see my first snow on a motorcycle ride! At first as clumps of ice, then whole sheets of snow on the peaks on both sides of this mountain pass. I know this isn't a big thing to many people and I'll see a lot more in Europe, but there's only one first time and for me this is a real thrill. I've reached above the snow line on a bike ride from Singapore! On a secondhand Japanese bike that seems to just go on and on despite all the abuse. There's been electrical failure, sandstorms, crap roads and gradually more and more loading as Boss fills Bumblebee with shopping, but the Suzuki just keeps going.

Going over these mountains there are snowfields on both sides reaching up to the summits. I can see I'm not the only one caught up in the moment. Several cars pull over and families enjoy something one doesn't often associate with Turkey: a snowball fight. Delighted squealing children in bright pink winter clothes and thick scarves, running and gambolling in the snowdrifts. Flasks of hot tea shared with

The V-Strom seeing snow for the first time

a madly grinning Chinaman on a grimy, dust-covered bike. It's the typical random moment of bliss; this really is the most wonderful way to travel through a country.

As the road winds over the highest peaks the snow covered grasslands give way to vast plateaus of bare rock, literally frozen in time. I notice innumerable piles of stones stacked up neatly over rock outcrops. Some are made of huge boulders that must have taken some serious lifting, others just a few inches of small flat stones piled together. I haven't seen these since hiking in Dartmoor years ago. Up there they're called cairns, I think. What this has to do with a very flat, hot, coastal town in Australia, I haven't a clue. In Dartmoor they represent some form of pre-Christian pagan worship but here some of them look distinctly recent. I suppose they mean different things to different folks. It may just be a simple way to mark the effort of hiking through here.

As I crest over the last of the hilltops the majestic Lake Van comes into view, surrounded by a ring of mountains. I find myself saying out loud to no one in particular, "Well this is a big surprise then. The largest lake in Turkey is ... turquoise." It's hard to keep my eyes on the road. The lake seems to have a colour all of its own, and with the clear blue sky the effect is quite hypnotic.

The coastal town of Van, on the eastern shore of its eponymous lake, is not what I expected. It has a distinctly Mediterranean feel with its long beaches, al fresco cafés and luxury apartments along the coast. There are long promenades with hand-holding couples, girls in sun hats, bikini tops and very tan legs. After weeks of modestly covered women, it's a welcome change. Van seems to have recovered completely from the earthquake that destroyed much of its downtown area just three years ago. Like I've said, this is a tough old place. People have a way of just getting on with things.

The next day is a long one to the medieval town of Mardin, some 500 km away. Normally I would worry about the distance but I find that I'm strangely chilled about the whole thing. As Mike would put it, "What happens next, well, happens next." I'm on my own now and rather unexpectedly, this has made me less worried. I think a lot of the stress I was feeling before may have been due to trying to keep up. Here there's no one to try and keep up with, it's riding at my own pace.

The scenery is definitely helping. Keeping Lake Van on the right, the road follows its southern coast. It passes several fishing villages but on the whole it's a sweeping coastal road between rolling golden fields of wheat that stretch all the way to the mountains to the south. The houses here are few and far in between, alternating from isolated farmhouses to far more lavish summer homes.

The roads are entirely empty and again I wonder why there aren't more bikers. It's not always fully tarmacked, but there can't be many prettier places than this. With these rolling hills, gentle curves and that bewitching turquoise water to the right, this place is a rider's paradise. It feels like I'm living inside one of those later Van Goghs. What lies ahead is even more enticing.

Today I'll be reaching the county of Batman, near the headwaters of the Tigris River. Some of the communities here actually pre-date even the earliest Chinese settlements we went through in Sichuan and Ganxi. It's a matter of some debate but many believe that this is the northwestern edge of what was once Mesopotamia.

At Tatvan I take one last look at the lake and take the left turn towards Batman. Once again the road leads upwards into a series of passes through the hills. This ancient land is dotted by hamlets eking out a tenuous existence on the hillsides. The rocky soil and precipitous slopes mean that there isn't much cultivatable land, although I do notice large herds of sheep and goats grazing on what vegetation there is. The villages themselves are simple places: one or two road junctions, a gas station on a main street.

Just before lunchtime I find what I'm looking for: a shady spot by a café with a large Coca-Cola banner out front. Cold Coke in hand I head for the shade of a broad chestnut tree. The tree's too good not to be shared out. There's already a group of old regulars here, their cigarette stubs almost blotting out the pavestones under our feet.

It's the same in villages all over Iran and Turkey. There are always these groups of old men and young children hanging about even in the middle of the day. They're curious about the bike, the rider and the riding gear. The slits in the riding jacket are what really get them. Who would want air coming through a jacket that's meant to keep you warm? The smaller kids are fascinated by the Velcro flaps on the riding boots. It's always only old men and boys. I guess most of the men of working age are at their jobs or in the fields. I wonder where the women go for their chinwag? Indoors, I suppose.

Pretty soon a small crowd gathers around me and the regulars bring out more chairs from the café. Here I am in

Sharing the shade in a village in Batman. After a while, I got used to the goldfish in a fishbowl effect.

this Turkish village surrounded by strangers and not for an instant do I feel anything but a curious welcome. Not a word is understood between us, and the innocent curiosity of the young boys really makes me wish I could reach them somehow.

I'm hoping there might be some English from school but no luck. What do I know about their world? In a moment's inspiration I recall one tenuous link. Turning to the oldest, a spunky, bright-eyed, skinny kid in a football jersey, I point to the patch on his chest and say, "Galatasaray?" What I get in return is priceless. A perfectly gestured left middle finger pointed upwards. "Yuck! No Galatasaray! Fenerbahçe!"

For the older men, there is a tried-and-tested way of breaking the ice. Out here everyone smokes. Mostly cigarettes or small cheroots, but occasionally the odd beaten-up pipe.

As I take my own pipe out of the jacket I feel like one of those street mimes. The act of filling and patting down the bowl keeps the audience I've gathered raptly attentive and by the time it comes to looking for a flame – I've never ever had to light it myself – some match or ancient gas lighter is produced and with the first puff comes the kindred spirit. I get the older men patting me on the shoulder, offering their own tobacco packets.

All I've brought is a beat-up packet of Blend Eleven from a petrol kiosk in Malaysia. The locals keep theirs in leather pouches or occasionally an ancient pewter flask. In this small village in Batman I finally take the chance with some greenish powder proffered by the leader of this male gathering. They must have asbestos-lined throats to puff this stuff – it burns all the way down but I manage to keep an appreciative face. Approving slaps on the back from all around.

At the first puff I instantly feel very, very happy to be here. Everything seems to look better right away, my troubles all disappear and I feel wonderfully relaxed, maybe even a little limp. I wish I had this in Thailand instead of the Prozac. My pipe gives a familiar odour that reminds me of another leafy café near the Rembrandtplatz in Amsterdam. There is a profound sense of appreciation to all my new friends. I also suddenly feel very thirsty, and one of them brings me another bottle of Coke. In my new chilled state, we watch the town life roll by in its languid pace.

I could stay here for much longer – hey I could keep coming back to this spot if they keep that green stuff coming. The leader of the group says something to another one of the regulars and he gives me some of it in a white envelope to take on my way. Soon it's time to get going. Once again as I secure the kit, I wonder if it's the bike that has made the difference. I don't think arriving by car would have the same effect.

Just south of Batman the road runs along the banks of the Tigris River. I spend the afternoon going past irrigated farmlands that may well be the oldest cultivated land anywhere.

The town of Hasankeyf sits in a bend on the Tigris River. As I round the corner it comes up without any warning, as though I've been transported to a place forgotten by time. The Tigris is serene here: its greenish waters flat as a glass, reflecting the walls of the city, the dome of the mosque and the minaret that dominates the town. The walls of the city blend imperceptibly to the rocky landscape, like different patches cut from the same cloth.

As I cross the bridge over the Tigris into Hasankeyf, to the right is the old Artukid Bridge, or what's left of it. Its pylons are all that remain, their massive bulk testifying to the historical significance of this city on the banks of this most ancient of waterways.

Written records date back to 1800 BC. It's a magical, timeless place, a working web of cobblestoned streets and a towering minaret surrounded by a walled city of stone. How the city juxtaposes on the banks of the Tigris is especially enchanting. There is a mystical relationship between the river, the surrounding fields and Hasankeyf itself. Maybe it's the nature of things that have been interdependent for so long. It's lived through nine civilisations, all of which have left their mark in architecture, artistry and religion.

It's been here since the time of the Assyrians, but it will not survive us.

I cross the river into the central square of the town and without warning, find myself completely gridlocked. The place is packed with tour buses disgorging yet more day-trippers to the crowds lining the central part of town. Tour guides in coloured straw hats lead their herds up to the Mosque or the old Fort. Long queues wait for a seat in the open-air restaurants on the banks of the river. Both sides of the narrow over-packed streets are lined with a permanent open-air market, selling miniature El Rizk minarets. It's the usual tourist thing: T-shirts, paperweights, fridge magnets, tea towels, and cheap wool carpets. Not quite my scene.

I leave the bike in low gear and take the first narrow street leading uphill, away from the central square. Very soon I've left the crowds behind. It's obviously not the touristy part of town: buses can't make it up these narrow streets, lined on both sides by high stone walls separating individual houses. After a few minutes this leads to another smaller square lined by more modest mud cottages with zinc roofs. There is the odd bunch of children playing street football, but other than that only silence. Many of the houses have their gates and front doors ajar, their small gardens overgrown. There isn't a single car on the streets, not so much as a bicycle. It takes me a few minutes before I realise just what kind of town this is, away from the touts and planned tours.

I pull over at the next intersection and get off the bike. Hasankeyf is emptying, whether it likes to or not. More than half the population has already been compelled to move. The Ilisu project plans to dam the Tigris and over a hundred

Hasankeyf the way I want to remember it, with its twin bridges and minaret bathed in afternoon sun

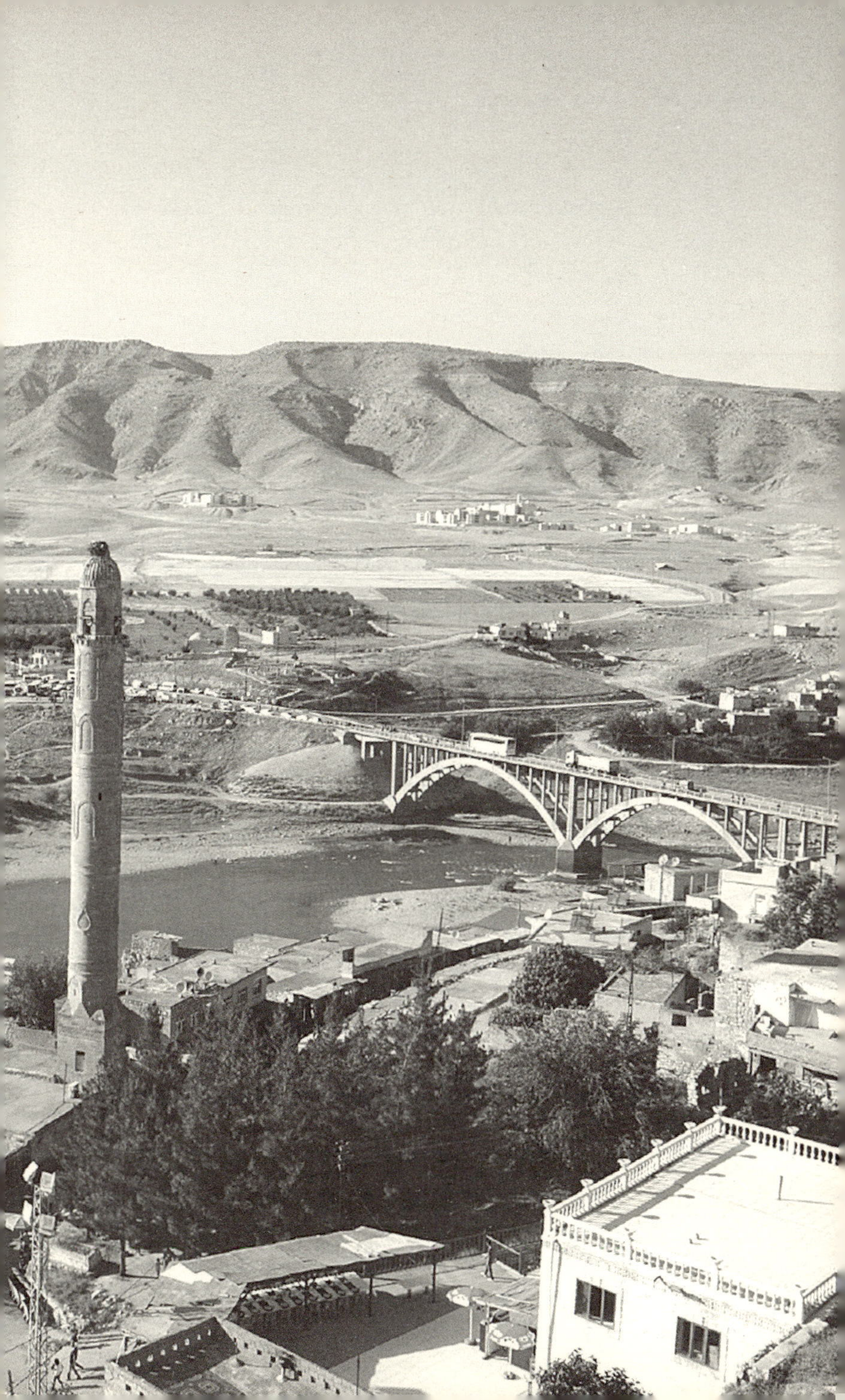

villages — most of the towns that I've ridden through since Batman — will soon be underwater. As for Hasankeyf, neither its minaret, its fort nor its mosque will save it. I take off the helmet and look at the silent streets around me, the empty houses. Hard to believe, all this gone. Nine civilisations! This town predates *Moses*, for crying out loud. I can think of several places that I've been through recently that almost deserve to be drowned, but this?

I side stand the bike and find a shady bench by an overgrown vineyard laden with grapes. Can't help but wonder how many generations have tended to these vines. It doesn't seem right. Nothing for it, I guess. *Alea iacta est*. I pat down the last of green powder in the pipe bowl and add the flame. Even this doesn't lighten the sense of doom.

MARDIN IS A CITY set on a hill that cannot be hidden. It is a magical place. Not only has there been a settlement here since Roman times, but it has by and large managed to keep its identity. There are modern amenities (mostly of the more expensive variety), but the walkways and buildings have retained their original plan. While many cities try to blend with their surroundings, Mardin has gone a step further and successfully blends with its past.

Part of its charm comes from the way it sneaks up on me. Mardin is set on a hill that faces southwards and I'm coming from Batman in the north through the desert. The road into town starts with a gentle incline. The first sign that I might be coming to something special is luxury hotels that start springing up on either side. Most of them have large tour buses disgorging blinking, blinded tourists into the bright desert air. Based on my instructions from the minders I've got a hotel right up the main street of Mardin. With the GPS missing, I hope this won't be too difficult to find.

Turns out I needn't have worried. There is only one main street, which is the real problem. It's mid-afternoon and the desert sun is unflinching. The traffic is completely gridlocked with a shambles of heavy tour buses, hotel vans and private vehicles. I'm melting over the overheating bike engine. Strained radiators and tempers are not helped by the increasing incline after the first junction. Crowds of tourists on the narrow pavements on both sides of the street spill over between over-revving engines. I take my cue from some locals on scooters and take to the pavement to make my way to the centre of town. It's a bit dangerous and not very polite and my bike is the furthest thing from a 90cc scooter but I figure when in Mardin ...

The hotel is a winner though. Everything in Mardin is set on a southward facing slope. After spotting the hotel sign I take the bike down a truly precarious nearly vertical downward ramp to the right, off the main street. This leads to an equally steep cobblestoned footpath with walled medieval houses on both sides. Each has its own stepped entrance, with a shaded garden and a small fountain. The hotel is nothing more than a collection of these terraced homes converted to separate guestrooms.

The room is pretty average and as I bring the panniers in off the bike I don't see what the fuss of Mardin is about. Then I step out to the southward-facing balcony and that wondrous view, and the reason is clear. Mardin is literally a terraced city. The front porches and patios of individual homes are roofs and ceilings of the houses below. The balcony that I'm standing on has someone's living room underfoot. Many of the porches are linked by walkways between the homes. While tourists sweat it out on the streets, the locals walk the rooftops.

In the distance is the featureless Mesopotamian Plain, leading off to the horizon. Mardin is an island surrounded by a sea of sand. The buildings drape down the hillside, regular cubes of light brown blazing in the sun like a child's building blocks, interspersed with sprigs of green from rooftop gardens. There is the occasional domed roof of the numerous grand madrassahs that dot the city. To the right is the towering 12th century minaret of the Great Mosque of Mardin, standing out from this island like a lighthouse.

Looking backwards over the roof of my room, Mardin stretches upward to its citadel at the summit of the hill. It might look a little cluttered and there is definitely the mark of age, but Mardin is by no means run-down. Even as I threaded my way up here I could tell that the main street is lined by upper-end restaurants and boutique hotels. The kind with smoothed-down white tablecloths, wine lists and four kinds of bread before mains. In the few cramped car parks were Mercs, Beemers and I think I spotted a Maserati. Mardin is where well-heeled Turks come to dine and play.

There's lots else to see here: a modest but very reputable museum, the bazaar further down on the southern slopes, madrassahs and restored villas, and to add to the quirkiness, one of the grandest post offices anywhere. I decide to spend the day just wandering the streets, getting a much-needed laundry load done and playing pavement football with some of the kids. It's way too hot for me to try anything else.

Walking this working medieval city is quite restorative. For one thing, it can only be appreciated on foot. There are no streets beyond the main thoroughfares. Cobblestoned walkways and near vertical stairways provide the only access to the town proper. The steep slopes and narrow passageways means one essential necessity remains unchanged through the centuries: All the rubbish is collected by teams of donkeys, which I keep running into. This is all done by morning and after a brief rest, the same working animals are dolled up with bells and ribbons, providing rides through the town for children.

As night falls the al fresco dining begins in earnest: rooftops fill with the sounds of live bands and people having a good time. *Shishas*, thick woollen carpets under the desert sky, and equally starry-eyed couples retake the now nearly empty streets. The minaret is all lit up, resembling more than ever a lighthouse in a sea of darkness.

Next morning I'm sitting on a stone bench under the shade of a Roman archway by one of Mardin's museums. The morning's been spent with the laundry, oil change for the bike and a visit to the bazaar. Now it's lunch with a *kebab* wrap and Coke. The sun's up properly now and great sweating, fanning herds of tourists make their way to the museum. I'm not entirely sure it's worth the jostling; I seem to be getting my fill of antiquity just walking the streets.

That's when I hear it. At first I don't believe my ears, but it's the unmistakable sound of a Beemer GS coming up the lane. For a mad moment I think that Mike and Pierce have accomplished the impossible, got the Beemer fixed and made their way back from Ankara. As I've said before, I'm

The city of Mardin, facing the Mesopotamian Plain

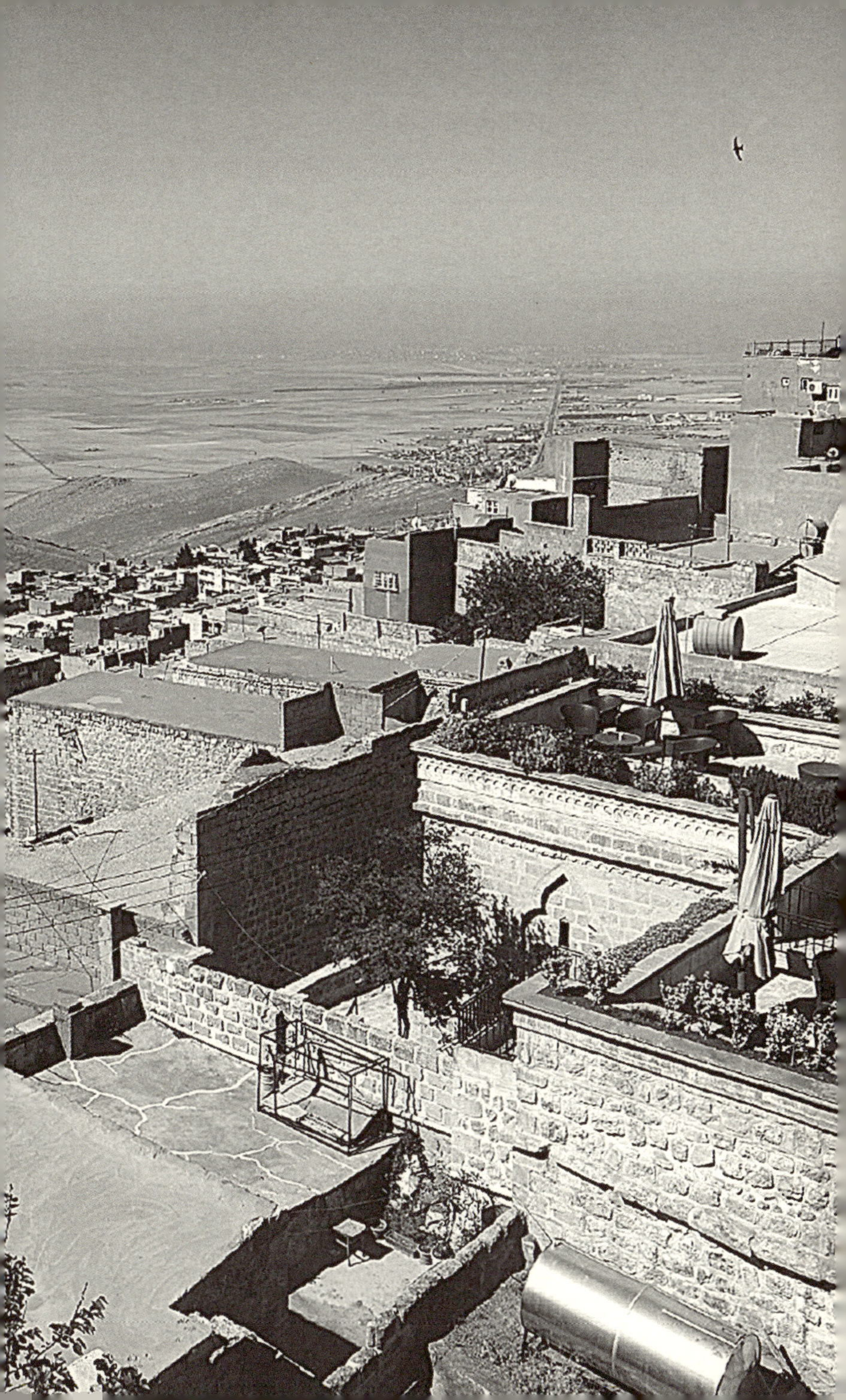

not the kind who likes these solo rides and I do miss having them around.

Not a chance. This is a lovely new white GS with Turkish plates. It belongs to Berat from Istanbul who's doing his first epic solo ride, taking the long way to visit his parents in Erzurum on his new BMW. Berat notices the riding boots I have on and soon we're sharing the bench. Between two bikers conversation is never going to be a problem.

Berat's an engineer working for the government and he's been saving up for this Beemer for years. He says that he's glad he's taken the time because he's been able to get the newest model, the first ever liquid-cooled GS. He tells me that touring bikes are a big thing in Turkey and these new babies arrived here sooner than anywhere else outside of Germany. I tell him we don't even have them in Singapore yet.

After years on smaller bikes the best thing, Berat says, is getting on this beast and just going. No planning, just go. I think about the preparations it took to get me here and realise that he's on a 3,000 km ride without even taking his passport. For all that's available in Turkey I can see why biking is big here. Since arriving in Turkey all I've had is fabulous country roads, breathtaking views and mouth-watering food. As for cultural distractions, this country has UNESCO World Heritage sites like they grow on trees.

"There's only one thing you really need to worry about out here," Berat says.

"What's that?" I ask. I'm expecting Kurdish separatists, Syrian refugees, over enthusiastic policemen, or traveller's diarrhoea.

"Sheep," says Berat. "They're killers." Then his mobile phone rings and he excuses himself before rushing back to get on the bike.

"Sorry my friend, they have just confirmed my hotel room but I need to get over there right away. Watch out for the sheep. Make sure you get to the shepherd quickly." Then he was gone.

I return his wave limply. I've been sitting in the shade for a bit now so I'm sure it's not the sun. He clearly said to look out for the sheep. Skidding on sheep dung? Kamikaze sheep dashing on to the road? Goats chewing the plastic and rubbers off the bike at night? Wait, no, he clearly said sheep, not goats.

Next morning I discover that like a true beauty, Mardin is even more beautiful at dawn than she is at night, and much more difficult to leave. It's completely still except for the *clip-clop* of a pair of donkeys coming up the lane. Most of the shops are still closed and there is a chill in the air, but I am keen to get on my way before the tour buses come back.

Today's ride will take me to something quite special. Nemrut Dagi, or Mount Nimrod, is just over 250 km away and a climb to 2,000 m. We're booked into the Euphrates Hotel, which is just off the summit and is supposed to have one of the best views of the mountains.

I weave my way down narrow, dimly-lit streets past the main junction out of town, then into the flat desert at first light. At this time of the day the rising sun paints the mountaintops on the horizon deep orange and the adjoining sky the deepest azure. I'm all alone out here on this dark ribbon of road, surrounded by an inky blackness. Not for the first time I feel like I'm travelling on a magic carpet, flying from one mystical place to another through this most ancient of lands. As the last of the stars disappear I see the first road sign for Diyarbakir, where I'm to make a left turn and head westward for Siverek. This really does feel like an adventure to far flung lands.

After Siverek the sun's out with a vengeance and I'm into the hill roads again. Tiny villages with limestone houses bleached in the heat lie interspersed with windy bits with lovely hairpin turns overlooking the valley below. What traffic there is on these roads is easily overtaken and the V-twin below me chugs happily along in third.

Another sharp right hairpin with a sheer drop off the cliff to the left, keep your eye on the apex, drop down to second, use the camber, rev up out of the curve and wait for 5,000 rpm. The bike's just coming out of full right bank when I see it. Or rather them. Lots of them. A whole herd of them. It's sheep as far as the eye can see, on the road and coming up the cliff on the left and then clambering further uphill on the right. OK, stay off the front brake until you come up, right foot on stands on the rear brake but even as the rear wheel locks and loses traction I know I'm never going to be able to stop in time.

Miraculously, the sea of wool parts as the bike drives into it and I coast to a stop surrounded by a cacophony of bleating. Well, at least I seem to have survived my first encounter with Turkish killer sheep. Then I notice the sea of wool hasn't quite completely parted. They've left a triangular clearing about 10 m each side but dead ahead the sheep seem to be standing rod still, glancing at me with a sort of amused look as they chew the cud.

Standing at the apex of my triangle right in front of me is what I initially think might be rather too big for a sheep. It might be a dog, but it's doing a good imitation of a muscular bear. It's the same tan colour as the sheep, but that's not wool, it's fur, and plenty of scars. Underlining its soot black face are two rows of very large teeth, and a long pink tongue hungrily dripping saliva. It seems to be smiling at me, but not in a nice way. A corona of spikes radiate from a leather collar around its neck. Inside my helmet I hear myself uttering those famous last words altogether: Whaderfuckizat. Then we lock eyes. His message is clear: We're having Chinese today.

I remember Berat's parting words. Get to the shepherd quickly. I notice the collared bear casually ambling towards me with a gentle trot, licking in anticipation. The sheep seem to be chewing more quickly; that's just sheep for: This is going to be good. I wonder if he'll eat the bike before the Chinaman.

Out of the corner of my eye I notice a dark disheveled short bloke in a worn poncho and a pipe in his mouth riding a small donkey. Without hesitation I steer the bike towards him and grab his hand in a warm handshake. He shouts something to the bear who trudges away up the hill, clearly disappointed. I have survived not only killer sheep, but my first encounter with the Turkish sheep dog.

I'm used to some sort of sweet Border Collie. The next door neighbour of the farmer I used to visit in Devon had one of those. Responded to his whistles, loved diving into the brook under the stone bridge, its face the very embodiment of intelligence and bonhomie. In rural Turkey those collies wouldn't last a week. Sheep dogs here kill wolves and snakes for fun. The collar is to stop the second wolf from getting a grip of his neck as he tears up the first one.

In grateful relief I offer the shepherd the rest of my tobacco pouch. He opens the pouch, has a whiff and then returns it. He's friendly but the eyes say everything. Real men ride donkeys up hills, not bikes on roads, and we don't smoke that girly stuff. I decide to have a calming smoke myself and watch the huge herd of sheep go past before starting on my way again. I regret not getting Berat's number in the rush, he might well have just saved me.

After that I step up the pace. Soon the road starts to ascend in earnest from the surrounding plains. It's 40 km of vertiginous uphill on a narrow road surfaced with pavestones, sheer drops on either side. I'm not one for heights but the greatest threat to life now isn't so much skidding off the road as the breathtaking view that keeps improving as we get higher. After I get to the top there's still a 2-km hike to the summit, but what's at the top of this mountain is worth every gut-wrenching bit of cornering it's taken to get up.

On two terraces facing in opposite directions, with a huge man-made tumulus separating them, are colossal statues. Antiochus I, a pre-Christ king of this region, wanted to ally himself with other deities represented here as part of the imperial cult of the Kingdom of Commagene. These include Heracles, Zeus, Apollo and Tyche. It's a mishmash of gods not usually seen together, wearing their respective headgear and beards as befit Greek, Assyrian and Armenian deities. Their heads alone are some 2 m tall and curiously, all now lie separate from their respective torsos, overlooking the surrounding mountains and valleys. On the opposite platform is a crumbling statue of Antiochus himself, flanked by two eagles and a lion.

Why he should choose this spot is a mystery, as is why the heads now lie separate from their bodies, even more curiously with their noses chipped off. The reason for this glorious self-aggrandisement might be easier to understand. Perhaps in simpler times it just made people easier to manage if they thought of you as a god. Or could it be that Antiochus was simply expressing a basic human vanity: the need to be adored and never forgotten. Take this to extremes and you have self-deification with the Pantheon.

As I walk around Nemrut what strikes me is not so much the magnificence of these colossal statues, but the grandeur of emptiness that surrounds it. As far as the eye can see there are majestic mountains and valleys, under a limitless sky of blue and benign puffs of cumulus clouds. Try as he might, Antiochus cannot claim to have made them — there is nothing man-made within view.

Far from being a focus for imperial deification, this site

was soon largely forgotten until the late 1800s, when it was discovered by a German surveyor contracted to plan a railway line. So Nemrut's lesson may be that man's need is also man's curse. He is, in the end, mere flesh. And all flesh is like grass, the glory of man as the flower of grass. The grass withers, and its flower falls away.

The next morning it's difficult to leave the Hotel Euphrat, about 800 m down from the summit. Without the need to beat any rush hour traffic I head out to the bike after taking full advantage of the breakfast buffet. There was some worrying rattling from the pannier locks yesterday. Probably loosening from the increasing load and the pavestone punishment on the way up here yesterday. I duct tape the pannier frames to take up some of the slack and hope this does the trick.

Today it's over 500 km alone to get to Cappadocia. Boss says we can look forward to living it up at the high-end Cave Hotel, wandering about ancient troglodytic settlements and hot air ballooning. Riding in Turkey really is like this: one magnificent place after another. What I'm hoping for is that Mike has his Beemer fixed and we'll start riding to Istanbul in two days' time. There isn't any Wi-Fi out here and we've been out of touch for a few days.

Off the mountain and down in the valley it's a greyish day and I have trouble warming up. The wind's picking up and a glance at the mirrors reveals storm clouds coming up behind me. Solo riding usually means taking my time but today that might not be such a good idea.

I have to take petrol at Gurun and consider stopping for lunch but by the time I get back to the bike it's already starting to drizzle. I've lost my GPS the day I came into

At the summit of Nemrut Dagi, with the heads of the deities mysteriously separated from their seated torsos in the background.

Turkey and have my waypoints on a piece of paper covered with plastic on the tank bag because I can't read the maps without spectacles on. I realise that in the rain I can't make out what I've written either. Out here there are no road signs for Cappadocia as yet, but Kayseri is starting to show up. Medium term goal: Get to Kayseri and have another look at the map there.

Beyond Gurun everything changes completely. The storm is freezing cold wind and rain and dense dark clouds turn day to night. The flat desert road enters the mountains and soon it's twisty roads up to each mountaintop before an equally vertiginous descent down the other side. I'm sort of grateful I can't see the sheer fall on either side for the low cloud. By some mad coincidence the Turkish authorities have decided that now is a good time for road repairs, although in this crap weather most of the machinery is just left on the road as the workers find cover. Warning lights would really be helpful to know where the road disappears entirely. Great stretches of road are surfaced by loose sand, so whatever you do don't touch the brakes. An alarm goes off in my head: I'm starting to fixate on road surfaces again.

Despite all the gear I have on, I'm freezing. I can't even feel the heat of the engine on my legs and boots anymore. I don't know if the bike is twitching because of the poor surface, the constantly changing winds on these mountaintops or my shivering hands on the handlebars. I have to slow down just to reduce some of the wind chill. I remember what Mike had said about keeping warm on the bike. Put on as many layers as you have and keep twitching your toes. I've got three layers under this jacket but there's a set of long johns and woolies in the pannier. Trouble is, there's nowhere to change in this wilderness. So under a tree by the side of the road, surrounded by rain and lightning, the mad Chinaman takes off all his clothes to put on more layers.

That was a silly thing to do, it really was. Now I've four layers on but they're all wet and I'm as cold as ever. Starting to tense up and hold my breath. Looking down at the speedo I find that I'm having trouble keeping up 70 km/h. In the reflection of the headlights the patches of water on these darkened roads look exactly like ice.

Fearing that I might fall apart completely out here on my own I start the mental routines. *Is it true? Is that really ice? What would you do if it was just water? Right, do that thing.* On a straight bit of road I pick what looks like a dark sheet of glass and plough through it. *Only water. OK then, do that again.* And again. Mustn't let the erroneous thoughts take root, have to sort them quickly.

Is the bike really twitching? At the next bit of twisties I start leaning the bike over farther and farther, trying to breathe normally and not tense up. *Right, make smaller adjustments than that last time, that was a pretty crazy wobble. Do it again. Now faster, hit the brakes later.* These really are good wet tyres.

What is clearly not a cognitive error is the cold. I need to get warm soon and it's not just for the comfort. I'm starting to tire on this bike. Riding in this weather on this road with this mental state is hard going. And I made that idiotic decision earlier to ride through lunch.

Ahead on the horizon is a narrow strip of bright, inviting sunlight; otherwise it's all dark clouds above, around and behind. The end of the storm. I need sunlight to get warm, I think, or there's no way I'm going to last another 200 km in these conditions. It becomes a race for time, to get to that horizon before the dying of all that wonderful light. Trouble is, no matter how fast I go, that strip of light stays as far as ever. I see the milestones for Kayseri. I figure if I keep in at 70 km/h average I can make in two hours. Then rocks appear on the road, I shatter one on the front wheel and the bike skips before righting itself. It's not rocks, it's ice, probably from a passing hailstorm. Do we need to avoid ice blocks? They're everywhere on this road. I want that sunlight, so on I go through them.

The road has straightened out now, leading directly to that warm line on the horizon. There's no one else out here at all. It may be just in my mind, but if I just fix my eyes on that distant horizon I feel warmer, away from the dark and wet and gloom everywhere.

I remember reading that Cappadocia lies in a broad valley and soon the road starts descending from the mountains. It's not twisting like the way up, just a straight road leading down. Magically, that strip of light seems to broaden rapidly and the dark foreboding landscape that surrounded me for the last few hours is transformed in seconds into lush green fields separated by low rock walls, bathing in the golden sunlight. The rain disappears and I put the visor up to get the sunshades on as I ride into the sun. Clean, fresh wind on my face changes everything.

It's a mesmerising transformation from the dark icy mountaintops to the valleys below. The heat is all-enveloping now, drying the riding gear and warming my bones. Everything is golden! When I look over the left shoulder to take one last glance at the mountains I've come through, I see it — the most perfect rainbow in a patch of pale blue sky, surrounded by billowing dark clouds. There doesn't seem to be anyone here and it's a message that seems to be meant just for me: A real God doesn't really need to have statues on a mountaintop to show His abiding presence.

I get to Kayseri just after last light and that's where things start to go wrong. There's a ring road around this city that doesn't quite show up on the map. Not that I can see any of the map in this darkness. Soon I'm in the middle of fast-moving traffic, with no clue where I'm heading. The light's all gone now and I'm starting to get cold again. I'm not sure but I think I'm on the major expressway heading towards Ankara, which is not a good thing.

Then I spot a name I recognise from map-poring last night: Incesu. I remember I take that exit off the highway and then before reaching Incesu itself I'm to take another turn to Avanos.

It's pitch black when I get to Cappadocia. Right, how to find the Cave Hotel? The town is full of winding streets leading to blind ended footpaths, and almost every other building is a hotel. Then I remember the pictures from the website Boss had shown me. Now that I'm out of the rain and the traffic, the adrenaline's waned and I'm nearly blind with fatigue. I see what might be the hotel but have no idea how to get there, until I see a familiar figure waiting on a street corner, red bandanna in hand. Mike directs me up some narrow pathways to the hotel front and helps me off the bike.

"Knew that you would make it," he says with a big grin, "but we were getting a little worried."

I glance down at the dashboard clock. It's just after 10:00 pm. I've been on that bike for over 12 hours.

I give him a grateful hug. Some of the other four by four

The end of the storm on the ever-distant horizon –
I need to get there and get warm.

crews have stayed up as well. Hung Tuan looks as though he was about to send out search parties, but puts away the road maps when he sees me.

"You have no idea, man," is all I manage.

Nineteen
TRANSFAGARASAN HIGHWAY AND THE MANSION OF THE BEARS

I'M FINISHING MY SECOND round of draft beer in a rooftop café, enjoying the sunset in the shadow of the Blue Mosque in Istanbul. This truly is a magical city, made even more so by Viola and our daughter Jean joining us. Mike and I crossed the Bosphorus two days ago and have enjoyed the time doing the usual tourist things.

In geographical terms the Long Ride has crossed the entire Asian land mass, from the Straits of Johore to the European side of this city. More importantly, we have fulfilled all of our obligations made before we left Singapore, meeting and working with breast cancer collaborators throughout the continent. Well, almost all anyway. The only exception was the intended congress in Ürümqi, which we didn't make because of the major sandstorm around Tulufan.

> One for the family album: in the shadow of the Blue Mosque, Pierce, Jean, Mike, Viola me and Belgian beer.

Istanbul is a time of rest and recovery, to catch up with each other and our families now that the hectic part of the ride is over. Had this ride been a motorcycling holiday or even "adventure touring", as they are called nowadays, both Mike and I can name at least a dozen places where we wish we could stay longer. There is a small village called Gevas on the southern bank of Lake Van where you can just leave me and carry on, thank you very much. As it is all this is for breast cancer awareness, so we only had so much time, and had to make all those dates and places. Crossing Asia has been exhilarating, but the furthest thing from a holiday.

After Istanbul we're no longer a convoy. Boss and his four by four group have been poring over their own itinerary for the European leg of their journey. Mostly this seems to consist of dining at Michelin-starred restaurants, select vineyards and chateaus, and spending nights in converted castles.

As for the bikers' itinerary, this is the part of the journey that I had left for Mike to plan. That pretty much means not much of any plan at all, the way a bike ride ought to be enjoyed. The only deadline we have to make is Copenhagen where we are to meet Cynthia and her team of anthropologists from the University of Copenhagen, and of course, Karolinska Institute at the end of the ride proper.

Mike's about to introduce another change in our riding arrangements. At Cappadocia he had met a German woman called Angelica at the BMW mechanic's in Ankara. Her GS had broken down when she was wandering around Turkey with a BMW touring group, but from a far more common reason than Mike's faulty fuel pump chip. The details are a little fuzzy but it involved a sideswipe by a truck.

In any case her intended ride is pretty much over and she plans to head home as soon as her bike's fixed. The dates are fortuitous and Mike had offered her a ride back together into Europe, if that's alright with me.

I'm not sure what to expect. The last time I had thought of a German woman was in downtown Chengdu with those wonderful giant-sized posters of Diane Kruger. Would she be a distraction? Could she cover distance? Was her bike sound? Does she by any chance look like Diane Kruger? Heidi Klum? Claudia Schiffer? Mike doesn't give anything away. Find out for yourself when we meet in Istanbul, he had said.

One look now at our new riding partner as she comes up the stairs is enough. Angelica is a stout woman with the constitution of German armour plate. She has a grip like a vice, with calloused hands that look like they spend more time in biking gloves than out. She may have a year or two on us but next to her it's clear that we are the shaky old codgers on bikes. She comes up to my height, with friendly grey eyes enclosed by a broad, weathered face. Her sunburnt neck is covered with a dark scarf, and her thin brown hair is lined with grey and tied into a long ponytail.

She looks like those massive-mileage types who would rather ride through the night than stop and sleep. You sort of know things are going to be alright when your new riding buddy shows up in riding boots and kit. "They're the most comfortable clothes I have," Angelica says, "like a second skin to me now."

Turns out those heavy-duty off-road boots have saved her leg, Angelica says. The truck had destroyed the pannier and racks on one side and bent the rear of her Beemer's sub-frame. She had lost a foot peg on that side but except for some bruising and tenderness everything was fine. I hadn't noticed any limp when she walked up. I don't think it's the boot, I think to myself. Angelica's asbestos, she's indestructible. I wonder what the truck looked like after their brief encounter.

As for her riding credentials, we needn't have worried either. She's done the gruelling Alaska to Argentina ride and covers most of Europe and even northern Africa with regularity. The wife is well pleased. Angelica is just the ticket to get Mike and I through Europe safely, or at least until Germany when she peels off for home. Viola's very good at this: "Of course I'm sure you'll be alright, dear, but Angelica looks just the thing to make sure."

Transfagarasan Highway and the Mansion of the Bears

Angelica showing me a better way into Europe before we leave Istanbul

The next morning we start off at the hotel with the unfamiliar setting of an additional rider. Mike's plan is to cross over into Bulgaria at Edirne. That is the most straightforward route but Angelica's done this before and suggests the quieter, nicer roads through Dereköy, and then to the Black Sea Coast. This is the better route but we're here at the wrong time of the year. We're entering Bulgaria about three weeks before summer and late springs here are wet and cold. Through the rain we stay on the Black Sea Coast to spend the night at the completely misnamed Sunny Beach.

Well, that's not quite fair. During the summer season there would have been techno music beach parties where the only dress code is soap suds and well-endowed girls vying for the Miss Wet trophy. Sadly when we show up, it really should have been called Pissing Down All Day Beach. The skies are overcast, we're drenched in thunderstorms twice a day, the rather sad-looking beaches are empty and hotels closed. We find a pension that's stayed open so that some of the rooms can be renovated before the season starts. It's so bad it reminds me of Brighton.

As we try to leave the coast the next day we find that most of the main routes recommended on Mike's GPS are flooded. Apparently the Danube usually floods its banks before draining into the Black Sea during this time of year. There is nothing blue about it and it wouldn't have inspired any of the Strauss clan. Unless they could compose breezy lighthearted waltzes from washed-out roads, bridges and farmlands. We eventually do cross the Danube in an improvised car ferry; the bridge indicated by the GPS just wasn't there.

Progress is slow and grimly silent, the elation of finally

arriving in Europe smothered by the damp weather. Around Bucharest we find ourselves on the city's ring road, which is a continuous display of grim Soviet-era architecture. I'm sure this city has a lot to offer but we decide to get out of our drenched clothes and boots, into a hot shower and call it a night.

After Bucharest we expect things to be different. Today we cross into Transylvania, then over the Carpathian mountains on the Transfagarasan, a highway considered by *Top Gear* to be the best road in the world. Better than German Autobahns and Italy's Stelvio Pass. What a remarkable television series that was. It's amazing what you can get done as long as you don't punch an assistant producer.

It's still raining when we leave Bucharest but soon the weather starts to play its part and by lunchtime it's bright sunshine through the Romanian countryside. This really is a pretty country. There's hardly any traffic on the roads and they're leading us ever upwards towards the mountains. We're surrounded by rolling green fields, with the occasional splash of bright red poppies, which seem to grow wild just at the edge of the country roads.

The houses here seem centuries old, with high-walled fortresses and monasteries dotting the landscape. There aren't so many of the tractors and other farming machines one sees on other European farms; much of the work still seems to be done by workhorse and elbow grease. Although some of the houses really do look like they could use a fresh coat, the gardens are meticulously maintained, with roses and sunflowers swaying in the bright sunlight.

There's hardly any traffic on the roads, and not a single traffic light for miles and miles, not even in the villages.

People seem to move about mainly by walking. There is the occasional man-pulled cart full of produce.

On one of the quieter roads I see a strangely familiar sight of a man walking slightly hunched over by the side of the road with a basket over his shoulder, a sickle's handle just visible over the top of the basket. He's wearing a beaten-up straw hat and worn out clothes. *An itinerant farmworker*, I think. A few steps behind him walks the wife in just as used clothes, a scarf covering her head and another wrapping a baby over the front of her chest. It takes a few minutes before I remember. I had just ridden past Henchard and Susan, and that would be Elizabeth-Jane she was carrying. The bike's a time machine. We're back in Thomas Hardy country.

As is our usual habit, as lunchtime comes around, Mike and I look for a provision shop for the customary Coca-Cola and chocolate bars. Angelica's not on our intercom so we need to hand signal to her what we're doing. She nods.

We finally find what we're after, a shop with an ice-cream cooler by the entrance and a cola fridge. Communication with Angelica doesn't always need an intercom. "You gotta be kidding," Angelica shakes her head gravely. Turns out she's been holding her peace for the last few days but this is where it stops. She waves us onward until we come to a proper country restaurant. "You people need to eat better," she says.

From here on in we're sitting at tables, being waited on and not on curbsides under the nearest tree. A bottle of wine at lunch, and proper coffee after. *Why didn't we do this sooner*, I think, as I carve into a most exquisite *cartofi*, a mixture of country potatoes cooked with bacon lard on a wood fire, with a side of pork sausages. It's hard to get back on the bike.

From Pitești the countryside changes dramatically. The broad trough of the Argeș River valley quickly replaces the rolling hills and farmlands as we head steadily northwards into the mountains. There are no farms here, the hillsides are far too steep, but we can still see the odd herd of sheep and goats. The road is nothing more than a narrow cutting into the rock face as it snakes upwards, with an increasingly disconcerting near vertical drop to the river below.

Now that we're here it really is hard to believe. The Transfagarasan! Before today my main perspective of this remarkable road was from above, where it's a dark squiggle through a lush green valley, snow-peaked mountains on both sides. On a big V-twin at asphalt level it's much better. Like that starting sequence from the first Italian Job movie. The one with Michael Caine and the Matt Monro soundtrack.

There are hardly any straight bits, just one hairpin after another as the road leads steadily upwards. So it's mainly staying on second, dropping till the foot pegs scrape, and then not quite recovering completely before dropping the shoulders and taking another 270-degree turn. I think it might be interesting how many of these I actually carve out before reaching Sibiu but stop counting at 22. I can't help the feeling that the whole thing must have been built by a biker. The distance between the curves is just right to get to 6,000 rpm on second, before closing the throttle and letting gravity and the engine do all the braking needed.

Then the rare bit of straight road between pine woodlands on both sides, kick up to third, listen for 5,000 rpm before switching to fourth but just before you need to … it's another

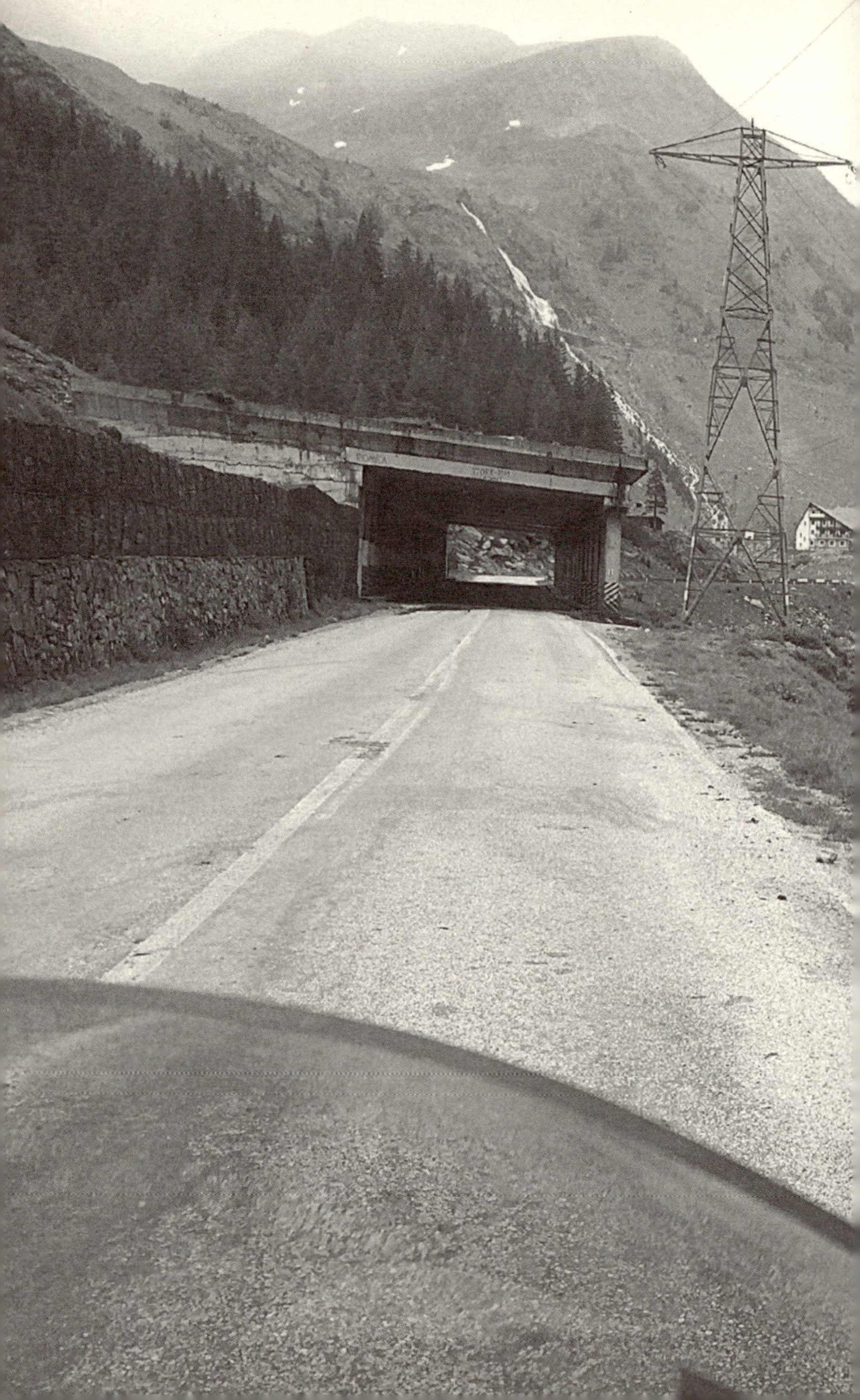

The Transfagarasan — the best road in Europe, with its life-threatening scenery of cascading waterfalls, towering mountains and the Arges River below

perfectly cantered hairpin so once again drop to second and watch the apex ... and on and on it goes. The few cars I catch up to can't keep up with this gradient and the bike leaves them standing. I may not have a three-litre Bavarian turbo-charged engine with an "M" badge, but I don't have much dead weight either.

The main threat to life here isn't the odd pothole, the sheer drops, or the occasional bit of slippery sheep shit that somehow deposits just on the perfect line to the curve. The most dangerous thing is the almost irresistible urge to take my eyes off road to take in the scenery, because the view here is just short of being to die for. Just on the basis of backdrop alone this stretch would have my vote for the best road in the world.

The Carpathian Mountains don't have that foreboding desolation of the Tian Shan Range in Xinjiang, or the regal majesty of the Himalayas, but it will steal your heart away. As a rule the road seems in perfect harmony with the mountains, following the contour steadily upwards towards the snow line. Now and then it leaps off from the mountain altogether and I find myself seemingly air borne over a deep gorge on a high arched bridge with the Arges running far below. I was to learn a little later just how much effort and sacrifice this road took to build, but for now I feel like a privileged guest. That's what the Carpathians are about, what makes them the loveliest place to come through on a bike. The mountains here are ... inviting. They may be majestic and windswept but you can still see trails leading up to the very top of these barren mountains and the odd mountain cabin for overnighters. Once again I wish that I had more time.

Through a series of tunnels that seem to cut through

the heart of the mountains I finally reach Vidraru Dam. Completed in 1966, this created Vidraru Lake and submerged an entire village under about 160 m of water. The dam is smaller than I expected, only 300 m long and shaped like the number seven between two vertical mountainsides.

What it lacks in scale is made up for in accessibility. You can literally walk on the edge of the parapet and no one's going to bother you about Health and Safety. Some kids are doing it as I turn into the car park. I suppose pointing out that you might fall and hurt yourself on the valley floor 400 m below would be the height of redundancy. I'm beginning to like Romanians. Maybe that's how they get all those fabulous narrow beam gymnasts.

There's some rather run-down coffee stalls to one side of the tunnel exit and that's where I find Angelica chewing down a corn on a cob. She tells me that Mike's gone ahead but says that he's going to take his time taking pictures on the way and he's sure we'll catch up. Angelica points to dark clouds blocking out the mountains on the northern shore of the lake.

"That's where we're going," she says.

"Well, I'm sure it'll clear up," I reply, sipping on the hot coffee she's given me. After a morning's ride like the one we've just had, it seems inconceivable that anything could possibly spoil our day.

"I've been speaking to some of the people coming the other way," she says, "they're saying the weather might be pretty cold up there, and there is a possibility that the road across the mountain may be closed to cars. Things will be safer tomorrow when the weather clears."

It may be the coffee talking, or that I'm not quite down from the rider's high yet. "Well, I think we'll be alright," I say, "can always turn back, I guess, if we have to. Besides, we need to catch up with Mike."

When I step off the bike I notice how cold it's suddenly turned. There isn't any real way to get warm on the top of an exposed dam, so I'm keen to get on a warm engine again. I notice a whole bunch of locals getting into their cars and heading downward on the highway. No one's heading up.

"Well, I'm in no hurry to get home," Angelica says, "So I'll ride on for now but if I see a place to stay I might spend the night here and wait for the weather to clear tomorrow. It's quite beautiful here. I can then catch up with the two of you in Sibiu, okay?"

I agree. One of the loveliest things about being on a bike ride without a strict schedule is flexibility just like this.

I thought it would be impossible to improve on the morning ride but the roads round the shores of Lake Vidraru prove me wrong. The woodlands come all the way to the banks of the lake. Several rivers drain from the surrounding mountains in a series of small waterfalls.

Through all the mad hairpins and hills the lake itself is this constant, serene presence over my left shoulder, sunlight glinting off the lapping waves. It reminds me of hiking the banks of Ladybower Lake in the East Midlands. That lake is man-made as well, drowning the village of Derwent with its spired bell tower. The legend is that on quiet evenings you can sometimes hear the submerged church bell and that if you do it's supposed to bring good luck. I guess it's a common enough folklore among submerged villages. It would take an

English sense of humour to put up that sign I remember by the entrance of the Ladybower though: "Derwent village, twinned with Atlantis."

Soon the road leaves the banks of the lake and starts to climb in earnest. I find Mike by his Beemer at the side of the road, packing up his camera and after a short update we head up into the cloud together.

Here it's suddenly very much colder and we're surrounded by a grey frozen muck. We've reached the apex of the river valley now. It'll be just mountains till the summit. In the gaps in the weather I can see the road winding ever steeper upward, the green grasslands giving way to grey shale and scree. Ahead of us the Carpathians have lost their inviting face. The mountains stand with their massive, frozen bulk, a tiny road just visible snaking up at an impossible gradient. This is first-gear stuff.

I don't think I have ever seen weather change this fast. As we round another hairpin we're on the windward side of the mountain and it's suddenly cold driving rain and bits of sleet. We seem to be staying on the windward side now, and soon we're over the snowline. Great snowdrifts cross our road and while it's fascinating that these Pirellis have taken everything from 40-degree heat in Thailand and crunching snow now, I also realise that they have no grip on this icy road. Belatedly, I realise that when Angelica bails, it has to be something pretty spectacular. Should I have stayed with her?

"Er, Mike," I call on the intercom, "this road's turned pretty crappy. How much further to the top tunnel?"

"Hey, Phil! Great to hear you! Isn't it wonderful that these intercoms can still work under these conditions?"

A thought hits me. Some sort of morbid curiosity, but he's the one with the multi-feature, German-engineered dashboard. "What's the temperature on that fancy thermometer anyway?"

"Oh, it's pretty cold."

Silence. We plod on. It's becoming not only a first-gear ascent, but also first-gear and try-to-stay-on-the-road kind of ride. I can't hear the engine for the howling wind. There's ice on these hairpins, but the good news is that with the weather this closed in I can't see how far I'll fall.

"How much further, Mike?"

"Oh, not much at all," he replies vaguely, "and this road is not so bad. Quite normal for Sweden actually, let's just keep going."

"Right ... normal for Sweden then, to ride in the driving rain and ice?"

"Oh yes, this isn't rain, just a bit of wet. Just stay off the brakes. You'll be fine."

Right then. It has to be sub-zero, the water's coming off the streams on the mountainside and freezing before it crosses the road. There's ice on my helmet visor and gloves. Everything that isn't in actual contact with the engine feels frozen, or feels nothing at all. I can't see any of the mountains on either side, it's all covered with ice and snow, with rivulets chucking all the melted snow and frigid water on to the road.

Soon I see the tunnel entrance at the head of the pass, a concrete arch framing this triangular blot of perfect blackness leading into the heart of the mountain. Mike's reached it before me and is having a look around. As I come up next to the Beemer and get off the bike it happens. This moment of perfect madness.

Out of the darkness, a couple of teenagers ride past us and down the road on bicycles, schoolbooks clipped onto their rear panniers. They're dressed in turtleneck sweaters, head socks, scarves, and without gloves. None of this heavy bike armour I have on. They're madly giggling in this maelstrom as only teenagers can giggle. One of the bicycles is girlie pink, with white pedals and gay yellow streamers, for heaven's sake. In this weather, like it's just the daily commute back from school.

"What the hell," I say, staring after them in disbelief as they disappear through the rain and down the mountain.

"See?" Mike grins, "Told you this is normal weather. All depends on your perspective. Come look at this, we've got other problems."

I walk over to where he is, just inside the entrance of the

Snowdrifts near the tunnel run as high as the traffic signs

tunnel. After adjusting to the gloom I can't believe what I'm seeing. The entire tunnel entrance has been sealed by metal boarding, with only a narrow door allowing passage of bicycles and walkers. We leave the bikes where they are and walk through the door. It's perfectly black in here, but quite warm and completely still. We see the light at the end of the tunnel, about 200 m away.

"OK," I say to Mike, "the other end of the tunnel is wide enough to take the bikes. The question is whether we can get them through this narrow door?"

We take some hasty measurements of the widest points of the bikes. With the panniers off and the handlebars at an angle we think the V-Strom should be able to make it. The Beemer, on the other hand, is 9 cm too wide — the twin opposing transverse cylinders won't be able to get through. The metal barrier's really zinc sheeting but we haven't anything to bend or cut through that. There's nothing for it. We'll have to turn around and head back and find another way through these mountains.

We turn back the way we came. Thankfully the weather seems to be improving on our way down and by the time we get to the Vidraru Dam again the skies are a clear blue. We still need a place to stay. On the way up I remember passing this pretty place which looked like a Swiss alpine lodge. I was a little preoccupied with catching up to Mike then and wasn't sure if it was a hotel or one of those Soviet dachas. Now as we come by it again I have the chance for a more leisurely look at it and it's even more inviting.

The main building is a three-storied lodge of elegant stone and pine construct. Stone pillars support its bevelled roof and a solid stone wall on the entire lower edge, topped with a large chimney. One glance and I know there'll be a massive stone fireplace on the ground floor, and I can just imagine a roaring fire through the warm glow of the ground floor windows.

Then comes the unmistakable whiff of burning meat. I'm suddenly very hungry, and to the picture of the great fireplace I add a massive boar sizzling on a spit. No words are needed. Mike has already pulled over. We're staying here for the night.

As we turn into the gravel car park we can see a children's playground, and rather inexplicably, totem poles. Out back is one of those obstacle courses one associates nowadays with "team building" corporate retreats. Beyond the playground there are smaller bungalows hidden behind the tree line, with the sound of the rushing river just audible in the still evening air.

In front of these lodgings two dozen or so locals in their forties are having a proper barbecue. There actually is a boar on a spit and at least two kegs of beer on a bar improvised by pulling together Coleman ice boxes and a few benches. People are obviously enjoying themselves, congregating beer in hand around two other fully-utilised barbecue pits. Curiously there aren't any children, just these people in their forties having this bit of forest to themselves. The whole effect is irresistibly inviting and I'm feeling thirsty now as well.

The hotel sign at the main entrance says Conacul Ursului. Ursa … that means bear, I think. I figure it must be the clear night skies around here. Maybe they named the place after the constellation because it was clearly visible in this night sky? We approach the reception and find it manned by a startlingly attractive dark-haired young woman. After complementing her on the beautiful setting of the place we ask if we might have a room for the night.

"Unfortunately we have just given away our last room. Is it one of your friends?" she asks, "a German woman on a large motorcycle?" she points to the tree line outside.

Through the glass we can just make out another GS, parked out of sight from the road. Angelica! Trust her to pick a nice place for the night as we struggled on the mountain roads.

"Ah, well," Mike asks as he turns to me, "should we look for another place?"

"I really would like to stay," I reply, "tell you what." I turn to the nice lady again. "Could we camp out next to the river? If there's a place to grab a shower we'll pay room rates?"

She says we can use the showers by the back of the bar and of course we could stay.

When we go out to get the gear off the bikes we find a small crowd of curious partygoers gathered around them. One points to the decal of the Singapore flag on my fairing and asks where we're from. When we tell them they can't believe it. That's one hell of a ride, one of them says, name of Dan I think. You must let us have you over for dinner and tell us about it.

It's happened again. Less than an hour ago we had no idea where we were going to spend the night or even how we were going to get off the mountain. Now here we are, guests of complete strangers at their party, in one of the prettiest valleys I have ever seen. I tell Dan that we'll set up tents before we lose the light and grab a shower before coming over to join them. He says our steaks and beers would be waiting.

After we get our sleeping arrangements sorted out we return to our new friends and discover that we've stumbled onto a college class reunion. These people have been meeting annually since graduating over twenty years ago, more often than not at the Conacul Ursului. Not all of them speak English, but through Dan we manage to answer their queries about why we're on this ridiculous ride, about breast cancer in Asia and some of the highs and lows of the last two months. Good food transcends language barriers and pretty soon we are alternating between stories of the ride and tales from twenty years of friendships, loves gained and lost, jobs and family.

As night falls there's a nip in the air and the party retires to the main lodge with its massive fireplace. I recognise the usual scenario when we tell people about the Long Ride. At first there is genuine curiosity, then the usual questions,

Romanian bear bait, brought in fresh from Singapore

followed by polite attentiveness and after a while you find yourself pretty much by yourself as people go about their business. It happens wherever we have a chance to chat with strangers. At petrol stations, provision shops, lunch stops or here at this barbecue in Romania. Then, if we haven't completely worn out our welcome, we'll notice those who want a private moment. They'll be the ones who really need to get something off their chest. Cancer is the great leveller of men.

I first notice Cristi as one of the quiet listeners at the periphery of our ring of new friends. Most of us have let ourselves go a bit but he looks extremely trim and fit, with a hawk-like nose and clear grey eyes. He's wearing running longs and a thin red runner's tunic despite the chill, like he's used to these mountains. He seems to want a word as the others fade away.

Mike engages him first. "Hey, that's a nice Hasselblad," he says, pointing to the camera Cristi has in his hand, "from Sweden!"

What follows is a rather technical discussion I can't really follow, about True Focus and Medium Formatting. Mike and Cristi are getting along fine, but we can tell that there's something else. At a break in the conversation he comes out with it.

Cristi tells us that his father had been diagnosed with rectal cancer some years ago. It had been fairly advanced when they found it, and soon after the surgery had spread to his liver and his lungs. He had been in and out of hospital with one course of chemotherapy after another. There would always be a partial response, and then the scans would show new cancer deposits again. It was all extremely exhausting, not just for the effort of seeing to his care, but more so from seeing a man he loves dearly fade in front of him. His father had said that he didn't want any more treatment, but just to go home and let nature take its course. The doctors had said that there was still some hope in third line chemotherapy.

Cristi had consulted with the rest of his family but they had left it very much to him. He had anguished over it for months, realising that taking his father home to die would be to admit that all hope was lost, while accepting another course of therapy seemed more like prolonging dying than prolonging life. His father was still alert, but was suffering every time they introduced another course of chemotherapy. There wasn't much pain. I ask him what he's decided. Cristi wants to hear what we think first.

"Well," says Mike, "it's difficult. With stage four disease the doctors are usually no longer looking for cure, but palliation. What that means is trying to relieve symptoms and maybe prolong life by the month. Then again, if the side effects of the treatment is as bad as the disease itself …"

Cristi nods. "It is," he says.

I sense that he has heard enough professional opinions. What Cristi needs is a human response. Although he's too polite to say it outright, it seems to me that he's found the whole process of cancer care downright dehumanising: the discussion of treatment options in terms of months gained, this person reduced to a disease and becoming, quite literally, less and less of his father. More and more like some sort of numerical ratio, the probability of response to therapy per cost expended.

It sounds a little twisted, but I remember that my Dad had all his wits about him literally until the day he died. He had collapsed at home from a massive heart attack. On more than one occasion before he had told Richard and I just how he did *not* want to go. "No tubes, no goddamn IVs, not plugged to any machines," was how he put it. So when he became acutely ill at home we were clear on what his wishes were. There was time for us to get him to hospital, but he was still lucid for a few moments and again made us promise. No tubes. He died an hour or so later, in bed at home.

Well, not "us" exactly. I wasn't there. I was working in Africa when it happened.

"You know," I tell Cristi, "it's coming to 10 years and I don't think there's a day that goes by when I don't think of him, or wish I could just have another one of our chats. And that's something I really envy you for."

"What's that?" Cristi asks.

"I wasn't there at the end for my father. You get to be there at the end for yours. You get to take him home and respect how he wants to finish. I'd give anything to hear my father's voice just one more time. You get to have all those entire conversations. Believe me, that's not a little thing."

Cristi is silent for a moment, his gaze fixed on the gravel at our feet. Then he closes his eyes and stretches his slim frame upright. He looks like some unbearable, invisible load has been lifted. When he opens his eyes and blinks at us, it is as though he has come through some dark place and back into the light. Then we shake hands and he thanks us softly. He says that he would like a picture, with the bikes and us. Later during the evening he would tell us that it's the first peace he has felt for months about his decision. That is, to stop treatment and take his father home to care for him.

I'm not sure when the party ended. I was already freezing in my tent by then. Next morning I'm awakened by birdsong. Mike had set his tent a few feet away and we quietly pack things up to get on the road again. There are some long miles to make up for today.

The pretty lady is back at the reception desk, charming as before. Other than that the whole place is perfectly still. I think our new friends will be rising late. We thank her for the use of the grounds.

"Oh, there's no problem," she smiles, "I hear you helped some of my guests at their party last night. There is no charge."

"Well," I reply, "that's very generous, we're really glad to have met you. I didn't think I would be happy about turning around at the tunnel, but I really am."

"Oh," she replies, "and I am very happy to see you alive and well this morning, really very happy."

There's something in the way she said it. She really seemed more relieved than happy. "Er, why?" I ask.

"Oh, we get a lot of bears around these cottages around this time of the year. Especially after parties. Especially barbecue."

"What?" Mike says, wide-eyed. "What bears?"

"Oh, one that is like that … or that … or even that brown one, we have seen a lot of him lately."

We had not noticed them earlier. This Romanian woman has a way of making anyone miss out on the detailed finishings of any room she's in. Only when she points them out do I notice the row of stuffed bear heads that dot almost all the available space at the cornices.

"After all," she says, "that's what we call our hotel. Conacul Ursului: Mansion of Bears."

Twenty
THE MONK IN THE GARDEN

WE TAKE THE ROUNDABOUT way through the mountains and spend the night in the lovely medieval town of Sibiu. Here we part ways with Angelica. She has time to wander about the place since her Turkish tour has been shortened by her accident. It's only two days' ride for her to her hometown of Munich. We've got more distance to cover to Stockholm. In fact, looking at the map, I'm wondering how we're possibly going to make the miles.

Soon afterwards I discover that it really is possible. You really can ride through all of Europe in four days if you want to. When Mike was planning this part of the itinerary I didn't believe it when he said that a week was a luxurious pace. It's nearly 3,000 km from Istanbul to Copenhagen. That's eight countries!

Now I believe. We're putting in 130 km/h, hour after hour, on this perfect motorway just outside of Brno. On the overdrive the V-Strom is managing this at just 4,200 rpm, and I'm estimating we can cover 500 km before having to refuel. We've been doing this since we left Sibiu early this morning. That was nearly 800 km ago. It's been raining hard but it's a European kind of pitter patter, pussy-footing kind of rain, not the zero visibility Thai thunderstorms that we're used to, so we don't really need to slow down. Besides, the roads here are so well made that it's only the odd shallow puddle, none of the axle-tearing potholes that we've come through before.

We've been on the same motorway since crossing from Romania into the Czech Republic. There weren't even any immigration booths in spite of crossing borders at Hungary and Slovakia. We made one stop for fuel in Hungary, but that was it. Slovakia is the only country I have ever ridden through where I didn't even set my foot down. I think I may have changed gear once, when I thought I might have missed an immigration checkpoint only to discover that all the buildings at the border crossing were empty. Then it was up to sixth gear again and here we are.

Some might say that this is the wrong way to see Europe and they'd be right. With the limited time we have it was either Asia or Europe and we're living our choice. All I've seen of Hungary and Slovakia is a soggy motorway stretching on interminably ahead through the rain on my visor and behind me, through droplets on my mirrors. It may be my imagination but motorway speeds seem to be getting faster the nearer we get to Germany.

As we are about to enter Brno the sun starts to break through again and the skies clear. I notice one of those brown tourist advisories showing what the next exit from the highway brings. I click on the intercom to Mike:

"Hello Mike! Guess what! We're riding past Austerlitz! Remember Austerlitz?"

No reply. I check on the intercom to make sure it's working. I guess Mike must be zoned out on Black Sabbath. Or maybe Anticlimax, or Ebba Gron, or Rude Kids. He's let me sample some of his playlist before. It's the kind of stuff that blanks out the mind and makes my ears bleed, before removing the feeling in my limbs and my will to live. It's pretty toxic, but Mike appears to like it. Whatever rocks your boat, man, but this is too significant a landmark to pass up.

"Austerlitz, Mike! Where Napoleon demonstrated the principles of deception and force concentration against an enemy with superior infantry and artillery!" To generate interest I provide what I think is a fairly brief, broad summary of those principles. I'm encouraged by Mike's silence – this must really captivate him, we passed the exit miles ago.

Finally, Mike speaks:

"Once again, Phil. How one head can be filled with so much utter rubbish is a source of constant wonder to me," he says, "but at least there's one piece of good news."

"What's that?"

"We've been doing 140 km/h speeds through every conceivable kind of road surface. All the grooves and ruts and puddles and pissing rain and even the occasional bit of ice."

"Yes, so what?"

"You haven't mentioned any of it at all. I think your anxiety attacks are over."

I give this some thought. It's been some time since I needed to challenge cognitive errors. I'm actually out here just enjoying myself. I haven't really noticed how far or how fast we're going. It's just a nice ride. I guess Ah Chye was right after all. The most important ingredient for a successful ride is to enjoy it.

The next day we leave Brno for Prague. We'll be spending the weekend there with Pierce and his wife May but there is this one place we have to see right outside of Brno. When I asked a local for directions I was told to look for the monk in the garden. Anyone who's in our line of work needs to pay homage to the monk in the garden.

He wasn't always a monk of course. Before he joined the clergy he was already an experienced gardener. His father had wanted him to take over the family farm. Even after he joined the Abbey of St Thomas, what he really wanted to be was a certified schoolteacher. This he failed to accomplish, failing the board exams twice. They kept him on teaching lower secondary school for his sheer passion and enthusiasm. It didn't take up all his mental effort and he spent the time becoming an accomplished mathematician and botanist. And then for eight remarkable years, he studied peas.

We find the monk in the garden, his statue looking benignly over neat rows of pea plants, their yellow petals swaying gently in the morning sunlight. I notice each row notated with neat paper tags: F1, F2, G1, G2 ...

Over on one side of the garden, in a row of what looks like converted classrooms, is a small exhibit of some of his

> A giant of a scientist — the monk in the garden

work. In that burst of scientific enquiry over those eight years he would cultivate 28,000 pea plants and dissect 40,000 blossoms and 300,000 peas, meticulously recording his findings into a veritable library of log books. He would publish two scientific papers, gain promotion to abbot and then die in relative obscurity. His dissecting microscope is on display, its dials worn smooth by use.

Before Mendel's insights into the mechanisms of inheritance it was believed that any offspring would simply inherit a random mixture of traits from both parents. Breeding of plants and animals for optimal stock was very much a hit-and-miss affair. He changed all that.

Just how he started his scientific enquiry is a mystery to me. Going through the exhibits it strikes me that he didn't have a hypothesis. He had chosen pea plants because of their short reproductive cycles and how distinct traits could be studied, like petal colours, shape of peas and so on. Much of his work stemmed from just meticulous records and cross breeding of different lines of plants.

From his calculations he would derive his famous four rules familiar to any student in modern genetics. That paired alleles, or "particles" as he called them (the discovery of DNA was eighty years away), made up the genotype of the plant, and was responsible for their physical features, or phenotype. They were inherited independently from other pairs of alleles, and could influence the phenotype in either a dominant or recessive fashion.

I doubt that Mendel would have appreciated calling them rules though. That would suggest that nature danced to his tune. Through his meticulous observation and open-ended enquiry I have the impression that he saw himself more as trying to bring some comprehension to a great mystery, rather than one who thought he was embarking on an entire new branch of science. His careful, meticulous approach seems to come from more than just scientific training. There is a reverence and humility in not bringing any preconceived notions to his work, and letting the observations take him where they would.

It would be a matter of time before the study of inherited traits would find their place in human diseases. Like Mendel's peas, to detect such a trait would take large families, records of illnesses over several generations, an obvious phenotype and most importantly, significant inbreeding.

The royal houses of Europe ticked all these boxes, and are used in all basic textbooks as an introduction to inherited disease. The disease in question is hemophilia B, which is due to a deleterious mutation on the X chromosome. As it is a recessive gene, women with another normal X copy are unaffected carriers. Males, with only one copy of the X chromosome, have the disease phenotype. In hemophilia B the defect in the blood clotting leads to easy and uncontrollable bleeding, and in many cases, an early death.

Among this regal cohort, the earliest putative carrier of the mutated gene is Britain's Queen Victoria, whose daughters were married off to the royal families of Spain, Russia and Germany. What follows over the next two generations is a litany of misery among their male offspring. True to Mendelian principles, about half of them would be affected and die early deaths. Her son Leopold died after a trivial fall, her grandson Friedrich died of complications from bleeding aged 2 years; her other grandsons Maurice and Leopold were dead at 23 and 32 years respectively.

For the last afflicted male of this royal family, however, it really didn't matter if his blood clotted normally or not. This was the unfortunate Prince Alexei Romanov, son of Tsar Nicholas II and heir to the Russian throne. He was murdered with the rest of the Tsar's family aged 13 years, at the end of the Russian Revolution. Normal clot formers or not, they all bled out.

I remember how breast cancer predisposing genes had captured my imagination when the time came for me to get on my PhD thesis. These BRCA mutations were the first examples of highly penetrant autosomal dominant genes that led to the development of a common cancer. It would change everything, or so we thought.

The ability to identify breast cancer-causing mutations led to the start of our family history clinics in 1999. Women with a significant family history of breast cancer were referred to this clinic where they underwent detailed counselling about what genetics were, what a mutation test would entail, and how the results might be interpreted.

What surprised us then was just how uncommon these mutations were. They accounted for just about 10% of all patients who were estimated to have at least double the lifetime risk of breast cancer because of their family history. The second surprise was just how much having a mutation at these genes could increase the chance of cancer. Without the mutation the general risk of breast cancer is about 1:18 in Singapore. With the mutation this risk ranges from 1:2 to close to 1:1.

The third surprise was just how few of the patients who had a 10% chance of having a mutation actually accepted genetic testing. This is despite having financial subsidies to substantially reduce the cost of gene testing. About 1 in 5 of patients whom we could offer testing actually took it up. To many patients it all seemed too theoretical – the idea that family members could have such a contrast in breast cancer risk on the basis of a blood test seemed too much to take on board.

I remember a morning not long before we left when I met perhaps the ultimate pragmatic approach to genetic breast cancers. I'd known May for over 10 years. She first came to the family history clinic after she had been treated with breast cancer elsewhere after being diagnosed at the age of 28. Her mother had died of breast cancer in her forties, and of two maternal aunts one had breast cancer in her late forties but was still alive and living in Malaysia.

When May had completed surgery and chemotherapy she had been referred to us for genetic counselling. She was just married then but without children. We had gone through the benefits of gene testing. A positive result would explain why she and possibly her relatives had developed cancer at such an early age, and would also mean a higher chance of cancer developing on her remaining breast and possibly her ovaries as well.

If the gene test was positive, we would offer a preventive removal of the opposite right breast and possibly her ovaries as preventive options. It would mean that her two sisters and her brother could go for gene testing to see if there was any chance that they may carry the mutation and take necessary action. A negative test would be uninformative.

Although her husband was supportive of the idea, May was adamant against it because she had not spoken to any of her family or siblings about her cancer, although she knew that they were worried. As for the possibility of future offspring, May had undergone chemotherapy which had affected her fertility, and so May and her husband had already decided not to have any children of their own.

In that sense, she reasoned a genetic test would not be useful to children she was not going to have. As for preventive removal of organs which might be at increased risk based on a genetic test, May already found breast surgery to remove her cancer difficult enough to accept. She was not about to agree to a preventive removal of her normal breast as an option, much less her ovaries.

As genetic testing would affect the rest of her family we advised May to bring them into the discussion, so that a collective decision could be made, but she felt she could not put them through all that. Her family had already suffered through the experience of caring for so many loved ones with breast cancer and May could not bring herself to bring it up again. The process had come to a dead end.

So for almost a decade we screened with mammograms and MRIs and each time when I saw her with the results I would politely ask if she would reconsider genetic testing and each time she would politely decline. All the results would be normal and it did seem as though she was like any other cancer patient in remission.

What made me remember May here in Brno is that just before we left for this ride, May's MRIs had shown a suspicious mass in her remaining right breast. I remember I had been awake for most of the previous night with some horrid trauma case and had only traced the biopsy results at the clinic just before seeing her. Suddenly the weariness got a lot worse. The biopsy had confirmed another high grade cancer, just like the first. That morning with the help of the breast care sisters I told May the news.

May sat there and didn't say anything at first. I could tell she was thinking about that offer for all those years ago about gene testing, which may have led to her having this remaining breast removed and preventing this cancer.

"So ... I have a choice of operations again?" May asked.

"Yes." It had been discovered early enough that she did not need to necessarily have her whole breast removed.

"And ..." she said more dejectedly, "... chemo again?"

"For breast cancer that's come back, yes, very likely."

"Right," she says. It did not appear to be an unexpected result to her. There was no "why me?" or how this was all so terribly unfair, to have cancer in both breasts by the age of forty, or how she was going to bring cancer back to the family discussions again.

Instead, May looked as though she was gearing up. I remember the way she looked around the room, nodding slightly to herself as a climber would, deciding what to take and what to leave behind for yet another hill to kill. She knew this would be back, and here it was. She knew what was needed, and she knew that she had it. In case this really weary-looking surgeon in front of her thinks she's not up to the task, she'd better make it clear to him.

"Well," May said, "at least I did make one right decision."

I looked at her. I couldn't think of anything to say.

"At least I don't have kids."

Twenty-one
THE WALL AT THE END

THE MOTORWAY TAKES US northwards to the coast, and then the Scandlines ferry from Puttgarden to Rodby in Denmark. From here it's a mere two hours before we arrive at Cynthia and James' home in Hundige, just south of Copenhagen. We arrive in the bright sunshine, the air full of summer birdsong and that sparkling cleanness that comes from being by the sea.

The place is achingly familiar. Can it be less than a year ago that I spent a few nights here and we first drew up the plans to get Cynthia and her team of anthropologists involved? This was just after that utter chance meeting at the Coffee Bean at the Kent Ridge MRT station. It was less than six months before this ride started and so many things needed to be done. We worked on the dining table then, well into the night and wound up with an impressive to-do list.

What had James said when he finally saw what we were proposing? So much needed to go right for us to pull it off. He is familiar with what his wife is capable of and was confident that Cynthia could hold up her end of the collaboration. His main worry was me.

"Is this possible? Can you make all those distances in time? I'll believe it when I see you at my front door. OK?" he gave one of his hearty laughs.

Now I hear that same warm welcome again as we ride the bikes into his driveway. There are hugs all around.

"Right on schedule, down to the very hour," James beams, "this is just incredible."

I'm having trouble believing it myself. The last time we were together was in Luzhou on that dark polluted morning. I was thinking of quitting entirely. What was it I had wished for then? To be in Copenhagen in the summer where the air is clean and seawater is just seawater. I take the helmet off and look around me. It's hard to believe I'm here with Cynthia and James again, but it's the sight in their driveway right before me that brings it home. The sight of two bikes and Mike, in that bright clean seaside air. I'm having difficulty trying to get the thought to sink in: We've actually made it.

After settling into our rooms I grab a shower, change into beach clothes and head out to the sea, just 100 m down the lane. It's just as I remember it: clean skies, an uncluttered sea, and a perfect sandy beach with beachfront housing just beyond a thin stretch of marshland. It's another week or so before arriving in Stockholm but I feel that I've already arrived. All those months ago I had promised myself that the

The beach just south of Copenhagen, where the air is clean and the seawater is just seawater, with Mike and Jean.

next time I sit on this sand it will be after having ridden my bike across Asia, and here I am.

That night James and Cynthia put out a supper worthy of any homecoming. Their home is a library of published academic work. The furniture is arranged in little cloisters for the many postgraduate students who come for after-hour discussions. After the dishes are washed and put away Cyn shows us some photo albums of her work with the Orang Laut, a maritime race in Sulawesi where she had spent years for her doctorate work after she left Singapore. One series of pictures shows her in a crowded room of a fishing village, watching on as an accepted member of the community, as a mother holds her child in front of a traditional healer. That child would die that night, Cynthia says.

The next album has a disproportionate number of pictures of the wall of the child's room in the attap house. It looks perfectly ordinary to me, but the traditional healer had said that the arrangement of some items on that wall was the reason for the child's failure to recover. On it were a toy bow and arrow set with a quiver and some floral decorations. From what clinical history Cyn could provide it sounded like the child had died of untreated acute appendicitis.

It's been over twenty years since those pictures were taken but they haven't lost their poignancy. Acute appendicitis. Not something a lot of people die of nowadays almost anywhere in the developed world. It's the first emergency operation any surgeon learns and even if you can barely hold a fork and knife most people manage it, but that child didn't have a chance. For all sorts of reasons we can't understand, including items on a wall.

The problem with breast cancer is that there are different things on the wall. So many people we've met on this ride didn't think it'd happen to them or their loved ones. So many more decline screening or treatment because they don't really believe treatment works, or think that it's all up to fate. They don't even want to talk about it because that would tempt fate. Some blind, impersonal, illogical but no less potent force that renders us all powerless to its whims. We've got so much stuff on our wall we don't even know about.

The next morning we meet with our anthropology colleagues at the University of Copenhagen. Cynthia had brought them together from all over Asia, where they were already working in different communities. The funds we raised for our ride would support their further studies in the area of breast cancer behaviour. Like moles in some secret network, they are already embedded in their communities doing other work and have made themselves available for our project.

I ask them how long they had been in the field. In Turkey? Seven years. Mongolia? Nine years. Iran? Three years. It's called participant-observation, arguably how the highest quality anthropology data is obtained, through an intensive participation and acceptance within that community. Just like Cynthia's years with the Orang Laut.

How much longer will you stay among normadic Mongolian tribes for our breast cancer study? As long as we have good questions. Maybe with these people we have a chance of showing just what our breast cancer wall is like, and start to take some of those items down. It isn't our riding motorcycles that will give our effort any significance; it's these dedicated people.

THE NEXT DAY MIKE leaves for Stockholm to meet his family and get his home ready for us. I will be staying on in Copenhagen for a few more days. My daughter Jean will come up first and I'll take her for a biking tour of Denmark. In a few days the rest of my family will show up here and rent a car to Stockholm to spend a week in Mike's place before we all go back to Singapore.

On the last leg of the Long Ride Mike leads us through the streets of Stockholm before finishing at the Karolinska Institute. It's the first time for the whole ride that he's using the intercom more than I am, showing me the place where he trained, where he got his first flat with Mette, the intersection where he had his accident that led to him coming off his Harley and off motorcycles entirely until this mad ride came along.

There's still a half hour before we have to make our grand

entrance into Karolinska where our families are already waiting. There's national press and most of the surgery and epidemiology units waiting to welcome their mad Swede back. After we arrive there will be lectures to give, a press conference and all sorts of photo shoots.

Across the street from the main entrance is a park with a Subway eatery with stone benches out front. We get coffees and have a quiet moment before the madness begins. After this morning we won't be heading westward anymore, but home to Singapore. A few awkward minutes pass in silence. This is the final stop before the end of our journey. I'm having trouble finding the right words.

"Real ride, eh?" I begin. Maybe Real Men can do better, but it's hard for me.

"Yeah, quite something," Mike replies, sipping the coffee. Another few minutes pass.

"Well I guess we've made it, Mike," I finally get out, "I don't know how long it'll take me to put everything into perspective, but one thing I'm pretty sure of."

"What's that?"

"No way I could have made it without you. You've been absolutely wonderful. Thank you for the last three months."

"Not a problem. Been a pleasure," Mike replies. "Would I do it again? Definitely. Would I do it again with you? Absolutely, but next time, let's plan to do it more slowly. The riding and the dates was just a crazy way to do this. And as for gaining proper perspective …"

"What about it?"

"Maybe if you put it all into a book it might help. Who knows, someone might even read it."

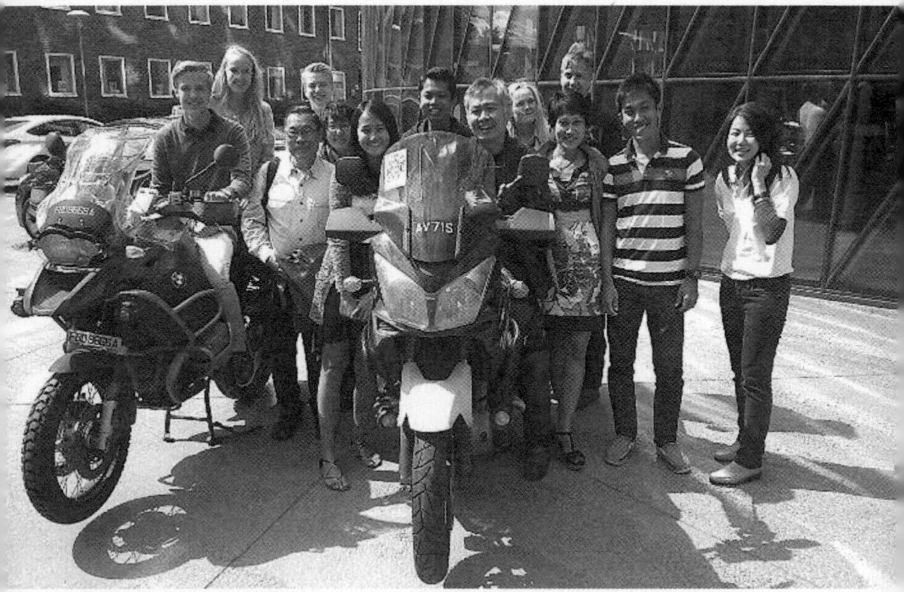
AV71S

ABOUT THE AUTHOR

Dr. Philip Iau is unaccustomed to referring to himself in the third person but understands that this might encourage you to buy this book. He has the papers to prove that he really is a fully qualified breast cancer and trauma surgeon, and is generally considered to be better at these things than long distance motorcycling.

Philip got his medical degree in 1989, completed his surgical training in 1996 and his PhD in 2004. He used to head both the breast cancer and trauma services at the National University Hospital, Singapore. This was up until 2014, around the time the events in this book unfolded.

Since returning to work he has been treated for colon cancer, taken up expedition kayaking and continues his mad love of long distance motorcycling. Due to his proclivity for thought retention he still has persistent issues with high places, dentists, grant application forms and train conductors. Small animals appear to trust him. He is married to Viola, has three grown children and a dog.

The Long Ride from Singapore is his first book, so be nice.

The Long Ride project was set up to benefit breast cancer patients and Asian women. All author's royalties go towards the Asian Breast Cancer Research Fund, administered by the National University of Singapore.

If you wish to support this effort,
please scan the QR code with your mobile phone.